Dragging Away

Dragging Away   Queer Abstraction in

Contemporary Art   Lex Morgan Lancaster

DUKE UNIVERSITY PRESS
Durham and London
2022

Printed in the United States of America on acid-free paper ∞
Designed by A. Mattson Gallagher
Typeset in Utopia and Helvetica Neue
by Copperline Book Services

Library of Congress Cataloging-in-Publication Data
Names: Lancaster, Lex Morgan, [date] author.
Title: Dragging away : queer abstraction in contemporary
art / Lex Morgan Lancaster.
Description: Durham : Duke University Press, 2022. |
Includes bibliographical references and index.
Identifiers: LCCN 2021055913 (print)
LCCN 2021055914 (ebook)
ISBN 9781478016045 (hardcover)
ISBN 9781478018674 (paperback)
ISBN 9781478023296 (ebook)
Subjects: LCSH: Art and society—United States. | Art—
Political aspects—United States. | Modernism (Art)—United
States. | Art, Abstract—United States. | Abstraction—Social
aspects. | Homosexuality and art—United States. | Feminism
and art—United States. | Art and race. | BISAC: ART /
History / Contemporary (1945-) | SOCIAL SCIENCE /
LGBTQ Studies / General
Classification: LCC N72.S6 .L36 2022 (print) |
LCC N72.S6 (ebook) | DDC 700.1/03—dc23/eng/20220512
LC record available at https://lccn.loc.gov/2021055913
LC ebook record available at https://lccn.loc.gov/2021055914

Cover art: Every Ocean Hughes, *Beyond the Will to Measure*,
2014. Wall-mounted ceramic, clock movements, and acrylic,
dimensions variable. Photography by Doyun Kim. Courtesy
of the artist.

For Garrett Morgan Lancaster,
whose memory drags on

CONTENTS

Plates

Abstraction is difficult to write about, and navigating this difficulty would have been impossible without the care and support of many people. First, I thank Jill H. Casid for their mentorship, unwavering confidence in me and this project, and many labors of care from reading countless experimental drafts to sharing the tools that sustain a queer academic life. For their advice and support during the first stages of this project, I thank Karma R. Chávez, Lauren Kroiz, Michael Jay McClure, and Ellen Samuels.

My thinking on the queer politics of abstraction has developed over a decade, and I have been grateful for the opportunities to present this scholarship at conferences and develop it through previous publications. A version of chapter 2 appeared in a 2017 article, "Feeling the Grid: Lorna Simpson's Concrete Abstraction," in *ASAP/Journal*, and I thank editors Amy J. Elias and Jonathan P. Eburne for their feedback and assistance in publishing this. I thank the editorial team at *Discourse: Journal for Theoretical Studies in Media and Culture*, especially James Cahill and Ennuri Jo, for helping me to publish "The Wipe: Sadie Benning's Queer Abstraction" (2017), which marks the beginning of this entire project and through which I worked out many of its central concepts. I am grateful for the generative discussion I had with Jared Ledesma, curator of the Queer Abstraction exhibition at the Des Moines Art Center (2019), which I also had the pleasure of reviewing for *ASAP/J* online. I organized and chaired a session titled "New Materialisms in Contemporary Art" at the annual College Art Association Conference (CAA) in 2017, with Anna Campbell, Linda Besemer, Sarah Cowan, and Joshua Lubin-Levy. Our conversations fueled my thinking on the importance of materiality to the queer operations of abstraction. I thank Eliza Steinbock and Cyle Metzger for organizing the panel "No Body, This Body: Marking Flesh, Figuration, Abstraction in Trans Art History" at CAA in 2019, and David Getsy for his feedback on my talk based on the third chapter of this book. I thank Travis English for organizing the 2018 Southeast College Art Conference session "Avant-Garde Echoes: Modernist Reverberations in Contemporary Art," where I received such warm feedback on material from chapter 1.

It has been my great pleasure to meet and speak with some of the artists whose works are featured in this book. For their willingness to welcome me into their studios and share their work with me, I thank Linda Besemer, Nancy Brooks Brody, and Carrie Yamaoka. Many of the images in this book would not appear without the generosity of many more artists: fierce pussy, Zoe Leonard, Joy Episalla, Ulrike Müller, Every Ocean Hughes, Lorna Simpson, Xylor Jane, Sheila Pepe, Shinique Smith, Tiona Nekkia McClodden, Angela Hennessy, and curator Jo-ey Tang.

I am grateful for the fellowships and financial support I received in the Department of Art History at the University of Wisconsin–Madison that allowed me to initiate this project. In the final years of writing this book, I was supported by the University of South Carolina Upstate, and I would like to thank the Office of Sponsored Research and Support, which provided course releases and a Research Initiative for Summer Engagement grant that gave me the time to complete it. I am grateful for the Teaching and Productive Scholarship grants I received to present this scholarship at conferences and to assist with the costs of publication. I thank my colleagues in the Department of Fine Arts and Communication Studies for their ongoing support.

It has been a dream to publish with Duke University Press. I thank editorial associate Ryan Kendall for answering all my many questions as I prepared the manuscript, and especially senior executive editor Ken Wissoker for his kind support and guidance through the process. Thanks to the two anonymous readers of my manuscript for your insightful suggestions and criticism. Thanks to Ideas on Fire, especially Cathy Hannabach, for their wonderful resources and editorial assistance, and for indexing this book.

The thinking and writing that has sustained me over the past decade would not have been possible without a crew of fellow travelers. There are too many to thank here, the dear friends and chosen family who wrote beside me, commiserated over coffee and cocktails, and cheered me at each hurdle. The list would begin with Rhian Brown, River Bullock, Ashley Cook, Jessica Cooley, Kiki DeLovely, Rique Hagen, Anne Helmreich, Taylor Henninger, Lisa Johnson, Carmen Juniper, Emily Kofoed, Claire Landis Davis, Lisa Marks, Robert Mebane and Jacqui Casey, Courtney McDonald, Teresita and Robert McPherson, Megan Milks, Lauren Miller, Megan Murph, Shannon Neimeko, Renu Pariyadath, Holly Rubalcava, Joan and Ron Short, and Emma Silverman. I know that those I have lost along the way, especially my father Martin King, would share in this great pride. My mother, Lily Lancaster, has always been by my side, carrying me with a boundless love.

INTRODUCTION

A dark line cuts through the white gallery walls. From afar, this thick line appears to float against and between adjacent walls, but it is heavy metal lead embedded directly into the Sheetrock. Materializing the measurements from its surrounding architecture, *West/South, 90º Line* (figure I.1) reorients and disorients our experience of the space as it shifts our perspective with this subtle intervention. This work is incorporated into the architecture and exceeds it at the same time. Moving around to view the line at different angles changes its length and thickness. We become aware of how the work itself is visually altered by our perspective, and how its relation to the space and other objects also shifts. Recalling 1970s minimalist-conceptualist works by Fred Sandback, who hung yarn from ceiling to floor to alter a gallery space; Sol LeWitt's restrained wall drawings; or Ellsworth Kelly's shaped canvases, this 2018 work by Nancy Brooks

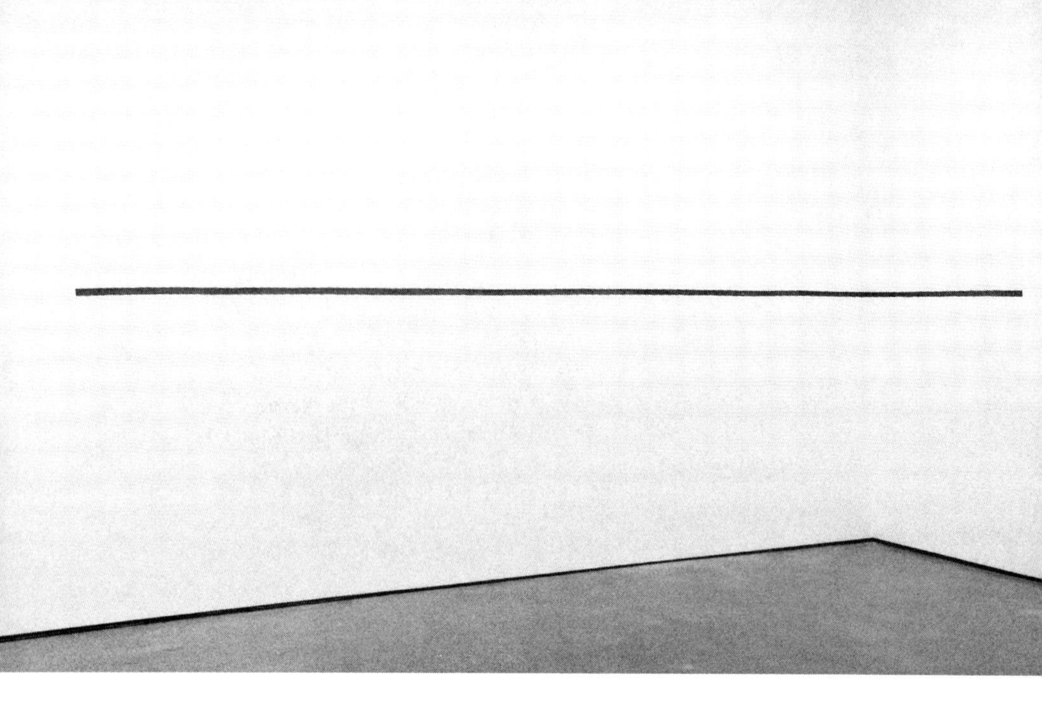

FIGURE I.1 Nancy Brooks Brody, *West/South, 90° Line*, 2018. Metal embedded into Sheetrock wall, 240 × 1¼ in. Chapter One of *arms ache avid aeon: Nancy Brooks Brody / Joy Episalla / Zoe Leonard / Carrie Yamaoka: fierce pussy amplified*, Beeler Gallery, Columbus College of Art & Design, 2019. Photo: Luke Stettner.

Brody drags on its own history of abstraction as it drags along the walls, by rendering the most minor of abstract gestures thickly material and playfully imprecise. Up close, the metal substance wavers with and against the sheetrock in which it does not exactly fit, and in relation, we are not sure where we stand.

West/South, 90° Line appeared in the first chapter of *arms ache avid aeon: fierce pussy amplified*, curated by Jo-ey Tang at Columbus College of Art & Design's Beeler Gallery (2018–19).[1] This series of chapters was dedicated to the work of four core members of the queer feminist art collective fierce pussy—Nancy Brooks Brody, Joy Episalla, Zoe Leonard, and Carrie Yamaoka—who continue to work together. Turning the corner from Brody's work, we encounter Episalla's *foldtogram* (2018) (figure I.2): a mural-scaled sheet of photographic paper manipulated to create cracks and wrinkles from handling, ripples and bubbles from light and heat exposure—abstractions created in a reproductive medium that the artist renders material and dimensional.[2] In another gallery, Leonard's series of *Sun Photographs* (ongoing since 2010) (figure I.3) turns the camera on the very source of light that is photography's medium, and its impossible-to-capture subject. The sun imprints itself as flaming white orbs against a grainy ground, demonstrating how photography can paradoxically destabilize visual perception rather than settle it. In another space, the viewer's body is mirrored and warped by reflective vinyl or polyester film cast in urethane resin by Carrie Yamaoka (figure I.4). These casts are produced in a chance-based process that yields undulating abstract objects that continue to change in an ongoing chemical development. Appearing still wet and fluid, shifting in our vision, these objects always implicate the viewer; by incorporating our image materially, they also imply the ethical responsibility of looking.

All of these artists engage in practices of abstraction, foregrounding the question of why queer feminist artist-activists would use such non-representational, abstract processes—a driving issue of this book.[3] These works demonstrate how formal and material processes of abstraction can *queer* (in the sense of an active verb) older modernist aesthetics by camping or torquing them; undermining the normative uses of media and materials to produce alternative processes and outcomes; using overtly representational media (photography) in ways that undermine easy legibility; refusing material mastery in favor of more messy, affective, unpredictable means of rendering an image or object. I argue that these methods of queer abstraction perform a *drag*—both in the sense of "temporal drag" (Elizabeth Freeman's term) that makes past aesthetics viable for the present, and in their pull away from direct representation in favor of active materializing processes that also exert a destabilizing pull on *us* as viewers.[4]

These artists' formal and material tactics in the studio and gallery are not divorced from their political strategies in the street. fierce pussy's collective, agitprop practices are often representational and direct in their use of language. Wheatpasted on public walls in New York City in the early 1990s, for example, their posters list and reclaim the terms commonly hurled as insults: "I AM A lezzie butch pervert girlfriend bulldagger sister dyke AND PROUD!" Photocopies of family photographs are juxtaposed with the

FIGURE I.2 Joy Episalla, *foldtogram (35'2.5' × 44"–August 2018)*, 2018. Silver gelatin object/photogram on Ilford Matte RC, dimensions of installation variable. Site-specific installation view from Chapter One of *arms ache avid aeon: Nancy Brooks Brody / Joy Episalla / Zoe Leonard / Carrie Yamaoka: fierce pussy amplified*, Beeler Gallery, Columbus College of Art & Design, 2019. Photo: Stephen Takacs.

FIGURE I.3 Zoe Leonard, *August 4, frame 9*, 2011/2012. Gelatin silver print, 23¾ × 17¼ in. © Zoe Leonard. Courtesy of the artist, Hauser & Wirth, and Galerie Gisela Capitain, Cologne.

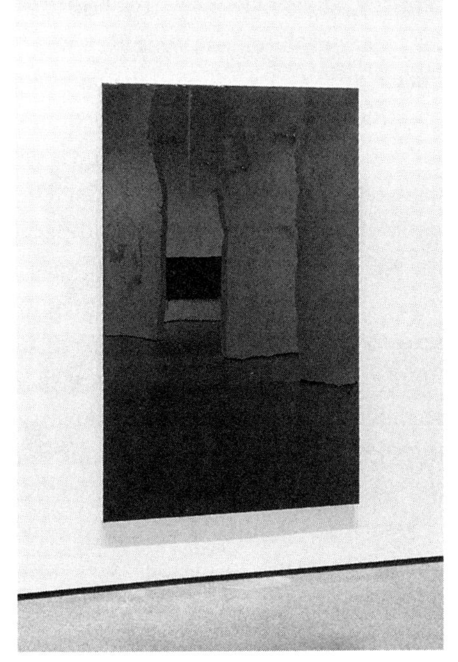

FIGURE I.4 Carrie Yamaoka, *72 by 45 (black)*, 2018. Reflective vinyl, epoxy resin, and mixed media on wood panel, 72 × 45 in. Chapter One of *arms ache avid aeon: Nancy Brooks Brody / Joy Episalla / Zoe Leonard / Carrie Yamaoka: fierce pussy amplified*, Beeler Gallery, Columbus College of Art & Design, 2019. Photo: Luke Stettner.

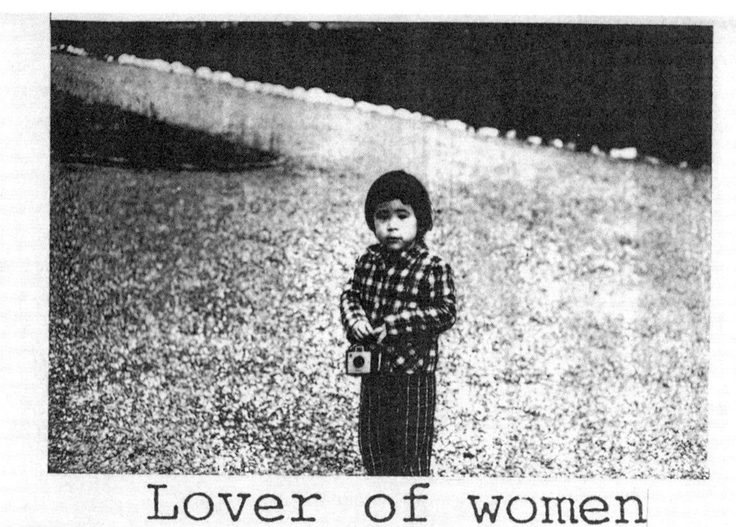

FIGURE I.5 fierce pussy, from the Family Pictures and Found Photos project, 1991.

phrases "Lover of women," or "find the dyke in this picture," as captions for seemingly benign images of children and friends posing for the camera (figure I.5). Reclaiming the language used for antiqueer violence— emotional assault that is never separate from material damage—fierce pussy confronts unsuspecting viewers with this language of oppression, which is disarming but also reactivated.[5] These pejoratives may abstract people into concepts (dykes and perverts), but fierce pussy reroutes the violence of that abstraction toward a language of pleasure and even pride. The words still have potential to harm, but when the terms are made tenuous through their exposure and repetition, their implications multiply so that pain and pleasure share the same space. Processes of abstraction can alter the terms and images we take for granted by expos- ing their contingency—the relationship between the work and every- thing outside of the work that we use to determine its meaning becomes obviously precarious. This strategy of taking on and torquing the forms that have harmed, forms that are seemingly "not for us" as queers, aligns with the difficult operations of abstraction that I will elucidate in this book.

When fierce pussy began working as an art collective in 1991, the AIDS crisis and racist, heterosexist legislation and censorship galvanized queer artists who produced radical work for the streets as much as for galleries. Along with fierce pussy, Dyke Action Machine, Lesbian Avengers, and ACT UP all used agitprop tactics and direct graphic posters to claim public space for queer identities. The culture wars era fueled the infamous 1993 Whitney Biennial that focused on identity politics and the ethics of representation, now understood to mark a significant shift in the art world.[6] Asserting visibility was a crucial political praxis: representations of queer people were used to insist that we exist, we will not be erased, we will fight for our lives. This insistence on representation and visibility is expected from queer political art. But the phenomenon of queer abstraction vexes our understanding of queer art, and, more importantly, what we think queering does socially and politically. It is the purpose of this book to show how queer abstractions make formal and material *processes* (and not just styles or appearances) evident as critical social and political tactics.

There are more examples of queer feminist artist-activists who produce abstract art, as well as artists who began producing overtly representational art and shifted to more abstract styles. For example, Carrie Moyer cofounded the lesbian public art project Dyke Action Machine! (1991–2008) and also produces abstract paintings in colorful acrylic and glitter. Every Ocean Hughes and Ulrike Müller, of the feminist genderqueer collaborative *LTTR* (a shifting acronym that began in 2001 as "Lesbians to the Rescue"), both began working in performance, video, and collective modes of art making, and later developed more abstract formal languages of geometry that speak to queer cultures (I discuss their work in chapter 1). It is usually not the case that these artists abandon all representation when they take up abstraction, but that abstraction is already part of their practice, and we are only recently beginning to notice how that abstraction might also do queer work. For example, Sadie Benning's famous early queer videos utilize abstraction, but were not considered in relation to abstraction until they were investigated in comparison with the later abstract paintings.[7]

Still, abstraction presents a problem for our conception of queer art, which is expected to speak directly to nonnormative sexuality and gender politics, often by picturing queer people or eroticized bodies. It is difficult to see immediately how abstraction can address sexuality, gender, and race, particularly because its content does not picture difference through figural representation or descriptive terms of identity. The assumed relationship between the form and content of the work slips, their binary positions breaking down.[8] These objects are difficult because they not only press our conception of what queer art is; they also demand methods of analysis that can account for how abstraction works queerly and politically. Another aim of this book is to develop such methods for addressing some of the central questions raised by these recent art practices: How is abstraction useful for queer, feminist, antiracist, genderqueer, and crip politics? How can abstraction address difference, injustice, or marginality when its formal and material processes actively refuse bodily legibility? Further, how can formalism—a traditional, seemingly conservative art historical methodology—intersect with queer methods?

Queer abstraction describes a recent movement in art practice as well as scholarly and curatorial endeavors that trace the increasing viability of abstract formal tactics for queer art. These practices of queer abstraction focus on formal and material invention, rather than transparent visibility. Abstraction has become a tool of queer resistance by undermining the demand that artists who are marked by difference must "show up" in ways that are expected and by creating a site to generate alternative spaces and worlds. David Getsy writes that queer abstraction addresses the persistent political desire to work from queer experience and revolt, but that "its priorities often emerge from a suspicion of representation, from a striving to vex visual recognition, and/or from a desire to find a more open and variable mode of imaging and imagining relations."[9] Abstraction can be dangerous, but it can also be a useful way for minority-marked artists to undermine the viewer's or critic's demand that their work bear the burden of representation. Julia Bryan-Wilson describes queer abstraction as "a resource for all those in the margins who want to resist the demands to transparently represent themselves in their work."[10] Queer abstraction has thus emerged as a crucial site of experimentation and resistance in contemporary art, but it does not have a singular definition or agreed-upon style. Rather, this contested terrain is marked by active tensions between methods and materials that reference the body and those that exceed it; images that represent specific cultural positions and those that undermine or explode beyond singular or binary situations; the explicitly political and the impossibly abstract.[11] These tensions are activated at once by queer art practices and readings of those practices, including mine.

In this book, I argue that abstraction—along with all of its historical and political baggage—offers visual and material tools for queer resistance via processes of dragging. I develop this book's driving concept, "dragging away," from the queering potential in the origins of the term *abstract* (particularly its verb form), derived from the Latin *ab*, away, and *trahere*, meaning to draw, pull, or drag. This drag performs in various senses of the term as a pulling force or friction that impedes or obstructs and leaves a mark; a temporal slowing down; a performative troubling of surface categories; a difficult labor; and a resistance. Queer abstraction drags in multiple aesthetic, material, historical, and political ways; this site of scholarly inquiry also drags in that it resists definition and raises contradictions. Below, I will outline three problematic paradoxes or irresolvable tensions at the heart of this book. These are tensions and difficulties that will remain active throughout the book, as their friction accompanies the risks of writing about queer abstraction. And yet, as I demonstrate, the difficulty of drag in multiple senses—its tediousness, its resistant material pressures, its imaginative projections—does not produce an impasse but creates multiple opportunities to expand our conceptions of queer art.

Between Abstraction and the Body: Nonrepresentational Politics

While abstraction is one way for artists to avoid the surveillance that accompanies the demands of visibility, there is also a tendency to interpret abstraction as a kind of closet when it is deployed by queer artists, particularly when earlier historical conditions seemed to demand it.[12] Abstract form is often read as an implicit bodily reference, reducing abstraction to a signifying content—a phallus here, a breast there; "feminine" curves or wounded flesh—in order to locate its queerness or its social efficacy.[13] Viewers are not likely to identify with abstraction in the way they would with figural representations, and yet, how we engage with this artwork has real ethical implications for how we engage with others in the world. Perhaps some viewers have trouble identifying with abstraction *without* thinking about rich painterly surface in terms of flesh, or thick sculptural heft as anthropomorphic. But abstraction presents more generative opportunities to explore queering beyond the figure or the encoded image of a body. Taking abstraction seriously as a dragging away from representation, I investigate how queering operates beyond bodily legibility. In doing so, I also make a case that what we call queer is not always a representational look, nor should it be reduced to bodily signs.

So then, who or what does the term *queer* speak for? What might abstraction reveal to us that is useful in thinking about the politics of gender, sexuality, race, and disability, if not through the body? Moving away from a focus on the body may seem to ignore the lived realities of these categories. My analysis offers abstraction as a queer refusal of certain representational logic, but this is not to suggest that queer art and scholarship should do away with references to the body or the figure in all cases. It makes sense that so much political art is focused on the body because our experiences of the world are embodied, and our lives are conditioned by how our bodies are conceived as gendered, sexed, raced, and abled or disabled. And this is precisely to the point, as abstraction can challenge the ways in which representation aims to fix difference on the body's surface. I offer alternatives to this visibility politics by exploring how, for example, queer relations and eroticism can be active in artwork that exceeds or refuses a settled corporeal figure, and what this difficulty can do aesthetically and politically. My argument is that abstraction can take us further toward imagining queer, feminist, antiracist, genderqueer, and crip formational strategies and ways of relating if we do not reduce its operations to a clearly signifying *iconography*.

Queer abstraction might describe what it feels like when others attempt to define us in relation to categories that do not fit, or it may describe an unresolvable position and constant state of misrecognition according to available codes and the limits of language. This state of incoherence prompts my interpretation of abstraction as a complication of the signifying processes that also do violence. Queer abstraction creates a space for exploring the operations of certain unmanageable aesthetics and ways of becoming; for modes of desiring and relating across difference without securing or encoding a subject; for exposing the violence that abstracting can do while at the same time exploding processes of categorization and signification. I maintain that we should take seriously the ways in which identity is lived in and through the body while also taking seriously the political potential of abstraction to refuse the oppressive meanings forced onto certain bodies.

I consider how abstraction performs catachrestically to undermine notions of the real that would fix difference on the bodies of others, and in this I am indebted to Peggy Phelan's understanding of subjectivity as unrepresentable. In *Unmarked*, Phelan breaks down the assumed correspondence between representational visibility and political power, as representations of difference often reinforce injustice. And yet, the politics of performance, for Phelan, shows how identity is not stably fixed in a name or a body; instead, our identities are always already constructed in relation to the Other.[14] My thinking on the political usefulness of abstraction as a refusal of transparent categories of difference is similarly indebted to Édouard Glissant's demand for "the right to opacity." Theorized specifically as a postcolonial response to Western notions that understanding the Other hinges on an essentializing transparency, Glissant's *opacity* makes space for the unknowability and multiplicity of difference in excess of categories.[15] Queer abstraction deploys opaque aesthetics to strategically refuse representational visibility, sometimes rendering the mediated space of the canvas or screen as one where something appears but is *not* stabilized or fixed. Indeed, queer abstraction reckons with the unrepresentable.

I argue that abstraction is ethically, socially, and politically useful because it can distance the operations of form and matter from bodily coherence, and stage new spectatorial possibilities instead. The viewing experiences I describe are in fact material and embodied. In my analysis, queer abstraction helps us consider differences such as gender and sexuality in terms of their possible experiences, affects, or relational operations without signifying a body or securing a subject. And yet, I discuss artworks that may seem inconveniently to shore up the body. Accordingly, I reckon with the body's potential appearances and slippages in my analysis, not disregarding the fact that bodies might seem to appear sometimes for some viewers. I deal with the implications for nonnormative embodiments where they arise (chapters 3 and 4 especially), but I do so in the interest of theorizing abstraction in more expansive ways. We seem to take for granted that certain forms and materials correspond to bodies, but I consider how abstraction complicates this easy correspondence. I similarly do not shy away from symbols—discussing the triangle, and the rainbow flag, for example—in order to tackle abstraction's paradoxical limitations and press at the limits of its political potentials. Abstraction still inevitably maintains some associative ties, some referring capacity, in either the process of creation or the act of viewing and interpreting.

Between Abstraction and Description: Abstract Catachresis

When writing about abstraction, I am constantly pressed up against the limits of language and attuned to how words fail me. While abstraction drags away from representation, it also resists description and thus troubles my hermeneutic gestures. A dragging force that obstructs or makes difficult, abstraction slows us down and troubles the possibility of any interpretation sticking resolutely to its forms. The works I discuss in this book are never pure in that they resist essentialism, and they generate multiple interpretive possibilities that may be at odds. Different viewers will certainly bring different desires and demands to the work. While this may always be the case, abstraction challenges our viewing and reading practices in ways that direct representation does not, creating a particularly compelling subject for queer analysis. In this way, abstraction queers by challenging the notion of any straightforward, secure reading. It demands a different kind of spectatorship and scholarship, embracing the interpretive risks and the impossibility of securing one's argument (if that argument is to assign meaning).

How can I describe abstraction as queer? Queer possibilities proliferate and multiply through abstraction, which challenges our efforts to designate or assign identifiable queerness to the work. This also challenges our expectation that identities are settled and will always materialize clearly on the surface of something (a work of art) or someone. The queer potential of this work will not always be legible to all viewers. But if we say that this work is not queer because it is not always clearly legible as such, we reify the notion that the "truth" of a subject will always be revealed on its surface—a logic rooted in heterosexism, racism, ableism, and transphobia. Further, we should not limit the contexts or kinds of artists that will allow us to join the terms *queer* and *abstract*. Rather, I propose some possibilities for how this work operates queerly, to prompt further questions but never to settle them. At the same time, I am not at all suggesting that the spectator is always responsible for "reading queerness into" the work: I will demonstrate in each chapter the queering operations that are already there, showing how the work itself prompts particular kinds of visual and material engagement. My interpretations are generated at the intersections of the visual and material operations of the artworks that we can all see, and the particular analytic lenses I have chosen that others may not automatically bring to the work. The openness of abstraction to multiple readings and points of view is what makes it viable for queering in the first place.

"Queer abstraction" might seem a contradiction in terms, if abstraction is viewed as a generalizing mechanism that would erase difference in its move away from representation, and if singular specificity is viewed as a necessary investment for queer politics. I study contemporary deployments of abstraction that are not limiting or universalizing, but excessive in ways that generate runoffs and alternatives to singular or dualistic categories. These artworks demand that we take abstraction seriously as a tactic that deviates and estranges us from the realm of the recognizable, undermining a politics of visibility that settles otherness in an image and fixes identity according to binary categories of difference. Queer abstractions perform this refusal and generate alternatives through formal and material invention: form performs historically and politically in this work. Thus, the book is organized into chapters according to formal and material strategies of abstraction: hard-edge, the grid, color, and spatial tactics. The artworks I discuss range from the abstract*ing* work of photography that alienates viewers from a secure space of representation to the impossibly abstract forms of painting and sculpture (in both the expanded sense and often combined use of their mediums) that make no immediate reference.

Some would consider the terms *abstraction* and *nonrepresentation* to be distinct in relation to art, where *abstract* implies a connection to something from the "real world," *abstracted from* a figure or object, versus nonrepresentational forms that make no reference at all. My purpose is not to argue for what counts as definitively abstract, and I understand abstraction in terms of its effects and activation of formal elements. Rather than a look, I consider abstraction to be an active, often unruly, *process*; queer and queering similarly operate as fugitive processes rather than a fixed category or image. I argue that the works discussed in this book operate queerly through processes of abstraction, which may include recognizable imagery and objects. To develop new conceptions of how abstraction can operate queerly, we have to dust off, reconsider, and reclaim that old term *abstract* to make way for the active styling of a queer visual and material resistance. This is not an abstraction that blocks out connections to the real world of culture and politics, but instead one that uses form and matter to trouble normative categories and shift perspectives, perverting abstraction's overloaded history in its wake. It is precisely abstraction's baggage (as a modernist tactic, as a potential tool for homogenization) that makes it such a compelling queer tactic.

I consider certain abstractions queer in their unsettlement of binary categorizations of difference (male/female, hetero/homo), while they also address particular counterpublics and nonnormative affinities. I argue that this abstract artwork *queers* by bending the resistant materiality of abstracted form for political ends, undermining and exceeding the representational, surveilling imperative to appear in ways that are expected. I understand queer abstraction as a *catachresis* that exceeds categorical boundaries of meaning (visually and textually), extending the work of David L. Eng, Jack Halberstam, and José Esteban Muñoz, who insist on the catachrestic agency of queering. Queer then becomes an active verb, a force or vector that works beyond particular bodies and identities.[16] Operating as a catachresis, abstraction offers alternatives to stable representation, and does so specifically through formal and material interventions that produce disruptions and exposures within processes of signification. Remobilized in queer, postcolonial, and feminist theories, catachresis refers to an excessive use of language—a term intentionally misapplied or perverted in order to offer a different and potentially transformative description of life's positions and conditions. Catachresis is a moment when language and meaning breaks down, and thus can open space for alternative narratives by generating terms or images for that which is unrepresentable.[17] For example, consider the catachrestic use of language in fierce pussy's posters, where terms attach uneasily to images, building with intensity and near hyperbole. These terms, which are historically misapplied and now reclaimed in queer contexts, signal both the performative possibilities of language and the arbitrary connections between the terms and their meaning. As a radical disruption of signification, the queering process of catachresis paradoxically insists upon specificity while troubling the defining and definitive regimes of normativity. In the artworks I study, abstraction constitutes its own catachrestic displacement, gesturing to specificities without direct naming, challenging identification even as the objects remain open to fantasy and projection. As a catachrestic operation, abstraction constitutes matter without transparent reference, suggesting a version of catachresis that is visible but cannot be fully grasped.

Considering queer abstraction as both formal and material invention, I join feminist new materialist and affect studies thinkers such as Sianne Ngai in challenging the notion that "abstract" means "not real," and prioritizing the excessive agencies of sensual encounters between objects.[18] As a kind of material catachresis, abstraction shapes and acts; it is not lost to obscurity but is substantial. Catachresis can function as a formal property or technique that exceeds immediate reference or classification through a promiscuous deployment of materials that cross categorical boundaries, allowing a specific medium to perform in ways that depart from its normal function (sculptures that resemble the viscous qualities of paint, or photographs that are more haptic than representational). Catachresis might also refer to the strained use of an existing formal language of abstraction that shows it to be already arbitrary or brings out its perversely sensuous features.

To describe abstraction is not necessarily to claim that it produces a singular meaning; however, describing abstraction can also limit it. This book explores various interpretive models for analyzing the queer politics of abstraction beyond iconographic logic. My readings will necessarily put words to nonrepresentational forms, making some associative ties to particular operations, for example, between particular materials and how they might resonate affectively. I discuss the loaded forms of abstraction (the edge, the grid, color) as tropes activated by dragging to produce alternative political possibilities or relational models. I also deploy the terms that are used to describe supposedly stable abstract forms (edge) in experimental ways to explore the term's multiple operations and effects (edging). I am often reading with and against the feminist and queer proposals that the gendered and/or sexed body shows up in abstraction, and in some cases, when it appears to be made ambiguous. Rather than pursue bodily metaphors for abstractions, I pursue these other material and spatial dynamics that are nevertheless sensual. I attempt to use language in a way that will complement abstraction's openness, shifting between the general and the specific. The formal innovations of this work prompt my analysis, which could be seen to ironically force meaning onto the forms that resist it. This does not stop me from trying, acknowledging that my words will not always stick. Even as I offer one set of possible interpretive moves, these are not prescriptive as queer abstraction remains an open horizon of possibilities.

Between Identities and Theories, Subjects and Objects

One of the dangers of writing about abstraction in relation to categories we assign to identity, as I do, is that it may seem to obscure particular lived realities. Categories are always problematically limiting and yet often necessary for our survival. While I align the operations of abstraction with those of queering, I am not using the term *queer as* an abstraction in the sense of a generalizing term that would describe all aesthetics that trouble categories or visibility. Rather, I take the tension between specificity that speaks to difference and the potential for a more expansive gesture as a productive point of departure. That these queering gestures exceed the specificity of their positions to leak out and stain the ostensibly "universal" is one aspect of their political potential. I use *queer* to describe the ways that we might relate to abstract work more affectively, haptically, and sensually, activating the *form* in *performative* to demonstrate how this work forges alternative relations, perspectives, and spaces. I mobilize theory in order to describe experiences of abstraction, and sometimes this also aligns with *feeling abstract.* In short, many of us live our theories, and theory also helps us to imagine new possibilities from what seems given or self-evident.

There is a live tension in this book between my deployments of *queer* in relation to abstraction, and the artists whose work I include under the banner of queer abstraction. Abstraction is an important exploratory site for politically invested artists from historically oppressed groups, so I take their deployments of abstraction seriously as intentional, and I take their formal and material innovations seriously as vehicles for social and political engagement. My understanding of how queer abstraction works does not hinge on the biographies of the artists who deploy it, but it does proceed from an awareness of their artistic practices and political investments. While it is the case that what the art world views as acceptable for oppressed artists to make is changing, thus, abstract practices by queer artists and BIPOC artists are increasingly embraced, this book is not concerned with defining the circumstances of that shift. Rather, I am concerned with how abstraction can operate in the service of queer, feminist, antiracist politics and theories. I suggest that abstraction can be called queer in the work of artists who are actively investigating issues of sexuality and gender in ways that forge alternatives to their categorical norms, even when the artist is not queer. This is not to say that the aims and identities of these artists do not matter, and it is usually the case that they are invested in queer politics and nonnormative ways of being due to their own social positions. Considering that the work an artist produces can operate beyond their own positions and continues to circulate in multiple contexts, I take their artistic and social practices as a starting point rather than the end point of my investigation.

While my analysis does not rely on forms of evidence linked to the artist's biography, the question of *whose* abstraction and *whose* politics still matters. The works I have chosen as central case studies, created by these artists—(in order of discussion) Ulrike Müller, Nancy Brooks Brody, Lorna Simpson, Xylor Jane, Linda Besemer, Carrie Yamaoka, Every Ocean Hughes, Sheila Pepe, Harmony Hammond, Shinique Smith, Tiona Nekkia McClodden, Angela Hennessy—also signal the core contributions of feminist work to the queer politics of abstraction. While abstraction has become increasingly viable for politically motivated art practices since the 1990s, a previous generation of feminist artists made significant strides toward this current movement, a lineage of art experimentation that I also understand to be at the heart of this current tendency. For example, in 1977, Harmony Hammond wrote in the first issue of the feminist journal *Heresies*: "If 'the personal is political' in the radical sense, we cannot separate the content of our work from the form it takes."[19] Filmmaker Barbara Hammer argued that "radical content deserves radical form," contending that conventional narrative cinema fails to address her as a lesbian spectator, and advocating for more abstract experimental cinematic forms that embrace play, complexity, multiplicity, and difference.[20] From the vantage of 1970s lesbian feminism, Hammond and Hammer contend that the radical political import of their art practices depends on a more expansive understanding of what makes certain forms and materials viable for political art and collective movements. Black feminist artists such as Howardena Pindell and Senga Nengudi have similarly expanded our conceptions of what abstraction can do in relation to identity and politics since the 1970s.[21] There are important parallels between categories of identity and difference that would describe the artists in this book, and the political strategies and aesthetic processes they deploy in their work.

Restating the terms of a politicized identity category that would describe many, though not all, of the artists whose work I discuss, I use *queer* to describe the formal and political resonance of their practices. Some artists included in my study, particularly Lorna Simpson and Shinique Smith, are not queer (as far as I know). When I describe an artist's *work* as queer, I am referring to the operations and interpretations of the work itself and the ways in which that artist's practice contributes to contestatory gender and sexual politics, which can be separate from a discussion of the artist's cultural position in that regard. Simpson's work has operated politically in relation to gender, sex, race, and even sometimes invokes queer content (gay cruising and John Waters in the work I discuss). Shinique Smith's work constitutes an ongoing political engagement with abstraction, and has been taken up by queer scholar Renate Lorenz as a form of "radical drag" that refuses direct access to bodily categories according to race and gender.[22] My project acknowledges the fraught histories of these terms as categories of identity while pressing off from that history to make space for the artwork to perform in excess of singular categories tied to their maker. It would not be politically advantageous to fully separate the work from its maker (that would repeat early formalism's claim to universal transcendence that does not account for difference); however, if I stopped with the artist's biography it would limit the potential of their work and disavow the powerful contingencies of its spectators. There are particular formal and material operations that politically engaged artists deploy through abstraction, and this book proceeds from a desire to investigate those operations.

I will argue that queer abstraction offers a contestatory site for refusing signifying logic that can be useful across multiple discourses and political modes of resistance. The visual and material processes occurring in the works I discuss align with certain intersections—between queer and feminism, between queer and trans (a position I would call genderqueer), between queer and critical race politics, between queer and crip. I do not attempt to theorize these different intersections of *identity* via abstraction; rather, I propose that abstraction offers new sites of experimentation that help us imagine alternative formations, and these align at various moments with ways of thinking of gender, sexuality, sexed embodiment, race, and/or disability beyond their singular embodied manifestations. For example, I attend to the genderqueer potential of abstraction when the work plays with seemingly gendered forms and materials; I attend to the crip potential of abstraction when I am discussing the work's deforming, destabilizing operations. These intersecting political sites of possibility are also sites of deep frustration and tension. Queer theory's embrace of a more expansive and nonspecifying understanding of *queer* as a verb cannot be so easily mapped onto other areas of difference. Queer cannot account for all nonnormative subject positions, and queer movements have their complicated histories of exclusion and misappropriation. I will not, on the one hand, ignore these potentially messy intersections in the interest of creating a falsely neat and tidy queer theory of abstraction; at the same time, I cannot fully attend to all of these complex intersections in a single book. I will attend briefly to each intersection below in order to highlight how I am building on scholarship in these areas.

Between Queer and Feminist

This book furthers some of the work of feminist art historians who have revealed the minoritized, heterogeneous, and ephemeral qualities of modernist abstraction. For example, Anna Chave and Ann Gibson have challenged dominant accounts of abstraction as a transcendent universal language, showing how abstract forms are nevertheless marked by ideologies and oppressive systems of power.[23] While these scholars demonstrate that modernist abstraction is not a universal language, the tension between seemingly unmarked aesthetics and the visual suggestion of certain minority positions marked by gender and race calls for further exploration in a contemporary context. I often cite the work of feminist scholars in my analysis of abstraction's potentially gendered implications (in both alignment with and departure from their readings). While queer and feminism are not so easily joined due to certain essentialist forms of feminism that maintain an investment in the category "woman," queer theory has also built on feminism's challenge to essentialized notions of gender and sexuality.[24] In my analysis, queer feminism refers to a social-political sphere and set of discourses and tactics that unsettle the categories of sex, gender, and sexuality in relation to embodiment and desire and the alternative possibilities and worlds that these tactics aim to create.

Between Queer and Trans

This book builds on the scholarship about practices of abstraction described as transgender, particularly the work by Jack Halberstam and, more recently, David Getsy, whose *Abstract Bodies* revises established narratives about 1960s sculpture through the lens of transgender studies.[25] In his other work, Getsy understands the queer and transgender capacities of contemporary abstraction to trouble taxonomic categories of gender and sex, as artists use it to speak from experiences of difference without recourse to the "evidence" of sexual acts or eroticized bodies.[26] Gordon Hall similarly finds possibilities in minimalist sculpture for theorizing nonnormative gendered embodiments and understands abstraction's willful silence to resist easily decipherable narratives of bodies.[27] While transgender studies scholars such as Eliza Steinbock and Jeanne Vaccaro have used the term *transgender* in expansive ways to discuss formal and aesthetic issues, the body remains central to this field as the primary vehicle through which transgender experience is understood.[28] Transgender studies scholars have also problematized queer theory's use of *trans* as a metaphor while ignoring the precarious material realities of transgender people (gender trouble, like abstraction, is not inherently liberating).[29] My insistence that queer abstraction's refusal of bodily signification is one of its most politically useful operations will not play out in the same way across queer and trans practices nor in the readings of those practices.

On the one hand, my insistence that abstraction should not be reduced to signs for the body may seem immediately at odds with transgender studies and its focus on embodiment. On the other hand, my discussion of abstraction as queer in ways that thematize gender variance in terms of nonbinary potential might seem to problematically subsume trans experiences under the banner of queer.[30] But some queer experiences also include gender nonnormativity. To say that queering can only speak to sexuality would foreclose queer experiences at the intersections of gender, sexuality, and sexed embodiment—the specific term *genderqueer* might get us closer to describing this experience.[31] Acknowledging that queer politics maintain alliances with, as well as distinctions from, trans investments, I discuss abstraction as a tool for queering that undermines surface legibility with reference to the ways we read both gender and race as transparently visible on the surface of the body (particularly in chapter 3).[32] My readings often make use of queer interpretive methods that focus on the relational possibilities of abstract form and matter, but I also consider how understandings of gender are as informed by relationality as queer sexualities and fantasies. We are gendered and raced by others, in relation to others, and that process or projection often involves some amount of desire, identification, or disidentification. My use of the term *drag* to describe queer processes of abstraction also implies the gendered or ungendering performances that make space for new possible becomings. Perhaps, then, something about gender is always at stake in my understanding of queer abstraction.

Between Queer and Black

Important foundations for understanding the politics of abstraction have been established by scholars and curators focusing on critical race perspectives and specifically Blackness in contemporary abstraction. My understanding of queer does not bracket out race, and concerns about race do not drop out when, for example, a Black person is absent from the image. Indeed, my conception of queer abstraction demands that we consider issues of race and gender without the presence of a body. Scholars and curators have countered the tendency to limit the significance of artworks by Black artists to what can be read as explicitly racial about the work, while Black artists' works are rarely the basis for formal and object-based debates.[33] Insisting on what Bennett Simpson terms a "freedom from representationality," or racially and biographically determined interpretations, new propositions for political tactics of "post-Black" art take up experimentation with medium and form as a crucial territory for resistance (departing from a focus on content and figuration).[34] Adrienne Edwards, who curated the exhibition *Blackness in Abstraction*, argues that "blackness in abstraction proliferates as a resistance to figuration and realism in visual representation, and in so doing it elides transparency, immediacy, authority, and authenticity."[35] Black is then not only a surface color (of skin), but a medium and mode of production and critical position for refusing a clear visibility or "authentic" portrayal of one's cultural position. (I explore the particular possibilities for color as a tool for queer abstraction in chapter 3.) Phillip Brian Harper's concept of "abstractionist aesthetics" demonstrates the possibilities for abstraction's distance from the sign to open space for reimagining the cultural codes to which it has such a difficult relation.[36] That is, in producing a distance between the sign and its ostensible referent, abstraction creates a catachrestic space in which the cultural conditions and positions otherwise defined by the visible signifier can be unfixed, multiply, and proliferate.

Between Queer and Crip

My analysis of queer abstraction often attends to the materiality of the artwork, and when the work's material operations are destabilizing and deforming, queering is brought into close contact with cripping, or disabling. Crip, like queer, reclaims an injurious term in the service of radical politics and unsettles fixed identities.[37] While queer theory and disability studies have been brought into alignment due to their shared critiques of normativity, the more theoretical crip approach to disability can be taken as a problematic obscuring of disabled people's lived experiences.[38] Thus, my own approach to abstraction as a refusal of bodily legibility may be taken as either a queer cripping (refusing bodily norms) or, more problematically, ignoring the ways disability is experienced in and through the body. Taking this risk, I will consider the crip perspectives offered by some forms of queer abstraction and their destabilizing effects. In *Feminist, Queer, Crip*, Alison Kafer offers a political and relational model of disability that is not inherent in particular bodies and minds (a medical model), but is a product of social relations. This makes space to lift off from the certainty of identity, from the abled/disabled binary, while offering more expansive ways of understanding disability as actions, events, encounters-between rather than inhering within a singularity.[39] Rather than ignore the crip implications of the excessive and unruly material trouble I often encounter in the queer work of abstraction, I attend to these possibilities in terms of how they affect the spectator. Disability studies scholar Jessica Cooley considers how crip works as a material instability and noncompliance in artworks, a radical potential which she theorizes as "crip materiality."[40] Here, the queer crip possibilities of abstraction are more about the experiences of being with the work, rather than the reduction of abstract form to a representation of disability.

This book aims to make a significant contribution to the scholarly conversations about the politics of abstraction, but it cannot and does not claim to make every contribution or fully address every intersection of difference in relation to these politics. Offering a centrally queer perspective and highlighting the work of particular artists is not at all to say that a political abstraction can belong to only one kind of artist or context. While I am focusing on the United States context in which most of these works and discourses circulate, some of these conversations and artworks cross national boundaries and appear elsewhere. Other studies might take a transnational approach or focus on different national contexts where queer abstraction may manifest in entirely different ways, and where conversations about modernism and the politics of form will also be different. It is my hope that dimensions of critical race, Indigenous, postcolonial, transgender, and crip politics will be taken up and developed further by other authors, and that this will be the first of many books to be written about queer abstraction.

Form Performs: Dragging and Camping

Abstraction may be defined as a drawing or dragging away from the real or concrete representations in art. But the performance of drag (as in drag queens and kings) also implies a stylistic play with gendered signifiers on the body; it is a strategic and often over-the-top reiteration of the masculine and feminine norms that we not only work to enact, but that also exert a drag on us via the everyday reinforcement of gendered behaviors. Judith Butler's now canonical theory of gender performativity posits gender as a compulsory repetition, but also shows how this repetition can create an opportunity to appropriate or exceed oppressive structures, and to throw norms of gender and sex into crisis.[41] Accordingly, I understand dragging as a form of critical recitation. Drag can draw out the oppressive strictures of gender and sexuality while at the same time exceeding and torquing those normative impulses in order to render them differently.[42] This strategy of torquing, also derived from the etymology of *queer*, is performed through various formal strategies: for example, a stable object or flat painterly surface projects outward as a radiant environment, or a photographic reproduction is rendered soft and fuzzy. Drag is often performed through an excessive materiality that oozes beyond its borders, or sensuous surface textures that invite touch and demand more intimate forms of spectatorship.

Rather than locate the queer work of abstraction through an exposure of the subject, I read abstracting as a political action of willful withdrawal, a dragging away. I use *drag* and *dragging* to describe the formal and material tactics of abstraction that undermine normative reading practices, which tend to depend on categorizing according to stable notions of difference. Artist-theorist Renate Lorenz deploys "drag" to describe queer artistic practices that create a distance from the body and normativity while still registering in terms of gender and sexuality, making connections to others without representing them: "What becomes visible in this drag is not people, individuals, subjects, or identities, but rather assemblages; indeed those that do not work at any 'doing gender/sexuality/race,' but instead at an 'undoing.'"[43] Drag both takes up and produces a distance from the norms determined by the two-gender system, whiteness, ability, and heteronormativity. That distancing, or the tension between distance and proximity, is precisely what makes these artistic strategies queer, catachrestic, and excessive. The drag of queer abstraction is a political strategy of denormalization that withdraws signifying conventions in order to make space for new spectatorial positions and possibilities.

The drag that abstraction exerts is not only a formal and aesthetic pull but is also a drag on its own history. This "temporal drag," to use Elizabeth Freeman's term, enacts a backward glance that puts the past into a disruptive and potentially transformative relation to the present.[44] Queer abstraction performs temporal drag by reworking recognizable traces of its history while also creating alternatives. Thus, while I examine the terms and incarnations of abstraction's continuation in contemporary art, I will also consider how queer abstraction retroactively transforms its own genealogy and does so with radical implications for the various forms and techniques of abstraction that it recites. This transformation is not merely the result of reading queerness back into certain historical forms, but a revision that can, just as Edward Said describes the dynamics of history, "dramatize the latencies in a prior figure or form that suddenly illuminate the present."[45] Rather than simply reuse the aesthetics of modernist abstraction or specific strategies associated with earlier movements, the contemporary works I study draw out the queer actions that are already there, and are made evident through this transhistorical exchange. Thinking with and against the history of abstraction in the field of art history, I consider the queering potential of this history, the mixed feelings and messy sensations that are reactivated by the drag exerted on them in the present. Contemporary queer abstractions may resemble formal tropes of the past, but they do not merely reproduce the same thing twice; rather, they produce something changed in the process of dragging. Though it may seem that recitations of a problematic history or canon would reinforce its power, the performative force of drag generates alternatives opening out from the gaps and spilling over from the excesses of repetitive gestures. Queering operates as creative praxis that *does* history: in this citational activation of past forms and processes, certain useful aspects of the past are made to perform differently, opening the past up to alternatives in the present.

Drag is closely aligned with the citational practices of queer camp and queer style. Queer practices of abstraction *camp* when they restyle older forms in ways that are eschewing (or actively skewering) the all-too-serious and the straitlaced in favor of the exaggerated, the over-the-top, the unnatural, and the humorous. Roland Barthes similarly views style as a citational practice which may reform or transform through excessive quotation or repetition with a difference. While style is normally taken as the superfluous aesthetic cover for the "real" or "truth" of content, Barthes understands the image as a proliferation of layers, where the "real" is not of depth, but of surface.[46] Style can operate as a queering gesture of camp, an aesthetic sensibility that resists identification even as it enacts a certain representational excess. Susan Sontag's 1964 essay "Notes on 'Camp'" defines this "sensibility" as a "mode of aestheticism," a way of seeing the world that delights in the artificial, the marginal, and the exaggerated. To practice camp is to understand the degree of artifice and excess present behind the seemingly natural or serious ("Being-as-Playing-a-Role"), and to be "alive to the double sense in which some things can be taken."[47]

An important feature of camp is its gratuitousness of reference, and the reiterative aesthetic practices of the artists whose works I study operate as forms of camping.[48] As Fabio Cleto points out, camp is an impossible object of discourse, working through semiotic destabilization in which the subject and object of discourse become collapsed.[49] The meaning attributed to the archive of referents to which the object or performance of camp gestures, then, fails to account for a legitimate origin point or historical progression, a truth of the subject covered by the artifice of the object. Instead, camp resists the notion of a substantive core or a stable foundation for its recitations, its multiple surfaces unfolding to reveal that its source of playful parody was never pure substance in the first place. By privileging the synthetic, the minor, the "low," or the frivolous in their stylistic and material recitations of abstraction's history, queer abstractions perform camp to produce alternatives from even the most difficult forms.[50]

Citations Drag: Queer Genealogies

Dragging, as an activation of material, visual, and historical relations, describes what the artworks I study are doing, and also how I study them. I consider how the citational practices of contemporary artists do not merely reproduce former aesthetics but work with abstraction's already perverse properties. My transhistorical reading practice produces queer genealogies of this work, tracing the strange legacies of aesthetic tactics that are both historically specific to modernism and expansive in postmodern contexts. This is not to claim intentional appropriations on the part of the artists, but to put this work into contact with older works in order to reckon with a burdened historical language of abstract form and how it might materialize queerly. My approach relies on an intuitive logic and relational charge that Eve Sedgwick proposes in the critical spacing of "beside," where new connections will emerge between objects, particularly those that seem incommensurate.[51] This approach is shared across other queer studies of contemporary art, such as the 2017 issue of *ASAP/ Journal* on "Queer Form," where the editors understand this comparative approach to have "pride of place in queer cultural studies," even while it is vulnerable to critique.[52] I put contemporary objects into contact with some of their potential relations from the past, exploring the possibilities that emerge from that encounter.

Abstractions are not neutral gestures—even nonrepresentational forms have histories. I show how queer abstraction attaches to and appropriates the dominant language of abstraction, which would seem to resist queering. To queer abstraction is, in part, to expose and reroute its power from a neutralizing and potentially violent erasure to a method for refusing fixity and materializing difference in unexpected ways. While abstraction is neither a modernist nor a Western invention, I am engaging with it here in the United States context as a legacy of modernism that persists in contemporary art. The particular forms that I focus on are modernist tactics that are also politically loaded and have been continuously reimagined in and for the present: the hard edge, the grid, color, and the readymade. My chapters are organized to build on one another in terms of the scale of the work and the scope of critical issues that I address. I begin with the detailed element of the hard edge in smaller works, proceeding with increasingly expansive deployments of the grid and color, and finally addressing large-scale sculptural installations. Several of the artworks utilize elements that appear in multiple chapters, so the hard edge of chapter 1 also appears in the grids of chapter 2, the grid appears in chapter 3 (on color), and color and the grid are important features of the sculptural works of chapter 4. (Color can also be seen as an important feature of the geometric abstractions in chapter 1.) I focus on particular formal and material operations in each chapter, but readers will see their overlap and dialogue across chapters. The chapters build in complexity as I address the import of queer abstraction for different intersections of difference, initially focusing on the queer eroticism of formal processes and then addressing the critical race, genderqueer, crip, and finally the queer national and decolonial potentials of abstraction's drag. In each of the four core chapters, I offer two or three key ways in which queer abstraction operates, and I use the works of several contemporary artists to offer multiple examples of the particular tactic under investigation (rather than an extensive narrative of a single artist's work).

In chapter 1, I begin an investigation of abstraction's political aims and operations through the unlikely aesthetic technique of geometry, particularly the hard-edged line. I consider how the geometric enamel objects of Ulrike Müller, Nancy Brooks Brody, and Every Ocean Hughes reconstitute the hard edge as a queer tactic. The dragging line here produces an indeterminacy and intimate friction—the bending and curving edge both refuses to contain a sign or subject and uses its hardness to produce an erotic edging. Putting Müller's work in contact with the modernist enamel works of László Moholy-Nagy, and Brody's work in contact with the shaped canvases of Ellsworth Kelly, I show how these lines of movement reconfigure the space of the picture plane in ways that not only exceed binary logic but allow for movements at the margins.

In chapter 2, I consider the grid as an aesthetic and political tactic in the photo-based felt installation works of Lorna Simpson and their refraction of Agnes Martin's iconic grid paintings. Carrying the difficult history of photographic grids, which produce raced taxonomies of their subjects, Simpson's grids refuse to picture bodies. I demonstrate that, far from only a tool of normalization and surveillance, the grid also operates as a vector for queer forms of relationality. These grids perform their drag through an infinite expansion and excess and produce spaces for transformation. I also bring grid paintings by Xylor Jane into contact with those of Jasper Johns to demonstrate how these seemingly closed systems for encoding information can disrupt it at the same time through their decorative surface and sensual tactility.

In chapter 3, I reconsider color as an unruly medium in the sculptural acrylic paintings of Linda Besemer, and I challenge conceptions of color as mere surface used to mark exceptional bodies as raced and gendered. Color's minor and deviant associations are activated and challenged in the genealogy I trace from Besemer back to Lynda Benglis and the op art (optical art) of Bridget Riley. By wrestling with the tension between the optical surface of color and its viscous materiality, this chapter attends to the fraught ontological implications of painting in the modernist tradition (as opposed to readings of paint as "skin" particularly in the work of women artists).[53] These chromatic abstractions drag via their performative surface play—seemingly synthetic and also resistant to signification, color can also exceed codes of race and gender. The work of color as a surface for imaginative projection is further activated in the work of Carrie Yamaoka, where the viewer is implicated in our own gazing.

In the fourth chapter, I focus on spatial and material tactics of dragging away: unruly and expansive installations that transform everyday matter. I consider how the threaded environments of Sheila Pepe, sculptures by Harmony Hammond and Shinique Smith, and an installation by Tiona Nekkia McClodden perform material processes that deform by unraveling, ripping, and cutting. The deforming processes of these large-scale works speak to vexed queer and crip formations that paradoxically resist fixity or material coherence. Reckoning with their foundations in minimalist and postminimal sculpture as well as the discarded readymade and associations with craft, these works drag the art object itself (the canvas or sculpture) to destabilize and make precarious that which seems established or given: the materials they alter, the spaces they occupy, and the perspectives and positions they elicit.

The epilogue reckons with that overloaded sign of queer "pride"—the rainbow flag—to test and push the limits of abstraction's political potential. Gesturing out from one of my core utopian propositions that we might yet find ways of being together in difference, the rainbow flag brings up issues of queer citizenship and homonationalism (Jasbir Puar's term) in the United States context and opens out to decolonial and global possibilities across borders.[54] I show how Angela Hennessy's *Black Rainbow* drags the flag by challenging the ostensible universality of our rainbow politics, dragging on a transcendent gesture of world-making to emphasize the unending physical and affective labors of abstraction.

In each chapter, I explore the continued political relevance of abstract aesthetics for United States–based contemporary artists whose work operates queerly. At the same time, I show how artists deploy and redeploy these forms and materials in ways that reimagine their own genealogies. Their redeployments remind us that abstraction is already political and demonstrate its viability for queer movements now. Locating queer invention in formal and material experimentation as well as reiterative practices, I am staging conversations between contemporary abstraction and the older forms and techniques of abstraction that they drag. Many of the abstract forms used by contemporary artists are borrowed from high modernism and many draw more closely from works created during the 1960s and '70s, a moment understood to be the start of the contemporary period. Working postmodernism through a transhistorical lens, I trace genealogies of queered and queering forms of abstraction through the work of midcentury painters such as Ellsworth Kelly (chapter 1) and Agnes Martin (chapter 2), iterations of minimalism and postminimalism and various forms of geometric abstraction from the grid to op art. Understanding that all of these artworks have their own citational impulses, and that my earliest examples are themselves reiterations of earlier modernist forms, some distinction can be made between the modernist discourses the artworks engage and the time in which those modernist forms were produced. For example, when I am discussing later works by Kelly or Martin, it is through that work that I also engage a longer history of geometric abstraction and its utopian political ambitions that preceded it by several decades.

The temporal framework for this project is not a linear historical narrative of modernism through postmodernism, but a close examination of current practices that stage specific conversations by redeploying certain abstract forms. The strange trajectory and genealogy of this book is created by allowing the work itself to lead me through these citational layers, without viewing US modernism as though it were a monolithic historical formation. In making these comparisons, I aim to show how the queer redeployments of these forms in contemporary art reveal new possibilities in the older works, suggesting that perhaps these queer capacities have been there all along but are now made active in the present. Modernism has never belonged only to those who dominate the canon, and my project seeks to show how some aspects of modernist abstraction continue to be operational now.

My queer formalist approach takes the material and visual qualities of artworks seriously as political and theoretical interventions. I conduct the kinds of comparative analysis that are foundational in the field of art history, while also taking the lesson from queer theoretical approaches to history that putting the present in contact with the past can transform both. In addition to Freeman's theory of temporal drag, my art historical juxtapositions might be considered akin to Jack Halberstam's "techno-topias": a collision of postmodern space and embodiment, sought by exploring new relations and shared aesthetics between avant-garde and contemporary subcultural visual practices.[55] My focus on the affective and relational charge of abstract forms across time also attends to the difficulty and tension of these relationships, between the potential harm of abstraction and the present work that attempts to retool it. This book is deeply indebted to the work of José Esteban Muñoz, who understands queering as an aesthetic praxis of refusal that does not simply discard that which is problematic and overloaded (in the case of this book, abstract forms that would seem to either gloss over difference or to mark for difference, such as the triangle), but rather works with and through those elements toward which the queer has a charged and ambivalent relationship.[56] This concept of a queer utopian aesthetic practice, as I understand it, is an extension of Muñoz's theory of *disidentification*, a practice that acknowledges the difficulty of identification and does not claim to dispel its shameful elements; "rather, like a melancholic subject holding on to a lost object, a disidentifying subject works to hold on to this object and invest it with new life."[57] Queer abstraction might similarly describe the ambivalent attachment to abstraction in contemporary art practices that claim abstract forms and styles in order to rework them while also acknowledging their potential for harm. In short, queer abstractions create mixed feelings, and my analysis attempts to account for this affective charge without resolving its tensions.

Dragging, Reading: Toward a Materialist Formalism

One premise of this book is that queer abstraction demands a retooling of older art historical methods that take forms and materials as fundamentally political, while also exposing the already present politics of these methods. Utilizing a process of formalism that is not opposed to matter or culture, I take form and matter seriously as their own social and cultural interventions.[58] Jennifer Doyle and David Getsy describe "queer formalism" as approaches to art making and art historical analysis that consider how gender, sexuality, and desire operate beyond their straightforward depictions.[59] Yet, a queer rejection of purity or essentialism runs counter to the universalism we typically associate with formalist methods. There are clear tensions between the terms of formalism and abstraction that describe earlier modern practices of making and analyzing art and the destabilizing operations that are now understood as queer. My approach to queer abstraction drags on this tradition of formalism that would seem to exclude investments in the social and political potential of art.

Just as abstraction is so often taken to bracket out the social, formalism as a method is presumed to be a politically "disinterested" model (often attached to more conservative positions). Some methodological debates would set formalist art historical approaches rooted in the legacy of Clement Greenberg, on the one hand, against identity politics taken up by cultural studies approaches, on the other.[60] But formal and social concerns need not be mutually exclusive. Forms can provide models for living otherwise, generating ethical and political alternatives via the queer practices called "world-making."[61] I am exploring the queer possibilities for formalist and materialist approaches here, and I will make an argument for why these are useful if we are to take abstraction seriously. But these artworks' capacities are informed by multiple factors, and other scholars may wish to focus on those factors that hinge more explicitly on the object's immediate context. Here, I am focusing on the social and political potential of abstraction that emerges from haptic forms and visceral material operations and how they speak with certain modernist traditions and discourses. I do consider form and matter to be suggestive of certain things rather than hopelessly undefined, but my readings consider how abstraction works queerly through affective, sensual, and material operations both within the work itself and in relation to the spectator.

My reading practices are aligned with a new materialist approach in that I take matter seriously as having its own unruly affective and sensational currents, and I consider how artworks queer through their performative materializing.[62] The central case studies of this book often transform certain modernist formal tactics by material means, so I attend closely to the haptic qualities of the artworks and their movements in the processes of taking form. Our visceral response to this work is folded in with its texture. Approaching textural perception in relation to affect, Eve Sedgwick's *Touching Feeling* records the flow of intimacy between textures and emotions, dragging with it the association with "touchy-feely," implying that "even to talk about affect virtually amounts to cutaneous contact."[63] The visceral is not divorced from the abstract; both are folded together and flexibly intertwined, as forms and processes of abstraction can also evoke or invite touch and have implications for ways of being in the world.

New materialist thought usefully reconsiders normative understandings of agency, which, Karen Barad argues, is not something possessed by a singular being, but an enactment, something that comes about through relational flows and responses that do not belong solely to the human. Barad's conception of agential matter that "feels, converses, suffers, desires, yearns, and remembers" aligns with my understanding of materiality as a crucial queering tactic that does not merely encode aesthetic form with stable bodily meaning, but produces an affective force both visually and texturally.[64] Offering a freedom from representation, abstraction is a performative force, a dragging away from signification or any kind of ontological certainty. Rather than a hardening or fixing of difference, abstracting materializes an active ongoing process, generates excessive multiplicities, and demands more intimate reading practices to account for the experience of these artworks.

I am utilizing these queer reading practices to attend to the ways in which form and meaning do not easily line up in the works I discuss. I would not say that abstraction is "inherently" queer, but its resistance presents such a generous site of possibility for the socially and politically motivated artists who use it and for queer analysis that can account for its visceral powers. The power is already there but is more fully activated by a formal analysis that considers the material interactions with and between objects. Dragging in a slow reading practice of close looking, I produce intimate descriptions of these objects to demonstrate their sensual and relational force. This force both amplifies and is amplified by a viewer's particular sensibilities. Cultivating this queer formalism by accounting for something excessive in the object also means staying attuned to how interpretation will always fall short—the catachresis performed when we try to describe how something feels, to translate the sensations that exceed description. I take a materialist approach to formal analysis by attending to the processes of formation and haptic vibrancy of the object, how media take form and interact, and how an object might feel to touch. These readings suggest that being with the work itself constitutes a queer experience. In what follows, I elaborate what queer abstraction might activate in this difficult space of encounter.

1   EDGING GEOMETRY

Glistening enamel forms unite on a small steel panel: a black half circle converges with white corners on the right, while deep teal meets pale pink on the left. The black enamel arcs down and fans sharply back out at the bottom, curving against its support and nearly spilling over the edge. The composition is divided in the center where triangular teal and half-circle black forms meet in a vertical line; they share an edge and are defined by the same cutting line on two sides, meeting a small red wedge at the upper center of the panel. The glossy surface of this object makes its darkest forms near-mirrors of the space around it; its lightest colors invite the play of light. The enamel remains suspended, but it threatens to flow over the edge of its support where it gathers thickly, pressing its borders. This vitreous enamel painting on steel by Ulrike Müller, from the series *Some* (2017) (see plate 1), demonstrates geometric abstraction as an unlikely aesthetic tactic for queering by contemporary artists. Dragging in a material convergence and resistance, these paintings suggest a tense pressure and ambivalence in both their formal visual language and their relation to the history of modernist geometry.

Müller has produced multiple series of these enamel paintings since the mid-2000s, reimagining the formal compositions of early twentieth-century painting, producing hard-edged, abstract geometric forms in a craft-based medium that also creates sharp lines and slick, swelling surfaces. The seeming impenetrability of geometry as a technique of abstraction, its resistance to aesthetic, material, or subjective excess, would also seem antithetical to the production of a queer visual language. The strict sharpness of geometric abstraction might not have the affective or sensual qualities we would expect of queer art—its austerity seems too closed off. The hard edge produces a sharp borderline that might define forms, mark a cutting division between figures, or produce a rift between the visual field and the rest of the world. The hard edge might appear to secure an undifferentiated subject, or a sign used to mark a subject (such as the triangle, which I will discuss at the end of this chapter). And yet, geometric abstraction and particularly its legacy in hard-edge painting is a vibrant site for recitation by contemporary artists, like Müller, who produce work in the service of collective queer feminist movements. In this chapter, I show how the hard edge performs as a feature of queer abstraction by dragging on a visual language of geometry to make strategic use of nonobjective forms, while also generating spaces for connection and eroticism. Exploring this temporal drag along with the fugitive formal drag of linear edges that refuse containment, queer geometric abstractions demonstrate the resistant possibilities of even the harshest or seemingly foreclosed abstract language.[1]

While modernist geometric abstraction is tied to radical political movements in early twentieth-century European art, geometry seems a strange aesthetic strategy for queering now, a century later, with the presumed exhaustion and failure of those utopian ambitions.[2] Geometric abstraction is historically associated with utopian aims and revolutionary politics—for example, constructivism utilized rational, nonobjective form in service of the Bolshevik Revolution.[3] But in contemporary art, viewed through our postmodern lenses, those ambitions for abstraction to serve collective political goals seem impossible. We no longer believe in the kinds of spiritual transcendence and universality that those earlier artists claimed for abstraction, and the art that we now invest with any hope for social and political change is typically the most didactic, narrative, and representational (because it seems the most transparent). So, what might geometric abstraction do for contemporary artists who are invested in queer feminist politics?

Ulrike Müller is not the only artist who uses hard-edge abstract geometry as a device of queering. This chapter includes the work of Nancy Brooks Brody, who creates enamel *Color Forms* that I consider to reimagine the shaped canvases of Ellsworth Kelly, a postwar artist associated with hard-edge and color-field painting. Brody's asymmetrical monochrome shapes are painted enamel on metal and are embedded into gallery walls rather than hung. Although their surfaces are hard, they appear liquid, fluid, undulating in the light. They are also very small, potentially handheld, so they are more intimate than the monumental shaped canvases. Sadie Benning similarly uses a language of hard-edge painting where two distinct shapes are paired to create sculptural wall reliefs. But the edges of Benning's paintings are soft and uneven, and their surfaces appear malleable.[4] Carrie Moyer's paintings stage visual conversations between hard-edged forms and gestural pouring in acrylic that often includes glitter. Paolo Arao creates geometric abstractions using textiles to explore queer spatial dynamics. If harsh lines are used to delineate shapes in the works of these artists, their excessive and unruly materials tend to produce edges that also activate another sense of edging that drags away. These works tend to render geometric abstraction in more fluid ways, through both mediums that seem to verge on spilling out beyond the confines of their support and their imprecise rendering of lines and surfaces.

While the work of several artists could be discussed in terms of queering geometric abstraction, the works of Ulrike Müller and Nancy Brooks Brody are compelling case studies due to their explicit citation of avant-garde modernist geometry along with their paradoxical material qualities that signal a queer ambivalence. They have the formal austerity of mechanical geometric aesthetics along with the handcrafted imprecisions and haptic fluidity that more readily elicit queer sensibilities. Müller's work has gained critical attention both for drawing on the formal history of twentieth-century painting and for the sensuality of form and suggestion of queer communal ideals for which the artist is known.[5] This could also be said for Brody's practice and extended association with the queer feminist artist collective fierce pussy.[6] Here, I consider the potential for their investments in queer feminist art activism to extend through formal and material practices. I demonstrate that Müller's and Brody's enamel paintings produce hard edges that are both cutting borders and active margins. These edges do the political work of shifting and challenging the limits of their physical borders and the limits of their formal histories in an edgy avant-garde aesthetic process. Considering the double edge of the *edge* that operates as both a noun and a verb (an edge and an *edging*), the lines of these enamel paintings drag away from the containment of borderlines by which the hardness of geometric abstraction might otherwise be understood.

Even as Müller's objects are specifically taken by others to constitute a queering of modernist forms, they are also assumed by some viewers and critics to reference the body.[7] For example, these abstract objects were included in an exhibition, *Figurative Geometry*, where the work was understood to "abstract representation" by referring to bodies through an abstract, geometric language.[8] In another exhibition, these works are similarly understood as abstract engagements with the figure.[9] Müller's work is understood to queer by camping a modernist formal language in ways that ostensibly bring it into contact with the body.[10] These readings interpret the queerness of this work only by way of reference and do not address the queering work of abstraction itself. I suggest, instead, that these objects do queer work precisely by dragging on the loaded visual language of the hard edge that can at once divide a space or mark a figure *and* insist on a margin that edges away from strict certainty and opens up to indeterminacy.

Scholars and critics have also noticed that Müller's enamel paintings have paradoxical material qualities: they have hard surfaces while they also pull away from the boundaries that their edges might seem to secure. David Getsy considers Ulrike Müller as an artist making abstraction from a queer perspective: "Müller's coupled geometric forms have boundaries and interfaces that blur slightly due to the material. Visual differences of color and line are all made inextricable from (and intimately related to) each other once the powdered glass becomes fused through heat into one solid matrix. Divisions become continuities. Such work reminds us how materials and processes can also be used to evoke the complexities of personhood and its accruals, transformations, and exchanges."[11] Getsy notes the play along a boundary that makes distinct and divides yet also blurs and blends. I am taking up the beginnings of this conversation about the queering potential of geometric abstraction in Müller's work in order to explore this indeterminacy, this slipperiness. These slick surfaces and dragging lines refuse a signifying, figurative logic. This work might seem to produce edges as clear boundaries, but they also edge away from figuration toward a fugitive edginess that actively opens up space on the peripheries of the expected or normative.

Müller has produced several series of these enamel objects utilizing basic lines and shapes that evoke a crisp Bauhaus aesthetic (generally mechanical, impersonal), and yet interact with one another and the borders of their compositions in ways that suggest an erotic proximity. Nancy Brooks Brody's *Color Forms* similarly evoke monochrome color field paintings and shaped canvases, yet their small scale and physical intervention in the architecture also prompt an intimate spectatorship. This eroticism is also generated by lines and edges that produce a sense of excess and movement into an unmarked zone, a wildness that refuses containment. Certainly, if we read these works according to a representational or signifying logic, we might find bodily associations, particularly if we are aware of Müller's previous body-based performance work or Brody's more representational projects with fierce pussy. But how else might we understand these objects to do queer work? Even if these works seem to ask that we read them as sexualized signs—they have the literal material quality of flat, shiny metal street signs—they do not reduce the queer to bodies and sex, nor reify what we might presume to "count" as a queer body or sex act. That is, if they appear as material signs, they do not point stably to a signified but instead suggest a site of connection between different forms or spaces. If they seem to direct us, they also move us toward a space of indeterminacy, where the undefined and undefinable finds expression without settling.

Rather than ask how sexuality or gender shows up in Müller's and Brody's works in the figural sense, I explore how their works reactivate a history of geometric abstraction to both destabilize processes of signification and yet still activate or speak to the kinds of networks and affiliations on which queer life depends. Rendered in an aesthetic language that evokes avant-garde geometries and hard-edge abstract painting, how might their objects posit queer challenges to the sign, along with readings that attempt to decode certain forms as legible signifiers of difference? Rather than an outdated aesthetic strategy, geometry's importance for modernist critiques of representational, pictorial convention is still useful for queer challenges to processes of signification. Here, the hard edge gives way to a transitory process of edging that unfixes and exceeds containment.

Dragging the Edge

While "hard-edge painting" designates a specific tendency or movement in late 1950s and 1960s art, I also use the term *hard-edge* more expansively to describe a formal device of geometric abstraction in general. That is, I will deal with the term as it is understood in the specific mid-twentieth-century context (exemplified by the work of Ellsworth Kelly) and also as a form or aesthetic with iterations in earlier avant-garde contexts (exemplified by the work of László Moholy-Nagy). In selecting these particular examples, I do not mean to flatten these movements by excluding the many possible influences or points of comparison one could make, such as the importance of women artists and designers of the Bauhaus who could be claimed as feminist forerunners. I chose these comparisons because they take on some of the most iconic operations of hard-edge geometry in earlier modernist contexts, and because Brody's and Müller's works take on some of the same formal and material qualities. By exploring their enamel work through queer genealogies and comparison to the avant-garde and the midcentury forms they drag, I will demonstrate how hard geometric edges can still offer a visual and political strategy for undermining an iconographic logic by which form is solidified into a bodily sign. It may be that hard edges and geometric abstractions have always had these capacities, but it is through their current deployments by artists such as Müller and Brody that we can now notice how they operate in ways that are useful for queer art practices.

The hard edge in geometric abstraction can perform as an opening, a pulling or dragging away that opens a space for the freedom of experimentation and play. The edge can marginalize; it can do harm as a cutting border. At the same time, it operates as a fugitive tactic that incites movement, giving an edge or power to a marginal space. Working with and through this historical baggage in a form of disidentification, queering redeployments of the hard edge activates its potential to generate alternative worlds, reimagining their own loaded visual histories.[12] This is not to generate a utopian space where the potential for the sharp piercing of the edge is lost or forgotten but instead holds on to the edge's difficulty and hardness while also producing alternatives.[13] This difficulty and ambivalence is precisely what makes the edging a queer strategy: the cutting margin also produces possibilities for alternate movements and undefined directions, a slipperiness that does not slide into settled singular meaning but can chart new territories for something like belonging or freedom.

While the hard edge might seem to foreclose the possibility for excess, blocking any expressive gesture, it can open out from the margins and produce an indeterminacy. The term *hard-edge* developed out of the 1959 exhibition *Four Abstract Classicists* curated by Jules Langsner, who used the term to describe California artists using clean edges, uniform shapes, and flat colors to produce total abstractions: "Forms are finite, flat, rimmed by a hard, clean edge. These forms are not intended to evoke in the spectator any recollections of specific shapes he may have encountered in some other connection."[14] The hard edge has historically worked as an essential design element in early twentieth-century geometric art: the line was both a primary means of mark-making and an industrial, accessible element of a democratized aesthetic strategy. Seemingly neutral and objective, the hardened borders of geometric form could speak to modern forms of social organization, uniting craft with industrial design (in the work of Bauhaus artists, for example). Forms of geometric abstraction that manifested in hard-edge painting and minimalist sculpture of the 1960s were similarly preoccupied with the mechanical and seemingly impersonal manufacturing of objects, the systematic structuring of space, and clean lines and surfaces that were undisrupted by expressive mark-making. While Langsner called this work "classical" due to its order and austerity—"form in a classical work is defined, explicit, ponderable, rather than ambiguous or fuzzily subjective"—Lawrence Alloway argued that "it is too schematic a method to make classical anything hard and precise, and romantic, anything fuzzy and personally autographic."[15] Alloway took up Langsner's term "hard-edge" instead, because the forms of color in this work "depend on the edge as a clear hinge, unsoftened by atmosphere, unbroken by overlapping."[16] Alloway also understood this work to be "systematic painting," a shift from expressionism to an interest in painting determined by formulaic order.[17]

Geometric abstraction would seem to produce no excess or ambiguity, but this discourse around the origins of *hard-edge* begs the question of why this fuzziness would necessarily be tied to subjectivity or autographic expression. The clean lines and flat planes might speak more readily to the mechanic or readymade mass-produced object that distances its production from the artist's hand. And yet, mechanical production does also produce some excess, something unexpected in the slippage of our encounter with that which would seem detached from the human. I want to explore how geometric abstraction can operate queerly, not as a necessary reflection of the body, not as a stable "look," but as an edging arc or process that generates alternative forms of knowing and being. It is not the case that these queered geometries merely reinsert the expressive gestural qualities that the modernist hard edge disregarded. Rather, they generate a more expansive, unruly edge or line that opens onto a void of uncertainty, edging away from the cutting legibility in rectilinear Euclidean terms that the hard edge would otherwise seem to enforce.

If geometry offers formulas for mapping the relation between signs and figures, the shapes and positions of figures in space, what might a queer feminist conception of geometry do differently? Considering that these forms of geometric abstraction might also offer alternative political possibilities, I am inspired in part by feminist philosopher Karen Barad's critical rethinking of feminist tools of analysis—positionality and intersectionality—as geometrically constrained and their understanding of identity formation as mutually transforming material processes.[18] The artwork in this chapter might produce a model for imagining queer relations and spaces—openings for positionalities and relationalities that exceed a strict geometric imaginary. I will consider primarily how their spatial and material operations produce these possibilities. These works configure space in ways that not only exceed binary logic but also allow for affective movements and trajectories across unsettled orientations and unsettling formations of difference. Pressing the margins, this challenging roughness offers a bending and curving away that both destabilizes and opens out.

Edging offers a tactic for opening up the queer possibilities that the notion of edge—as containment, border, or outline that fixes or holds—seems to refuse or keep at bay. Edging produces spatial variability within geometric formats that refuse singular definition or settled location, allowing for more expansive conceptions of positions and relations between subjects. Reforming that which is seemingly problematic beyond repair, the double valence of edge as a noun and a verb slips beyond the linear force of a cutting straight line. This indeterminate betweenness and uncertainty is useful, I would argue, precisely because it is not entirely clear of difficult associations or even terms of injury. In the following sections, I elaborate on the ways in which Müller's and Brody's queer feminist geometries drag the edge to produce different kinds of intimate encounters, evoking queer desire and eroticism while at the same time refusing the figurative logic that is often projected onto geometric forms.

Slippery When Wet: Erotic Edges

Ulrike Müller produces abstract geometric compositions across multiple media: enamel painting, drawing, prints, and textiles. I am focusing particularly on the enamel objects to attend to their severe edges and paradoxical material qualities. Their lines create both sharp divisions and slippery curves; their surfaces are hard and slick, yet they also appear liquid. They seem to be at once hardened dry and still wet, a protective coating and a fragile glassy substance. Enamel is both an industrial and craft medium, carrying connotations of mechanically produced street signs and jewelry making. A substance associated in the history of art and design with decorative surface, enamel is used by Müller to produce strict geometric compositions that link them to modernist and minimalist aesthetics. This proliferation of associations and operations that are often contradictory also produces a generative difficulty, a hardness, or a troubling of the expected in that they drag on some of the qualities of geometric abstraction in order to render it far more sensual and open. They are undefined and proliferative in their edging effects. The hardness of their lines and surfaces drags on the margins of a trapping, categorizing boundary to edge away from the expected foreclosure that might be produced by those same forms.

These objects operate queerly through this deviant lining and material excess: the slippery line and suggestion of wetness that produces an erotic experience, but one that might occur through the spectator's interaction with the object rather than an abstracted depiction of bodies and sex. The form and matter of the work itself might create eroticism that could potentially be experienced by a viewer. Müller's enamel paintings drag on a modernist geometric language that aimed to remove the signature of the artist's hand from the work (refusing a singular subjective meaning) while at the same time refusing the ostensible "purity" and essentialism of those aesthetics, making them look and feel dirty. They generate this eroticism without settling into bodily legibility; the choice of enamel medium is significant in this refusal of a surface that could be read in corporeal terms (a softer surface or conventional paint might be more easily reduced to skin). Yet even in their hardness, these objects do not foreclose a relational capacity.

Müller's craft-based practice and geometric compositions draw on Bauhaus aesthetics: crisp lines and stark geometric shapes that intersect and interact to produce abstract designs. Relationships between forms and colors are explored across multiple media and formats, both industrial and craft. Müller's enamels drag back particularly to the enamel "constructions" of László Moholy-Nagy. Their compositions are quite different: the colors and curves of Müller's are distinct from the straight lines and limited primary color palette of Moholy-Nagy's. And yet, they share a similar scale and surface facture as well as a certain playful tension between the handmade and mechanical.

In 1923, Moholy-Nagy exhibited a series of five enamel objects: pictures on steel that were manufactured by a porcelain-enamel sign factory. Moholy-Nagy described his vision of painting according to "objective standards" achieved through "neutral geometric forms"—Brigid Doherty explains that these efforts depended on the "smooth, impersonal handling of pigment, renouncing all textural variation."[19] This removal of the artist's hand from the facture of the work was achieved through an impersonal production process: Moholy-Nagy claimed to have ordered his work by telephone from a sign factory, dictating his compositions using graph paper and transmitting nonvisual information encoded by coordinate systems rather than a mimetic image rendered by hand.[20] Pursuing these "objective standards" to exceed the capacities of the human was also an effort to produce a universally communicable art: the idea of an image as a construction, as transferable data rendered accessible through the democratic promise of modern technology. In a Duchampian performance of the artist as generator of ideas rather than craftsperson, Moholy-Nagy's radical move to exhibit these readymade industrial products-as-paintings distanced the work from the artist's subjectivity in both their production and their abstraction.

Three of Moholy-Nagy's enamel works share the same composition: a vertically oriented white field, bisected by a thick vertical black panel to the left of center (see plate 2). Two sets of small perpendicular lines intersect at the upper center (yellow and black), and at the bottom of the composition (red and yellow), also intersecting with the black panel. They are simple arrangements of straight lines and primary colors: the lines are oriented vertically and horizontally, so that it is apparent they were composed on a standard grid and their colors selected from the company's chart. This standardized, mechanical production and appearance aimed to make art more utilitarian, essential, and in line with modern life. The fact that they look and feel akin to street signs and the slick surfaces of household appliances might draw on viewers' everyday experiences and associations. The precision of this work is presumably the opposite of ornament: straight lines, no decorative excess, no expressive or autographic marks.

Müller's enamel objects take on a similarly smooth surface facture and scale, but what this comparison makes evident is the way in which their seemingly "objective" medium or "neutral" lines are rendered through an emphatically handcrafted process that playfully asserts a sense of intimate contact and eroticism. Rather than the industrial porcelain-enamel applied uniformly across the surface by a machine, the vitreous enamel of Müller's objects is sifted across the surface by hand, producing varying thicknesses and degrees of imprecision. Rather than the coded logic of color charts and standard grids used to dictate a composition, Müller's compositions are more playful. They utilize the hard line differently, producing an interplay between straight and curved edges. In one example from the series *Curls* (2017) (see plate 3), a thick, vertical, peach-colored line appears to separate a black half circle on the left from a field of white on the right. But then, the black also extends to the other side of this central line, a small curve protruding into the white field at the bottom of the panel, and the white field extends and curls up over the line at the top of the composition. The peach color also fills the space at the top and bottom corners to the left of the black semicircle, while a small arc of teal blue appears at the top right corner over the white field. The interplay between forms creates some ambivalence. At first it seems that the peach color is the "ground" against which the "figure" of the black form emerges, but the curvature of forms and interaction between fields of color complicate this relationship. Just as one plane or shape emerges in relation to another, the lack of distinction between them further confuses figure and ground, as their edge is produced by the fusion of enamel. In Moholy-Nagy's work, figure-ground relations are not complicated—it appears as if the black, red, and yellow lines are set as figures against the larger white field. Müller's works are more ambiguous because figure and ground are difficult to parse. The edges of their forms fuse together so that, even in the boundary between colors that distinguish shapes, the line is deployed as both a visual division and a material space of contact and connection. This produces a sharp boundary that is also melding, a uniform material surface that is also inconsistent.

Lifting off from the vertical-horizontal orientation of Moholy-Nagy's work, Müller's use of line often diverges in multiple directions. Lines merge and conjoin and depart in curves and arcs that produce a suggestion of intimate touch, a brushing against, a friction of drag. Their compositions often divide vertically to produce a playful, or strained, relation between either side of the composition. They often suggest a multiplicity in the mirroring that occurs within as well as beyond their surfaces: the shining reflective colored glass creates a distorted mirror of the viewer's space. Müller's series *Mirrors* (2013) plays with this concept, but their surfaces are never really flat, they undulate and ripple so they may reflect light and create shadow but never a duplicate picture. That rippling surface also creates a sense of depth, even as these are thin, flat objects. Their wetness, along with the play between sharp cuts and arced lines, refuses the precision of a Bauhaus construction or an industrial product, insisting on a more intimate spectatorship.

The ways in which this work might both invite projection and create a topography in which we are oriented, and those orientations shift, suggests queer desire and eroticism. I am considering this eroticism in terms of a material sensuality and spatial orientation, and by thinking with Sara

Ahmed's understanding of sexuality as a spatial and directional formation, the "queer phenomenology" of how bodies and worlds are shaped in proximity.[21] In relation to these objects, our own positions might become precarious as they prompt us to move closer to their surfaces while also obscuring the very reflection we might hope to see there. If we think sexuality beyond the sex act—as a form of relationality belonging as much in the realm of fantasy as in the everyday, as a precarious positioning of ourselves in relation to others, and as a connection that is plural and has multiple vectors—we can also imagine how queer desire can be activated in our encounter with these objects. Renate Lorenz's understanding of sexuality as a medium, and queer sex as more than merely a bodily act, is similarly useful, particularly when encountering abstract work that does not project a figure or body but rather creates a space of desire and reflection between the self and the social realm: "standing before the work, beholders reflect on their own social positioning in the world and experience it as maneuverable."[22] Understanding sexuality as a medium, and desire as a method, we might consider how the slippery edges of Ulrike Müller's enamel objects both draw us in and shift our perspective through curving line and the oscillating spaces of figure-ground that create a disorienting composition. In contrast to the pristine, crisp rectilinearity of a Bauhaus aesthetic, these objects take on an artificial aesthetic (perhaps read as camp) that draws on and produces a collective fantasy, something excessive that is shared rather than singular.

The "edging" that this work performs also refers to a form of sexual denial associated with BDSM: keeping one in a heightened state of arousal for an extended period of time. Edging is both a form of control (self-control or consensual domination) and a boundary play between pleasure and pain. This quivering on the borders of withheld and extended pleasure also produces an excess; not a border control that prevents movement or moves only according to the normative logic of a linear climax, but a process of pulling away in order to push over the edge. The edging performed by Ulrike Müller's enamels might similarly suggest a cutting that wounds and a movement that drags out to sustain an intimate contact, or to exceed boundaries that produce pain and also give way to pleasure. Moving beyond the edge-as-border that might police boundaries between sexualities and genders, they do the edging work of moving away from containment. Evoking the uncomfortable and discomfiting aspects of intimacy, these lines that curve and bend also press the margins to suggest an opening out, a creation of space for nonnormative relations and life on the edges.

The intimacy of Müller's enamel objects also becomes apparent in their scale. All of these enamel paintings are roughly fifteen by twelve inches, but Müller has also produced a series of *Miniatures*: tiny, wearable enamel paintings (figure 1.1). They are each just two inches tall, with a metal ring piercing the top so that the object can be hung or worn as a necklace. These minipaintings are even more obviously handcrafted than the larger paintings. They relate most clearly to jewelry, but the enamel frit is more difficult to control at this small scale, so there is less precision. They begin to look messy and fuzzy with a suggestion of touch, as if their colors have been smudged. These tiny objects are more intimate in form and function: they suggest a keepsake one could hold in their hand, perhaps given by a friend or lover. At the same time, their ongoing multiplication suggests a collectivity or a communal art project. This furthers my understanding that queer abstractions often intimately involve an embodied viewer who potentially has a sensual material exchange with the object, but that the object need not be identifiable according to some figural legibility in order to do this work.

This shift in scale also relates to Moholy-Nagy's enamels. Three of the five "Telephone Pictures" share an identical composition, scaled to progressive sizes (small, medium, large) in order to study the effects of scale on color combinations.[23] It would seem that the repetition of an identical composition across three variations in scale would produce the same product, yet subtle differences emerge. We begin to notice the relationality of scale, how the largest picture relates more to a street sign, while the smallest could easily be held. While Moholy-Nagy aimed to produce a "pure" design, devoid of the inessential elements of expression, Müller's deployment of the same materials embraces the ornamental and is not at all essential or pure. At the same time, their abstract geometric designs are not removed from the everyday. There is something particularly queer about their smallness, their decorative flourish—minor and inessential qualities that are often assigned to the queer and the feminine. At once intimate and campy, these objects of care (of careful production, of something held close) transform the hardened borders of a mechanical, formal language of geometry into a slippery vector that drags up queer

FIGURE 1.1 Ulrike Müller, *Miniatures*, 2011. Vitreous enamel on steel, 2 × 1¼ in. Ongoing edition of wearable miniature paintings.

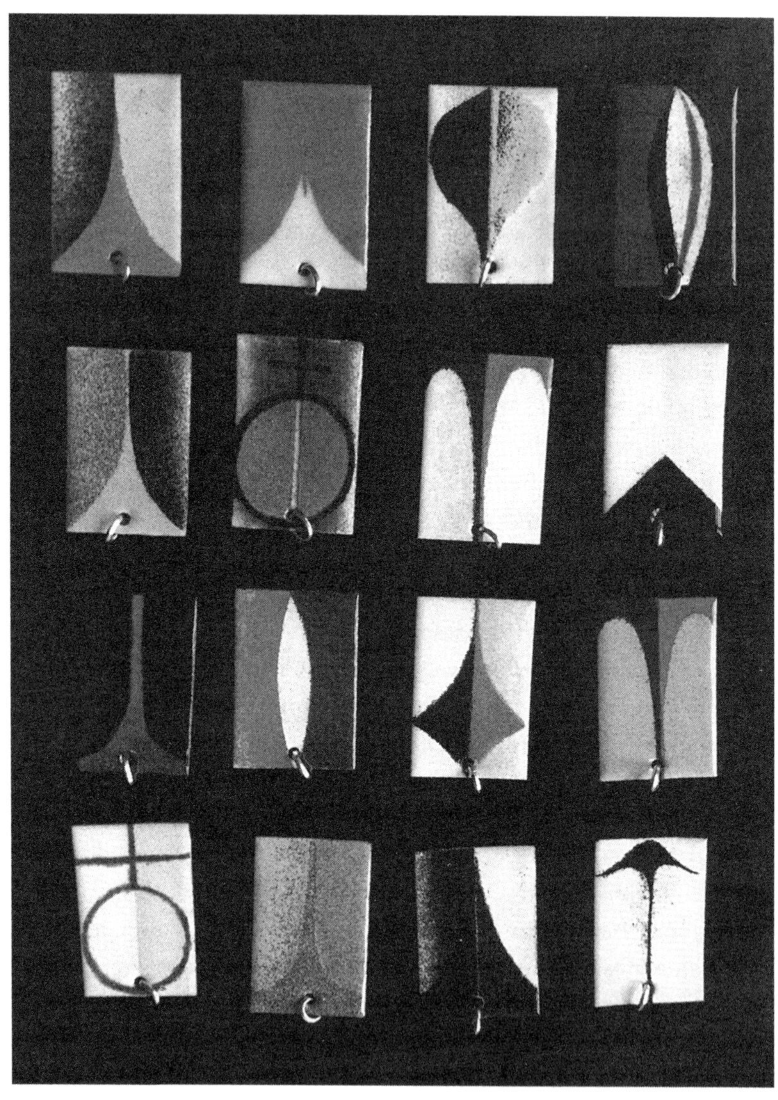

associations and desires. Not only do the curved lines of Müller's compositions suggest twisting; their small supports also curve in the production process. Bending out toward the viewer, these tiny, pierced paintings are about the same size as a razor blade; their edges advance toward us. Not the most comforting keepsakes, these miniatures also speak to the hurt of the minoritized as well as a movement out from the margins.

Abstract Transfers: Edging Onto

Nancy Brooks Brody's small monochrome *Color Forms* are also enamel paintings, but they produce a different kind of queer encounter.[24] Brody's geometric forms might similarly seem to assert cutting boundary lines; their hard surfaces and austere, understated compositions of basic line and shape would seem impervious to any form of excess. But they also demonstrate how the hard edge performs otherwise, pulling away from one surface to move onto another as a mode of transference, a volatile vector in both the formal and affective senses. Through a tactical comparison with some earlier manifestations of hard-edge geometric abstraction in the work of Ellsworth Kelly, I will consider the edge as a queer approach to space that shifts, expands, and drags away from the boundaries that would secure a marked subject position. Brody's enamel objects produce abstract transfers that edge out and onto another space of possibility—a space for difference, or one that we could occupy differently.

Reimagining high-modernist geometric abstract painting, Brody's work specifically recalls and furthers some of the formal concerns of Ellsworth Kelly. Kelly's paintings are often characterized by strict delineations between flat monochrome planes, with an emphasis on the tension between figure and ground. Merging painting with elements of sculpture in the mid-1960s, Kelly began producing shaped canvases. Dispensing with figure-ground dynamics on a rectangular support, he painted monochrome canvases that were large, flat, geometric shapes, and the wall became their ground.[25] Brody's work shares some notable formal strategies with Kelly's, as both use painted monochrome shapes with sharp geometric edges that boldly intervene in their surrounding spaces.

Brody's *Wild Combination* (2006) (see plate 4) is composed of three color forms embedded into a wall: one pale yellow, one bright red, and one green. The enamel shapes are arranged in such close proximity that they almost touch, the green form on the far right just barely grazing the red in the middle with a sharp point. The arrangement is eight by five inches overall, a very small composition intervening in a large expanse of white wall. The edges of these geometric shapes are not straight but irregular and visibly hand cut, pressing unevenly into the Sheetrock wall in which they are embedded. Rather than flat fields of color, the varying thickness of the painted enamel creates a rippling surface facture, catching the light unevenly. Ellsworth Kelly's *Red Panel, Dark Green Panel*, and *Dark Blue Panel* (1986) (see plate 5) is a series of three large monochrome canvases: a bright red triangular shape with subtle convex edges, an irregular dark blue hexagon in which no two sides are parallel, and a dark green shape like a bent rectangle that is folding or buckling in the center. The arrangement is ten feet high and spans thirty feet along the gallery wall. The monumental shapes are distanced from one another by several feet so that each shape could be conceived separately. The forms are placed with points facing downward toward the floor to create an unstable and dynamic sense of movement—they look as though they might roll to the left or right along the wall.

Ellsworth Kelly's geometric forms tend to be read according to a signifying logic. While Kelly's images are abstract, his shapes are derived from observations of natural and architectural forms, prompting art historians to consider these abstractions as references. Gottfried Boehm writes, for example, "Rather than engaging in a process of abstraction, he, as it were, reduces significant aspects of the visible world and extends them into his works."[26] Abstraction then paradoxically becomes a process of representation, through a transference of form from the world. Yve-Alain Bois has defined Kelly's motifs as "already made," transferred indexes rather than tampered-with representations. According to Bois, Kelly utilizes the index without the referent, approaching the sign as necessarily contingent and without pointing to what exactly the sign indicates.[27] In this view, the signifier is detached from the signified, and this does not produce representation but something still grounded in the natural or real; Kelly indexes the world around him, though the world is indiscernible in his work.

Nancy Brooks Brody's *Color Forms* might similarly prompt us to question the relationship between the abstract and the figurative. The repeated description of Kelly's works as *transfers* could also arguably describe Brody's work, as *Wild Combination* is based on memories of people: the shapes are "impressions" of the form that someone occupies in her mind. The *Color Forms* that followed this set were similarly drawn from the outlines of figures, though we would never know this by looking at them.[28] Brody's embedded lead line works (discussed at the start of the introduction) are more precise measurements of architecture, made thickly material and reoriented to a new location. It might seem that all of this work constitutes abstract*ed* references to real bodies and edges in the world. At the same time, their edges do not define solidified figures but instead demonstrate a wavering or an uncontained movement on the peripheries—Brody's lines are never straight, and even the convex curves of Kelly's shaped canvases prompt a dynamic movement. Considering these as *transitional* objects might acknowledge that they expand into the world beyond themselves and yet maintain certain associative ties contingent on their surroundings and viewers. Brody's process also seems to abstract a person, forcing me to reckon with the problem of a body losing meaning through abstraction (the violence that abstraction can do through suppression and marginalization). At the same time, these works are neither impersonal nor finite. Rather than read these abstractions as signs or figurative references, exploring what else their edges can do might open up more interpretive possibilities, making space for the contingency of unruly material encounters with this work.

I consider what kind of encounter these works produce in order to complicate the tendency to read abstract geometric forms as merely another signifying representation. Rather than creating a site for the viewer to settle meaning on their surface, I argue that these works produce edges that both drag away and draw toward in an unstable process of transference. The edges of these objects might transfer differently: not as a form of reference or relocation, but through enacting a different relation to the world beyond their borders, or a kind of transference encounter. These previous understandings of Kelly's geometric forms as abstract transfers might be complicated by the psychoanalytic concept of transference, a repetition of feelings for, or attachments to, someone or something in the past onto a new object in the present.[29] *Trans*ference is crucially not *re*ference; it moves affectively across objects, repeating yet appearing as if for the first time, enacting repetition with a difference. Encountering Brody's work does not involve a reading of edges as bodily contours, and it would be particularly difficult to view these forms as figures because they are so small. Rather, I imagine how they might feel to touch, the visceral contact between warm skin and a cool hardened surface that was once fluid and potentiate. Leaning in, the line of contact between the enamel support and the white Sheetrock produces a palpable tension; the objects never quite fit. If there is a body involved in this encounter, it is not a body represented, but my own immediate presence. I begin to feel more precarious in relation to my surroundings, my boundaries as insecure as these color forms that still look wet and threaten to flow out over their borders.

Abstract lines and curves can transfer by dragging across and away from fixed form, visually disrupting boundaries that would stabilize figure against ground, and producing new forms of attachment beyond the bounds of space and time.[30] In *Intimacies*, Adam Phillips discusses transference in terms of the preoccupation with boundary violations in the practice of psychoanalysis, the anxiety of the analyst who could commit a category error by forgetting or not knowing the difference between love and transference love. Recalling from Freud that "we are at our most insistent about boundaries when we sense their precariousness," Phillips suggests that love is nothing if not a boundary violation.[31] The edge again operates in this double sense of a boundary that also opens *onto*, a traveling line of connection—a space in which to transfer differently. I consider the edging boundaries in works by Brody, and by association, Kelly, according to intimate associations that do not settle direct reference, but violate the hardened delineations between categories across time, space, and bodies. That is, these edges can perform as vectors for contact and connection rather than to separate, secure, or fix. In associating Brody's work with Kelly's, I am also dragging back across generations through certain formal attachments and drawing out new formulations between and beyond them. If shapes and colors and forms are copied from the world onto their surfaces, they transfer or transpose in order to transform, abstracting in order to produce new relational models and forms of attachment.

The transferring edges of these objects work to exceed categorical definition by which singular positions would be secured. Brody's forms are sometimes multiple or doubled, and these are always proximal, pressed close to one another or sharing a line of contact—as in *Ginger and* MPA (2011), where black and light blue color forms share an edge, or in *Merce and Scotty* (2014), where light gray and deep blue forms come close, barely parted by a tenuous line of Sheetrock between them. And although they are set into the wall, all of these combinations of color forms can be re-arranged; they can take on other relational possibilities. These are not "impersonal observations of form," as Kelly once described his own work, but more like imprints of memories transferred across time and space, attachments that do not entirely hold.[32] Brody's edging suggests a practice of care through close attention to boundaries, carefully etching into the gallery wall to make space for these small objects. They are embedded materially in the way that form can become embedded in memory while also taking on the uncertainty and contingency of that impression. They do not hide their handmade processing as Kelly's work does, refusing that visual insistence on neutrality in favor of sensuous materials and processes. The intimate encounter prompted by Brody's work produces a relationality that is queer and also unspecified—their boundaries do not fix a figure but suggest that figure and ground mutually shape one another, the ways in which subjects orient and are oriented by their environment. These fields of color are not entirely fixed, but contingent on their surroundings; and alternately, their surroundings are also contingent on them. The play of light will always affect the shadows cast by Kelly's reliefs and the color and shine reflecting on the enamel surfaces of Brody's. Our viewing position and orientation will also affect their positions in space, whether they move closer or touch or change shape in our vision.

Considering the ambiguity of perception in these works, we can begin to see how they destabilize processes of signification while also producing affective spaces of contact. The figure-ground relationship in painting typically presents a perceptual dichotomy, a tension where the viewer could focus on only one form or the other. Kelly's shaped canvases are both figure and ground in one, but we could also read the entire canvas as a figure against the ground of the wall. Or, in the case of the three shaped canvases I described, we might see three figures against the wall or ground. Brody's objects relate similarly to the wall, but because they are embedded into their ground, they also become part of it as a material intervention. Kelly's objects are so large that they might take over the wall; Brody's are so small they subtly *become* the wall, the very architecture, merging figure with ground without succumbing to it. Brody's works occupy the same plane as the wall and yet do not settle there, oscillating through wavering line and undulating surface to produce a push and pull in our vision. The separation and distinction between them produce an excessive edging and fuzzy logic through vectors of transference that generate multiple possibilities (rather than bivalence or linearity). We might consider this relation between a marked figure and surface plane according to Judith Butler's formulation of the body as a ground of cultural inscription. She challenges notions of "the body" as a passive surface for discursive inscription and the assumption that materiality exists prior to signification and form. For Butler, signifying systems that mark the body actually structure the social field.[33] Systems (or grids, to which I will return in the next chapter) that make the body cohere according to predetermined signs still persist when abstract forms are read as code for a queer body. But the destabilization of boundaries between edge and plane also renders the sign precarious; we cannot be sure what it points to, as the position it might seem to mark is also one of contingency, of ambivalence.

The edges and spaces of Brody's *Color Forms* drag on the hard-edge color field to render it messy and far more contingent. Considered in proximity, Kelly's shaped canvases might begin to seem a little less severe, performing openness rather than constraint. The edging of border lines opens onto sites of excitement, erotic boundary crossings where places of containment might paradoxically produce a sense of excess or freedom. This boundary violation speaks to queer attachments, involving a certain amount of precarity, or anxious ambivalence.[34] Attachment to the very things that are not supposed to be "for us"—such as hard-edge painting— is itself a queer feeling. Boundaries of association are uncertain; they oscillate like the lines in Brody's *Color Forms*. Considered together, Kelly's objects also push beyond reference. If these are transferred impressions, they are not the direct inscription of signs. Rather, they speak to the precarity of signs moving across time and space, the oscillation of dissolving boundaries between bodies and worlds. Rather than transcribe an associated reference, encountering these objects calls for a different form of association that allows us to hold onto contradictions as generative. The hardness of these edges is also a difficulty that presses out beyond bivalent Euclidean logic, a bending that alters what the line can do in relation to surface plane.

These objects do not represent things in the world but instead generate encounters in order to engage the world. This is the performative potential of queer abstraction. The queer attachment to geometric abstraction is ambivalent due to the violence it can do to either mark or neutralize a subject. Brody's work engages with the legacy of hard-edge painting in a process that we might see as reclaiming it for queer subjects. If we do take that line-drawing process into account, it still does not mark a subject in order to make a body legible, nor does it produce a pure or universalizing form that would erase difference. Rather, they prompt material interactions that are intimate, sensual, and particular. Brody's color forms are each specific—they are visibly handmade, their surface facture varies, and they appear in different locations. These objects play on the borders of association in ways that suggest not a direct equation but an approximation, an estimation, that comes near without a claim to mastery. The lines and borders of these geometric abstractions bring forms close yet refuse the precision of a coded signifier. The linear boundaries in these works—the lines that separate planes or mark surfaces—strategically operate to create spaces of intimate contact. When hard edges also edge into and onto something else, lines do not merely separate or produce distinctions but open up spaces of vibrant movement rather than foreclosed spaces of the symbolic. While geometry historically moved away from painterly gesture that was tied to subjective expression, here, the hard-edged line is visibly produced by a gesture of drawing. Material excess and affective boundary crossings work to refuse oppressive formulations of center versus margin, or figure versus ground, that would measure the "other" and the different against the natural or normal.

Stigmatic and Reparative Edging: The Triangle

Ulrike Müller and Nancy Brooks Brody utilize abstraction in ways that refuse to settle into an easy process of signification. Müller's work does, however, utilize certain recognizable symbols that draw on associations with queer and feminist movements: the triangle and the gender sign for "woman." Varying iterations of the circle above two crossed lines shows up consistently across the series of *Miniatures*, while the triangle appears across enamel and textile works. These geometric signs have been deployed as both terms of categorization and injury and have been redeployed in the service of radical collective politics. Here, I want to consider how the loaded geometric form of the triangle is deployed by Müller and Every Ocean Hughes in order to consider the energetic work of the double-edged tactic of edging that presses off from merely a marked category of difference. It is notable that Hughes and Müller were both members of the feminist genderqueer artist collective *LTTR* (active 2001–2008), so their work is already connected by queer communal practices. Producing a sense of community as well as agitation, the triangle form carries its painful edges and histories of injury while at the same time reinvesting that hardness with possibilities for connection and eroticism. These works might allow for a reimagining of a symbol or sign for identity in ways that prompt us to think differently about how the form itself operates.

The triangle already carries a double edge, weaponized as a badge of shame in Nazi concentration camps and reappropriated as a badge of self-identification and pride in queer countercultures in the 1970s. The upside-down pink triangle used to mark deviant sexualities, and thus mark for violence and death, was reclaimed as a political symbol by gay rights movements. During and in the wake of the AIDS epidemic, the hot pink triangle, turned to point upward, was reappropriated by ACT UP's Silence = Death Project to shift a sign of humiliation to one of connection and resistance. But this triangle was not transformed from a "bad/anti-" to "good/pro-" symbol; rather, it drew a connection between Nazi genocide and the illness and death associated with certain bodies and sex acts. The poster that founding members of ACT UP designed and pasted on the streets of New York featured the hot pink triangle and Silence = Death logo as well as the message: "Why is Reagan silent about AIDS? What is really going on at the Center for Disease Control, the Federal Drug Administration, and the Vatican? Gays and lesbians are not expendable . . . Use your power . . . Vote . . . Boycott . . . Defend yourselves . . . Turn anger, fear, grief into action" (figure 1.2). The pink triangle became a call to action, a queer aesthetic tactic and form of politics that held onto its history of harm, at the same time that it pointed to a government responsible for the deaths of those deemed not worth saving. The hard edges of a flaming triangle could both account for that violence while at the same time using its cutting power to incite social-political movement and call for collective response and repair.

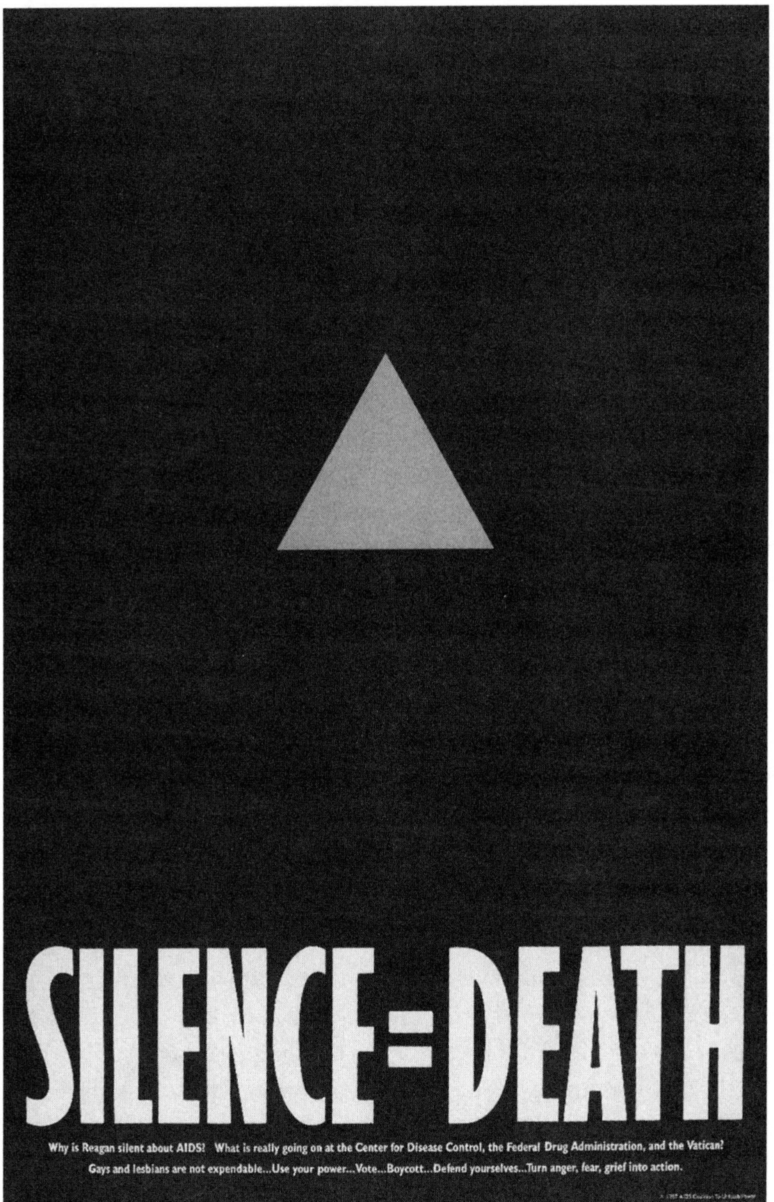

FIGURE 1.2 Silence = Death Project, *Silence = Death*, 1986. Poster, offset lithography, 29 × 24 in.

Considering two works by Müller and Hughes, I would like to conclude by exploring the edging power of the triangle that might mark a subject position but that also opens a space to inhabit. Müller's *Rug (con triángulos)* (see plate 6) is a large tapestry, a woven wool composition of eighteen triangles in various colors set against a burgundy ground. The triangles are arranged in rows, but they are staggered so that the triangles are not stacked on top of one another but move in a zigzag pattern across the surface. The triangles themselves are tilted, oriented so that they point left and to the upper and lower right. Their multiple colors—shades of pink, fuchsia, yellow, black, red, and brown—also recall a chart of Holocaust identification emblems used to mark subjects as particular types (Jewish, criminal, immigrant, queer) according to their color.[35] The historical associations of violence are alive in this work. At the same time, the pattern produced by the triangles is dynamic rather than static, suggesting an uncontained collectivity, an edging that mobilizes the margins. The rug itself was designed by Müller and then woven in an artist's workshop in Mexico, produced in a collaborative process across national borders. This production process also blurs another edge, that of national bounds. Their deployment of the triangle shores up the power of its edges to categorize and police the bodies it marks as other. That is, using the triangle does not erase its symbolic power to harm. At the same time, the zigzagging movements of these edges rendered in soft wool on a domestic, crafted object that might offer a foundation at one's feet also edges out onto a different space—one that can hold the hardness of its cut *and* open up to a space for living on the margins.

The triangle is also deployed by Every Ocean Hughes, who draws on its resonance with past collective movements and potential for edging toward imagined futures. Hughes's *Beyond the Will to Measure* (see plate 7) is a row of royal blue ceramic triangle clocks, inverted, with the top line of each triangle forming the edges of a continuous wave. These synchronized clocks might evoke Felix Gonzalez-Torres's identical readymade clocks—*Untitled (Perfect Lovers)*, 1991—but, rather than a couple, Hughes's work forms a collective and a multiplicity. Along with the hard edges of the triangles, this installation produces a traveling edge: not a straight line but an undulating pattern that dips and peaks in sharp waves. These wave-triangles were repeated across Hughes's exhibition at Participant, Inc. in 2015, *If Only a Wave*: standing alone, coupled, or lying on the floor, this hard-edge geometric form evokes the pink triangle—the pink walls helped to make this connection—as well as the deep blue of the ocean beneath the waves. The porcelain surfaces of this form produce a similar effect to Müller's and Brody's enamels; they are slick and shining, appearing still wet and reflecting the light.

In the poetic text accompanying the exhibition, Hughes writes: "How can we build a structure to be alive inside? To to to-wards a building of space and commons that privileges movement and margins."[36] The wave-triangle edge adds to the triangle sign a sense of movement, drawing on associations with a social-political movement and pressing out to make waves, a transitional effort across time and space. Beyond measuring, the edging work of this triangle might move us into the realm of what Hughes calls the "uncounted"—uncounted experience, uncounted futures. Queer feminist experiences and futures are unaccounted for, but they are also myriad and incalculable. *Beyond the Will to Measure* reimagines the triangle marked by stigma to demonstrate its reparative potential to refuse measurement and incite movement at the margins.

Queer feminist edging drags away from signifying logic and toward multiplicities and collectivities—connections that also acknowledge the sharp cut of the hard edge. Demonstrating how this form performs, Müller and Hughes convert the triangle's power to determine the fate of those it marks and marginalizes, mobilizing that power to different ends. These edges are not stable borders to mark subjects, but they instead perform a provocative edginess, insisting on the curving and bending movements of an edging away that makes space for the uncounted and uncountable to move in and inhabit. This dragging allows for movement at the borders of difficulty and harm, an energetic line of sight and struggle that drags away while also dragging toward a future—the seemingly exhausted forms and aesthetics of the past remobilized for the possibilities they work to imagine. Lifting off from the hard edge that edges beyond the margins, the next chapter considers how the queered form of the grid further challenges oppressive geometries of signification.

2 FEELING THE GRID

Lorna Simpson's *The Park* (1995) (see plate 8) is a photograph of a city park at night, blown up and screen printed onto a large grid of six felt panels. Approaching the image, our perspective is destabilized, even rendered sublime: we look down through the small forest of trees at a clearing of grass illuminated by scattered spotlights that suggest a walking path. In the distance, rows of buildings and skyscrapers create an expansive grid of windows that echoes the larger gridded structure of this felt canvas. The large image is flanked by two narratives.

To the left, a small felt text panel reads:

> Just unpacked a new shiny silver telescope. And we are up high enough for a really good view of all the buildings and the park. The living room window seems to be the best spot for it. On the sidewalk below a man watches figures from across the path.

And to the right:

> It is early evening, the lone sociologist walks through the park, to observe private acts in the men's public bathrooms. These facilities are men's and women's rooms back to back. He focuses on the layout of the men's room –right to left: basin, urinal, urinal, urinal, stall, stall. He decides to adopt the role of voyeur and look out in order to go unnoticed and noticed at the same time. His research takes several years. He names his subjects A, B, C, X, Y, and O, records their activities for now, and their license plates when applicable for later.

Accompanied by the perspective-shifting projections of these texts, the gridded image becomes the scene of observation and seriality. The grid of felt tiles offers an analogue of the sidewalk's squares of pavement and the side-by-side rectangular openings of stall by stall. The shiny new telescope, which both enables voyeuristic habit and beckons toward the years of a sociologist's research, suggests a sense of duration—a dragging—that corresponds to the boundless intervals of the grid itself. Although no one appears in the images, the scenes offer multiple viewing positions from which to project narratives of private and public acts; such implied acts, like our spectatorship, are at once intimate and impersonal.

An image about the erotics of serial looking, *The Park* is one piece in Simpson's *Public Sex* series. In all of these installations, black-and-white photographs of public spaces are blown up and screen printed onto separate felt panels arranged in grids. Pictures of uninhabited places become the implied locations of sexual and voyeuristic acts described in narrative text panels: they present a landscape, a city, a staircase, a theater, or a hotel bedroom, but they are devoid of bodies. Rendered abstract and fuzzy in their expansion to the large felt grids, the images depict scenes of sexual encounters we never see. The absence of bodies in this series may seem a departure from Lorna Simpson's previous work, which characteristically features unidentified figures who are presumed to be Black women. Since the 1980s, Simpson's conceptual photography has undermined the correspondence between identity and representation, particularly as it applies to raced and gendered bodies. The bodies that do appear in her previous work are usually cropped to the point of abstraction, often framed by different versions of the grid format. These figures typically turn away from the camera, or their faces are obscured, in defiant resistance to our gaze. Simpson's *Public Sex* series continues her ongoing investment in challenging viewers' expectations of representation, and undermining photography's assumed transparency.[1] The narrative texts and grid formats of this series also call to mind the absent bodies, and the oblique, abstracted body that appears consistently throughout her work. The encounter between text and image that populates these scenes and renders them as sites of sexual encounter and sexualized looking is notable for its recourse to the grids that mediate their installation.

In the context of *The Park*, the grid enables certain forms of relationality that I understand to do queer work. Not only do the narratives reference the gay cruising sites of public parks and men's restrooms and the voyeur(s) who observe them, but the gridded image further references the grid's ambivalent capacity for both surveillance and association, which the texture of felt makes all the more sensual. This chapter explores how the grid's latent capacities for queering are drawn out by Simpson's work in ways that prompt a reconsideration of the grid in the earlier paintings of Agnes Martin. I make this transhistorical comparison in order to show how Simpson's contemporary iterations of the grid allow for different readings of Martin's iconic work and the queer potential therein. I will demonstrate through a reading of Simpson's work (and considering its refraction of Martin's) that the abstract formal strategy of the grid is far from merely a figure of standardization or a panoptic tool used in the interest of bodily surveillance. The grid features instead as a vector for queer forms of relationality, a mediating structure that brings aesthetics and politics into intimate contact. In particular, I consider the grid's visual and material *excess* as a strategy for undermining categorical divisions its form might otherwise seem to secure. These works drag on the grid's overloaded significance in modernist discourse in order to expose its potentially oppressive power while making strategic use of its resistant and transformative potential.

In her seminal 1979 essay "Grids," Rosalind Krauss defines the grid as *the* emblem of modernism, and one that is profoundly contradictory and ambivalent. The grid serves this iconic function in part because it seems to declare art's autonomous visuality: "Flattened, geometricized, ordered, it is antinatural, antimimetic, antireal. It is what art looks like when it turns its back on nature." The modernist grid is precisely *not* a mapping of mimetic representation (not the premodern, perspectival grid) but the literal surface of the canvas—"it is the result not of imitation, but of aesthetic decree."[2] Yet Krauss and other scholars, such as Meyer Schapiro, have noticed that even as it withdraws from the real, the grid also acts as a kind of window that pushes our vision beyond its frame, opening up to a larger spatial continuum, a universal field of which it forms a subset.[3] This modernist, purified, and universalizing model of the grid might seem a dangerous cruising ground for queering and antiracism, to the extent that specificity rather than universality is viewed as necessary for these politics. And yet the geometry of the grid offers a queer model of relationality that does not foreclose multiplicity or settle around sameness. For example, considering the grid in avant-garde utopian thought, Andrew McNamara argues that the grid was never aimed to solidify the immutable "specificity" of art, but to expand its possibilities: "The grid format shifted emphasis to systems of relations—that is, a proliferating and seemingly endless network—which in turn suggested the futility of attempting to shore up the sanctity of the aesthetic."[4] This chapter explores the continued political relevance of the grid as a network of relations and as a formal and material excess that drags beyond its own borders.

Dragging the Grid

The grid carries many difficult and often contradictory implications, both formally and politically. As a form of geometric abstraction and a fraught object of modernist discourse, the grid presents certain problems and possibilities for artists such as Lorna Simpson who are engaged in contestatory politics of gender, race, and sex. On the one hand, the taxonomizing function of the grid might seem to foreclose, to block or contain nonnormative identities; and yet on the other hand its antihierarchical focus on two-dimensional relations also opens up to more utopian possibilities, as in the work of early twentieth-century European avant-garde movements such as De Stijl, Bauhaus, and constructivism. In the case of Piet Mondrian's paintings, for example, the grid's "universal plastic language" aimed to produce a united, nonhierarchical field in which no single element is more important than another.[5] As an avant-garde utopian strategy, the grid was considered to exhibit a democratizing logic; its infinite extension and repetition would convey "a collectivity without boundary or hierarchy."[6] This model of the grid is at once politically useful and problematic, as it can generate a commonality or affinity across difference as easily as it can homogenize and control.[7] The grid might seem to produce a trapping binary situation, but this form is interesting and viable for the artists in this study precisely because it is not neutral.

The grid is most often understood, however, to be predicated on this latter kind of homogenizing binary spatial logic and totalizing worldview. The grid is particularly resonant as a dominant matrix for modernity, for instance, because it was central to industrialism and colonialism and because it offers a visualization of the assertive rationalism that structures actual and virtual spaces, from urban landscapes to power grids.[8] The capacities of the grid for systematic regularization came to the fore in conceptual art of the late 1960s and 1970s. Works by artists such as Sol LeWitt took on the "look of information," as Eve Meltzer has written, their logic coinciding with structuralist understandings of human subjectivity as a product of preexisting systems rather than a sovereign consciousness. Yet it was precisely in understanding that modern humans are inescapably governed by the territorializing order of the grid that both conceptual artists and structuralist theorists turned to grids for "a revolution in signifying structures."[9] Along with a generation of artists engaged in postmodern methods of deconstruction and pastiche in the 1980s and 1990s, neo-geo (neo-geometric conceptualist) painter Peter Halley, for example, used a self-reflexive grid to evoke and critique contemporary human conditions of confinement: the grid and the rectangle became prison cells and conduits for technological power.[10] Jack Williamson similarly notices a shift from utopian modernism's validation of the visible mathematical coordinates of the grid to postmodernism's claim for a reality beneath its surface—a surface that is understood to obscure or cover over actual political scaffolding and material life.[11] These artists, along with a chorus of postwar scholars, have noted how the grid's rationalizing coordinates can reveal themselves differently, visualizing the very things they would seem to repress, such as randomness, variation, and precarity. Understanding the grid as inescapable and far from universalizing, contemporary artists have subverted and converted its parallels and meridians to alternative ends.

For this reason, the grid's ability to construct and transform its environment and to resist containment (even as it appears self-contained) still holds radical potential for queer, feminist, and critical race movements.

The grid remains especially compelling because it resonates ambiguously as both an object and an operating system, demonstrating the unruly capacities of formal elements that are seemingly benign, such as a series of squares or intersecting lines on a canvas. Precisely because the grid can function as a panoptic apparatus of surveillance according to which bodies are organized and made ever more visible, it also can function to reveal that apparatus by making abstraction itself undeniably perceptible. An oscillating form and conduit for power, the grid works both in relation to sign systems that make bodies appear and cohere as raced, gendered, and sexed objects *and* in relation to material realities that resist the logic of these systems and render their abstraction discernible.

Thus, while grids can organize space in order to map deviations or to homogenize a field of observation, in the work of some artists, grids also have the potential to subvert and exceed regimes of representation that demand that bodies be abstracted into encoded forms recognized by a hegemonic system. The order of the grid still does not screen out the glitter of possibility for politically engaged artists whose work makes visible its divisive space-making operations while at the same time converting the grid's function for affective and even erotic channels of intimate contact. The work of such artists is sometimes interpreted in bodily terms, or codified as subjective expressions of the artist's life.[12] Harmony Hammond, an artist engaged with abstraction and lesbian feminist politics since the 1970s, has recast the minimalist grid in fabric ("soft grids," which I discuss in chapter 4) and more recently produced a series of monochrome grid paintings.[13] Frayed strips of canvas and grommets create a gridded pattern of holes and layered fabric and paint that tend to be read as bodily topographies.[14] Betty Tomkins's 1970s grid-centered "Fuck Paintings" and drawings have similarly been discussed in terms of a "feminist formalism" where body politics and the politics of painting itself are engaged simultaneously.[15] In this criticism on Hammond and Tomkins, the grid can operate as feminist or as queer precisely because it is somehow embodied even as their work does not cohere or fully appear as such. These interpretations consider a political formalism to necessitate a reclaiming of a gendered or sexualized authorial position through bodily metaphor.[16] But such a perspective limits the material topographies of Hammond's and Tomkins's works to biography, and abstraction is then read as another form of representation or iconography. I argue that the grid is made to work queerly as a form of resistance when it is shown to subvert a symbolic structure's power to cohere a signifying form or body and instead taps into the excessive and relational capacities that scholars have shown to be already operational in grids themselves. The grid is queered when its excessive and materializing capacities are radically deployed, dragging with it the weighty repressive implications of the grid that still persist and cannot be discarded.

The grid emerges in contemporary art as an emphatically material form, disrupting its regularity or cold austerity in favor of more haptic abstractions that not only invite touch, but also project out to touch us. We can see this continuation of the grid in the printed felt serigraphs of Lorna Simpson. We can also see it in works that play with queer spatial tactics, such as the "Hot Lesbian Formalism" of Sheila Pepe's crocheted installation environments (also discussed in chapter 4) or A. K. Burns's multimedia installations and performance work.[17] The grid appears as an illusory optical play of color in the paintings of Xylor Jane and Linda Besemer (see chapter 3) and in Nancy Brooks Brody's *Glory Hole* grid paintings. The drawings of Edie Fake utilize the grid as a structure for imaging queer social spaces.[18] In all of these examples, the grid is not simply the background framework, but an actively sensual, relational, and excessive materializing force. While I will focus on Simpson's work as a core example here, these particular iterations are also part of a larger trend of contemporary deployments of the grid that do queer feminist work. Refusing to foreclose the grid's capacities for charting nonnormative affinities and decorative excesses, these artists mine the not-yet-exhausted political potential of this modernist strategy.

I am particularly interested in how the grid works both in relation to and in excess of sign systems that make certain bodies appear and cohere as raced, gendered, sexed, or disabled. Charged with difficult implications of state power structures, the grid maintains its ability to make visible a minority-marked otherness and to shame it at the same time. Even as these structures are inescapable, contemporary artists work with and through the grid's injurious charge in order to exceed it, all the while holding on to that difficulty. Utilizing the potentially exhausted or failed aesthetic strategies that might otherwise be repressive can reshape the loaded visual language of abstraction, allowing these seemingly outdated or depoliticized formal devices to perform differently. While the repressive implications of the grid will persist (indeed, we cannot disregard them), this form is queered in work that refuses to limit the pleasures and affinities that emerge when its excessive and materializing capacities are radically deployed.

A medium for channeling power in multiple capacities, the grid generates live wires of connection that produce a commons or commonality among people and environments. That is, while the grid would seem to be one of the most formulaic and absolute forms of modernism, producing an endless repetition of lines that demarcate and divide, this particular technology for organizing space can in fact generate intimate spaces of contact that do not collapse the specific into the general.[19] This allows for relations and affinities across difference while at the same time refusing the universalizing tendencies that suggest difference is stably fixed on the bodies of others. While the grid functions in art practice as a process of bringing parts together to form a whole, the serial arrangement of distinct areas does not necessarily produce a coherent picture or a settled signifying system, but rather, it exceeds calculated borders. This chapter focuses on two particular operations inherent in the grid that demonstrate its queering operations: *relationality* and *excess*. As a political tactic of abstraction, the grid can operate simultaneously as a mechanism for queer relationalities and a site for affective attachments, while also exceeding the configurations of difference that would signify or settle around an encoded sign.

This map, this system of interlocking integers—this grid—then becomes an excessive spatial arrangement that can sustain, rather than resolve, contradiction, and with the capacity to hold in tension what it would seem to visually repress. Its expansion points us continuously beyond the picture plane, beyond the sign, to what is not there and will not appear in a fixed image: unrepresentable, unimaginable, and irresolvable tensions. The grid operates here in a gritty, even dirty, capacity to obscure rather than organize and to press up against borderlines that otherwise insist on either equivalencies or strict separations between spaces and forms. Subverting a modernist project of commensurability—transcribing human experience into a shared or universal frame of reference, a common language—the queered grid produces a space of incommensurable contact, not in an act of resolving into sameness, but by putting forth approximate relationalities that do not demand equivalence.

Relationality: The Grid as Production Site
for Intimate Contacts

Lorna Simpson's work demonstrates the potentialities of the grid as a queer technology of association. While the grid structure is especially clear in the *Public Sex* series, grids continuously appear throughout her work as framing structures for her photographs. Through the expanded medium of photography, her work deals with intersecting issues of race, gender, and sexuality, often employing photographs that are fragmented, repeated, and juxtaposed with text.[20] While the photographs usually depict what we assume to be Black women, these representations are always contingent, complicated, and never easily decoded. Simpson's strategies of abstraction work to complicate or withdraw legible signs of difference. Her subjects often turn away from the camera and refuse to appear in ways that are expected or easily codified. These works notably combine reproductive technologies and gridded systems that have historically produced human types and taxonomies by which a person's inner character could be interpreted through their body's outward signs. Consider, for example, how the photographic documents used to justify eugenics in the nineteenth century often place certain physical "types" together in grid patterns to evoke comparison and produce the very raced, disabled, or otherwise deviant bodies they depict.[21]

As an instrument of association, the grid brings figures and bodies into close contact, producing separations as well as comparisons. At its most oppressive, the grid represents what Judith Butler identifies as the signifying systems that structure the social field, producing "a social space for and of the body within certain regulatory grids of intelligibility."[22] Following Butler, we can understand this field of visibility as racialized as well as gendered and sexed, and according to Maurice Wallace's understanding of a racial gaze that fixes the Black subject within a "rigid and limited grid of representational possibilities."[23] Systems or grids that bound and mark the body according to certain codes of cultural coherence are precisely what readings of abstraction as coded reference (and attendant methodologies of visual decoding) continue to enact. My discussion of the grid necessarily reckons with the danger inherent in this form that is used to reproduce and stabilize minoritarian positions. Even in linguistic form, the grid potentially reproduces power arrangements and enforces certain patterns of relationality upon which they depend: GRID was once an acronym for "gay-related immune deficiency," an early term for AIDS. These patterns are disrupted, however, by queer deployments of the grid as a tactic of abstraction that draws distinct elements close without drawing direct correlations, and with the capacity to maintain the spaces of contradiction that its borders might otherwise claim to resolve.

Lorna Simpson's *The Rock* (1995) (see plate 9) is a large-scale installation of twelve felt panels arranged in a grid pattern on the wall, accompanied by a narrative text panel on either side. While the overall image is a single enlarged photograph of a large boulder and a stream surrounded by trees, the scene is fragmented by the panels that separate the print into equivalent rectangular segments, and further abstracted by the felt material foundation and oversized scale that render the image fuzzy. The print is black and white, so that light and shadow define the forms, and flecks of light in the trees, water, and pebbles enhance the pixelated effect of the felt fibers.

To the left of this image, a text panel reads:

Female Trouble: Divine has just left home after an argument over a Christmas gift, and storms out of the house. She is picked up on the highway by an auto-mechanic (played by Divine). They approach a wooden area and have frantic sex on a mattress, by the side of the road.

And to the right:

Driving all day long, has induced a hypnotic state upon both of us. It is definitely time to pull over. I recognize the state park that we are now in the middle of, and can endure a few more minutes of this drive in order to find the same spot I went to last time I was here. Hoping that this search will not turn into another journey, since I didn't make any mental notes of the surroundings during my last visit, I'm ill prepared, and not really wanting to appear too familiar with the area. I make an effort this time to commit this trip to memory. But here we are, sick of driving. We get out of the car and start to hike to find a spot and it will probably replace the last one, completely. Haven't seen any week-end hikers for a while and since we are miles away from any rest stops it seems plausible that we will not be patrolled. I asked, "How's this?" "Is it secluded enough for you?"

While the grid sometimes silences, this structure brings multiple narratives together in Simpson's work. These stories transform the environment that is represented, implying intimate relations that occur within the scene, or just outside of it, or are perhaps entirely separate from the photograph. There is no direct reference in the text panels to this particular printed image, only a generalized secluded wooded area. *The Rock* confuses our spatial as well as our temporal location, suggesting scenes that may have occurred in the past, or might in the future. The narrative on the right panel oscillates between present and past tenses, creating an opening, an approximate spacing of contact in both time and space. It is unclear when and where these interactions occur, and whether voyeurism gives way to participation. As the "you" and "us" of Simpson's right text panel suggests, we are already there. This grid not only maps a space but opens an infrastructure for our projection into the scene—we might project alternative narratives or map our own bodies into this opening in time and space. It activates and unsettles the spectator, an unsatisfied voyeur with nothing to see but much to fantasize.

This felt grid becomes a cruising site for what remains unrepresented and unresolved yet still shared or "public" through a multiplicity of imaginative projections and participatory events in which we, the spectators, are implicated. The text points to what is not seen in the image, what remains just beyond the frame, but still tempts and teases us with indirect reference to a space of intimacy. While the right panel describes what seems to be a personal narrative, the left panel references John Waters's high-camp, cult-classic film, *Female Trouble*, and his muse and star, the drag queen Divine. The sex scene described here is between Divine and an alternate persona played by Divine, so that intimacy occurs between two versions or performances of one subject. The trouble in this case is not only the illegibility of gender, or perhaps that multiple genders are performed by a single subject, but that the intimacy described between these two aspects of a self is also alienating, decidedly impersonal sex. Something is shared, in common, but intimacies remain suggestive and anonymous. So while the grid is a site of intimate contact, it is also one where nonnormative relationalities are activated without containing or fixing the subjects it would seem to describe. This grid refuses to produce the bodies of others.

Something similar occurs when we look at *The Park*. The photograph is taken from a vantage point high above the trees, and the "we" of the left text panel suggests that the viewer occupies the position of the voyeur in a high-rise apartment building with a shiny new telescope. The right text panel describes a sociologist recording the "activities" in the men's public restrooms—cruising sites. This voyeur within the park also occupies several subject positions: a sociologist, a voyeur, and perhaps a sting operator (who records license plates). The various forms of looking described by these narratives are at once erotic and insidious. As spectators, we are implicated in the scene and the systems of oppression that are implied by both the form and content of these images. Simpson's previous work that depicts bodies clearly implicates the spectator, but the absence of bodies in the *Public Sex* series also opens up a space for the viewer's projection. In this way, we are drawn in more deeply by the abstraction of these images. While there is no figure with which to connect or identify, this absence also disallows the spectator's own refusal—the "not me" that distances us from the position of Other and at the same time affirms their otherness.

While intimacies are most clearly suggested by the textual narratives, the linear separations between panels and austere geometric format of this installation potentially alters the kinds of affective encounters that serial logic might otherwise produce. The grid operates as a support structure that imposes a linear system and repetition onto the landscapes depicted. Simpson's work plays with two seemingly opposed functions of the grid in two-dimensional art. In a 1972 essay, John Elderfield points to two uses of the grid—as either "structures" that serve no mimetic purpose other than to map the surface itself, or "frameworks" which organize pictorial elements or serve as a background scaffolding for representations.[24] Simpson's felt grids both declare the "surfaceness" of the work (their tactile fuzziness draws us to the surface) while they also serve as demarcating frameworks for her images: the grid both coheres and fractures the surface, defining and dividing the space. This mapping of a represented space through the repetitive system of the grid offers a queered form of seriality that does not reproduce a signifier in order to reinforce its relation to a stable signified.[25] Rather, this is a deployment of seriality that fragments and abstracts a space of representation, an infrastructure in which bodies are never figured forth, but relations of desire are still active. If, thinking with Butler's theory of gender performativity, repetition stabilizes the categories upon which representations of difference depend, then perhaps Simpson's grids alternately refuse to fix bodies on solid ground or chart a territory for sanctioned sexual practice.[26] Rather, this fuzzy landscape, divided and multiplied by the lines and planes of the grid, produces a ground without figures that nevertheless manages to activate intimacy and materialize queer forms of eroticism. Simpson's work frames absences in many ways, but considering her work in terms of the grid brings into focus the ways in which their formal interventions are also political. The grid is not merely an organizational tendency to produce rigid taxonomies; it is more crucially a process of abstraction that drags on the categorizing and controlling power of this form, converting its capacities for affective and erotic proximity without letting go of its difficult history.

Simpson's grids ask us to rethink the importance of repetition and seriality. Repetition is crucial to the production of categories such as race and gender: repeating patterns and formulas do not often seem to have the capacity for producing difference or multiplicity. But seriality can also create points of contact between distinct entities that avoid a pure unity in the interest of creating relationality between them. For example, feminist theorist Iris Marion Young proposes a useful rethinking of gender as seriality to avoid the problem of taxonomic reductionism that would define women as a generalized and isolated group in ways that gloss over their differences of race, class, sexuality, or disability. Young understands the series as a structure defined by each member's individual orientation toward objects and their material possibilities as well as their constraints, linked indirectly rather than through mutual identification or sets of attributes that would define membership in a group.[27] Our lives are conditioned as gendered, sexed, raced, abled, or disabled through a vast complex array of objects and materialized histories that structure social spaces. And it is the normalizing physical models of space created by gridding that produce disability in particular, if we can understand the body marked as deviant precisely in and through built environments and patterns that restrict them.[28] But this model of serialized existence also allows us to imagine how individuals move and act in relation to objects and within structures that position and constrain them. This model of seriality inflects the grid as a system for mapping spaces that nevertheless allow for mutability.

We can think of the grid in this case as the cruising ground for intimate queer relationalities that place strange and disparate bodies and worlds into contact. This proximity brings them close and in common, but still acknowledges dividing forces of social and historical constraints and possibilities. I am using a conception of relationality that extends the work of José Esteban Muñoz, particularly his formulation of the *incommensurate*: a proposition of queerness as a sense and a sharing-out that moves beyond the individual subject (following the work of Jean-Luc Nancy). If, for Muñoz, queerness is about the incommensurable, a "sense" of the world that is incalculable and excessive and also shared through proximity, then the geometric format of the grid offers a method for sharing the unshareable, for thinking beyond the register of the singular subject to produce a "map of life in which singularities flow into the common." In the grid, "irreconcilable integers" can also allow us to think beyond the register of the individual subject and to conceive a commons (rather than equivalence) of the incommensurable, even as crisscrossing trajectories of singular beings remain violent and traumatic.[29] I imagine these trajectories in the form of intersectionalities that modify identifications and positionalities. Lifelines travel in both parallel and intersecting capacities, moving with and beside, crossing and connecting, touching consistently but not constantly. This is a fuzzy system in which membership exceeds binary logic of either belonging or not belonging, and indeed opens out to infinity.

Excess: The Grid as Textured Surface That Exceeds the Canvas and the Sign

Even as it promises a clear division of categories and creates a closed sense of space that might suggest equivalence, the grid also has the capacity to place things into intimate proximity, bringing disparate aesthetics and media into close contact. Simpson's work crosses the minimalist geometric format of the grid with reproductive photographic imagery, furthering the question of how abstraction relates differently to the sign or exceeds signification. While the grid has a different history in painting than it does in photography, I compare Simpson's felt works with the paintings of Agnes Martin to consider excess as a strategy for undermining categorical divisions that the grid might otherwise seem to secure. Martin's work exemplifies a continuation of the modernist grid in 1960s minimalism and could be positioned on the border between modern and contemporary. Bringing the two artists into contact demonstrates the affinities that emerge across their handling of the grid surface. The excessive relational capacities and erotic tensions already latent in the modernist icon of the grid thus emerge through its continual redeployment and transhistorical associations.

While linear time may be mapped on the grids of our calendars, the excessive repetition of the grid evokes an infinite temporality—the dragging of slowed queer and crip time along with a resistant pull against the settled image. The grid often cannot be fully grasped as an object, and in this way, it exceeds representation. Briony Fer usefully shows how Agnes Martin's grids refuse a single totality: "the work of repetition marks the impossibility of completion."[30] Martin's work may seem self-contained through her formulaic and meditative process, but this "infinite line" also marks "incalculable differences," exterior as well as interior alienation.[31] In some ways, the grid is an impossible object of art; neither Martin nor Mondrian ever produced a perfect modular grid, nor was this perfection ever necessarily the ambition.[32] Scholars have already noticed that the modernist grid is not exact, but excessive in its infinite extension (material and virtual), and that its repetition also gives way to variability, to difference.[33] I explore these excessive capacities of the grid by bringing Martin's work in contact with Simpson's, particularly their material and textural qualities.

As a mathematical partitioning of the canvas surface, the grid maps the literal space of the picture plane. A flat surface is broken up into equally measured segments that organize a "real" space that is also represented. The modernist grid mapped the surface of the canvas, an already gridded textile, and ultimately emphasized the flatness of painting.[34] In the case of Simpson's work, however, the particular medium of felt creates a surface that is compressed rather than woven, its precarious fibers interacting randomly. Simpson's literal division and multiplication of panels, cut and juxtaposed, produces a picture plane that is unbounded, the interlocking grid unraveled. The intimacies are not represented but felt.

The particular materiality of felt is crucial to understanding how Simpson's deployments of the grid also exceed or trouble its oppressive capacities. Fabric, for Gilles Deleuze and Félix Guattari, constitutes a "striated space" of intertwining and intersecting elements, necessarily delimited and closed. Felt, on the other hand, constitutes an "anti-fabric" of entangled fibers: "An aggregate of intrication of this kind is in no way *homogenous:* it is nevertheless smooth, and contrasts point by point with the space of fabric (it is in principle infinite, open, and unlimited in every direction; it has neither top nor bottom nor center; it does not assign fixed and mobile elements but rather distributes a continuous variation)."[35] Further considering felt as both a tactile sensation and affective experience, trans studies scholar Jeanne Vaccaro points out that this "anti-fabric" cannot be calculated mathematically, or mapped in the way the space of fabric is: rather, "It is the result of the destruction of the grid." This composite material, "fibrous and fleshy," challenges the spatial and corporeal division of interiority and exteriority.[36] In Simpson's *Public Sex* series, the nongridded anti-fabric offers a queer and antiracist logic for alternative calculations and mappings of space and bodies. The composite and compressed matter produces a picture plane that is not the ground of representation but becomes a fuzzy and unruly site of contact. This work refuses the force of the grid to settle bodies and spaces, and instead uses the felt to connect affect with materiality, pointing to the textures of feeling that structure queer associations and relations.

Concerns with the material qualities of surface and space bring Lorna Simpson's felt prints into close contact with the grid paintings of Agnes Martin. Simpson's gridded images are produced through a silk-screening process, bringing her photographs closer to the realm of painting. Their abstracted qualities also take on the facture of drawings, graphite sketches rendered by hand, akin to Martin's delicately drawn lines. Simpson's prints are muted in tone; black, white, and gray, they share with Martin's a subdued palette, drawing attention to the surface qualities of their supports. While Agnes Martin's deep engagement with the materiality of painting would seem at odds with the ordered system of the grid and her formulaic process of rendering, the surface terrain of the fabric on which she painted is doubled again by the woven structure of her pencil lines and paint strokes. In Martin's 1960 oil painting *White Flower* (figure 2.1), the grid is punctuated by symmetrical white dashes that enhance the woven pattern of fabric. While the tight grid pattern extends to the painting's borders, the dashes are maintained in the center, and where

FIGURE 2.1 Agnes Martin, *White Flower*, 1960. Oil on canvas, 71⅞ × 72 in.
© Agnes Martin Foundation, New York / Artists Rights Society (ARS), New York.
Photo: The Solomon R. Guggenheim Foundation / Art Resource, NY.

they end, the lines of the grid appear like the cropped and frayed ends of a woven textile. Moving "with the grain," her grids seem to constitute the fabric itself, which moves and responds in turn to the artist's touch.[37] Redoubling the pattern of her fabric supports, Martin's painting does not figure forth, but produces a second ground. Simpson's and Martin's works are environmental in scale: Simpson's felt arrangements exceed six feet on either side, and Martin was devoted to square canvases that were six feet per side. They relate directly to the viewer as a landscape one could enter; at the same time, their gridded surfaces bar us from getting too caught up in an illusory depth. They demarcate in order to call attention to their surfaces as material planes on which a picture is both rendered and abstracted.

Considering how "nature" or the natural is alluded to in the work of both artists also demonstrates how they exceed signification. Much has been made of Agnes Martin's titles, which characteristically allude to landscapes—*The Beach, The Desert, Garden, Field*—and prompt readings of her grids as, if not representing nature, projections of the affective experience of nature, as a transcendence also connected with the artist's interest in Buddhism.[38] Rosalind Krauss posits the grid as a closed system in Martin's work, which is formally and materially bracketed and closed off to readings of the "abstract sublime" or the social context of the work.[39] Alternately, Jonathan Katz has asserted the importance of the context, particularly Martin's biography, for reading geometry as encoded personal reference to closeted lesbianism in her work.[40] Strangely, both readings mark the grid as a closed system, a signifying practice—a /cloud/ or a /closet/—even as it refuses the figure (the diagonal slash here marks and contains a signified).

But the fluctuation between figure and ground operates both visually and materially in these works to frustrate notions either that the grid would bracket out the concrete or that understanding its cultural or political operations would necessitate a contextual biographical account. The "nature" in Martin's titles may seem to specify a subject (as in *White Flower*), but it corresponds to a boundless geography of coordinates that exceed two-dimensional mapping of longitude and latitude. The excessive material dimensions and the vibratory effects of figure-ground oscillation in these grids trouble a settled reference, or even a settled point of reference. The landscapes pictured in Simpson's *Public Sex* series along with their titles similarly seem to specify a particular place (*The Park* rather than *A Park*), and yet, as I have shown, the thick materiality of their felt supports creates a ground on which no singular figure is fixed or naturalized. The linear slash of figure-ground might evoke a nearness of meaning or a conflation, but it is also a pause that does not enclose but maintains tension without resolving into meanings that are entirely either abstract or concrete. That distance produced by a dragging pause opens up time and space for intimate contacts or erotic tensions that still maintain, without resolving, their difficulties and differences.

In Lorna Simpson's *Public Sex* series, dragging the grid also performs a boundary transgression between public and private spaces. In both Simpson's and Martin's grids, passive viewing or voyeurism gives way to participation and projection as the textures and tactility of their surfaces seem to demand that we touch (or imagine touching). The surfaces of both artist's works beckon us, but Simpson's printed felt is erotically charged as a vehicle both for the abstraction of the photograph and for the bristling contact of skin and hair.[41] While a /bush/ is never depicted, certainly the public is in proximity to the pubic, where sites of intimate contact exceed the borders of the individual subject or distinctly gendered body. Both corporeal and representational boundaries are unfixed by these grids that generate textures of charged affective attachment and demand more intimate forms of spectatorship.

Gilt and Glistening Grids

The materiality and surface textures of Simpson's and Martin's grids are crucial to their queering operations, and two works in particular introduce the excessive effects of color and light by rendering the grid in gold. Agnes Martin's paintings are already notable for the atmospheric quality of their surfaces that also appear to shine from within. Departing from her typically muted color palette, *Friendship* (1963) (see plate 10) is a gilded canvas that, taking the luminosity of her work further, literally reflects light from the gold leaf that covers it. Gold leaf is an incredibly fragile medium—thin and sensitive to touch, it demands a delicate application process. Martin incised the lines of this grid by hand, damaging while also decorating the gold surface. Rather than duplicate a layer of woven, gridded lines on woven fabric, the canvas is covered with a shimmering matter, which is then scored and visibly altered by the etched lines. Process is not only visible, but texturally felt. The formulaic and meditative process for which Martin is known becomes increasingly devotional in this work; even as the canvas measures six feet on every side, this work has the material qualities of an intimate religious icon. As we become absorbed in it, the golden matter also reflects and shines back at us, exceeding its own surface.

Lorna Simpson's *Curtain* (2011) (see plate 11) depicts an empty public setting in large format serigraph across a series of felt panels. This photograph of an empty theater, taken from the vantage of the balcony, is printed in monochrome gold so that the large curtain over the stage produces a shimmering field of golden light. A spherical light fixture hangs from the ceiling like a disco ball, transforming this theater without bodies into a performance site for a show that has perhaps yet to occur, or long ended, but still glistens with possibility. The expansive potential of the grid, its extension out into the world, would seem to operate only on flat horizontal and vertical planes, but the gilded surface and shimmering gold materiality of these grids project outward toward us. This proliferating network of lines becomes inflected with light from its immediate environment, so that the grid's organization of an abstract surface also affects a lived space of contact—and even if that contact and its implied intimacies are indirect, the textures and materiality of gold produce an affective immediacy nonetheless.

These golden grids perform an alchemical transformation of matter in which the canvas or the felt support for an image is not only a screen for our projection—a meditative surface in which we insert ourselves—but one that projects back on us. In both works, the horizontal and vertical lines that divide the surface do not function as a figure that comes forth; rather, the golden planes between them swell out with a material thickness as well as a shining light. Considering projection in the psychoanalytic sense, visual culture theorist Jill H. Casid elucidates the important associations between alchemy and projection in Freud's work, where "to project the projections of the past not surpassed is importantly *not* to dispel but rather to recast the disavowed as mattering in and for our present."[42] Casid's point is that this contact—between us and the Other that we disavow or cast off, between the past and the present—matters both imaginatively and materially. I think of these particular grids—*Friendship* and *Curtain*—as alchemical projections that not only transform the mundane grid into gold, the subtle into the spectacular, but more crucially point to the capacity for this technology for organizing spaces and bodies to do something other than categorize and separate us from the disavowed Other. These gesture toward the queering potential of abstraction both to alienate us from forms that are otherwise straightforward (we might think we already know what the grid is and does) and to reconfigure that projective technology into something profoundly rematerialized; the grid as fuzzy and flaking, glittering and reflective, and as contingent as the spectator who encounters it.

Returning to what is at stake in the exhausted or failed that is dragged by this work, I turn to the queer form of the mirrored grid projected over a sphere: the disco ball. Transforming the already utopian associations of the grid, the disco ball projects what Muñoz calls a "wish-landscape" or queer aesthetic practice that shines out and reflects the world back at us, but also inflects the world with dazzling sparkle.[43] The utopian potential of queer aesthetic wish-landscapes might also be considered, as Casid has written of landscaping as a verb, "material process involved in making or 'worlding' the 'worlds' they might otherwise seem merely to depict."[44] We might take the rotating figure of the disco ball as an object that is both associated with the celebratory, gay, dance-party magic and a technology for projecting the glitter of light to transform a space, expanded to account for both what is there and what may yet come to be. The unruly spatial boundaries of this reflective grid illuminate the incoherence of form, subverting the dominating possession of spaces or bodies. Similarly, the glittering gilt surfaces of grids by Lorna Simpson and Agnes Martin cannot be disregarded as mere deviant excess but can instead be taken in a performative capacity to transform their spaces.[45] They do not operate as abstract aesthetic cover that obscures the real; rather, they materialize another space through the proliferating projection of light that, like the disco ball, reflects back at us a landscape or spectatorial space that it also radically alters.

While the queer seems diametrically opposed to gridded surfaces that might immediately foreclose affective, sensual, or erotic possibility, Lorna Simpson's work reimagines this formal device to map the queerly projective spaces of intimate contact as excessive sites for relations across the bounds of difference. Placed into intimate contact with the grids of Agnes Martin, we can see how this contemporary formal device also draws out the inherent queering capacities that are now activated, retroactively, like the retro activities of our disco-grid-inflected dance floors. The magic of this queer alchemy renders the grid as flexible rather than stagnant, staging possibilities and affinities yet to emerge from behind a glittering curtain rather than settling a space by and for certain bodies. This queer form performs by producing a space for intimacies to exceed bounds of difference, of public and private, of historicizing coordinates of here and now or then and there. The grid remains a problematic form of modernism, but these felted and fractured, gilt and glistening deployments of the grid also show it to be already shimmering with transformative potential.

Grids in Color: Pattern and Decoration between Jasper Johns and Xylor Jane

Gesturing out to consider how other deployments of the grid might undermine its signifying function, I will conclude by considering the ostensibly straightforward sign systems that structure the grids of Jasper Johns, alongside the current paintings of Xylor Jane. Jasper Johns's *Gray Numbers* (1958) (figure 2.2) is the first figure in Krauss's "Grids" essay, and yet this lead image is not discussed, although Johns's number and alphabet paintings are mentioned as grids that expand human-made sign systems somewhere between the abstract and the representational.[46] Johns may not be considered a foundational grid artist, but it is significant that his number grid is juxtaposed with Krauss's initial claim that the grid is the emblem of modernism, and perhaps this painting seems to demonstrate the flattened and ordered nature of this construction. *Gray Numbers* is literal indeed, a seemingly self-contained aesthetic field determined according to the order of numbers 0–9, progressing in sequence along the lines of a grid. Johns is known for postexpressionist painting that draws attention to the material support of his canvases, incorporating everyday materials such as newsprint along with thick encaustic to build up surfaces that were at once gestural and pulled from the readymade and banal stuff of the world.

Discussing uses of the color chart in painting of the late 1950s and early '60s, a grid that could be both rational and fetishistic, Briony Fer notes the important point of connection between colors and numbers: like the color chart, "numerical sequences offer readymade serial systems for encoding information," and this combination occupies a prominent place in art of the mid-1960s. This also brought the random operations of chance into play, for within a mathematical system, the random effects of color combinations could emerge—and it is this interplay of serial and sensual that revealed them to be precisely not opposite—"Jasper Johns had already shown how easily numbers slipped into alphabets and into body parts and into colors."[47] Johns's work might seem to call for decod-

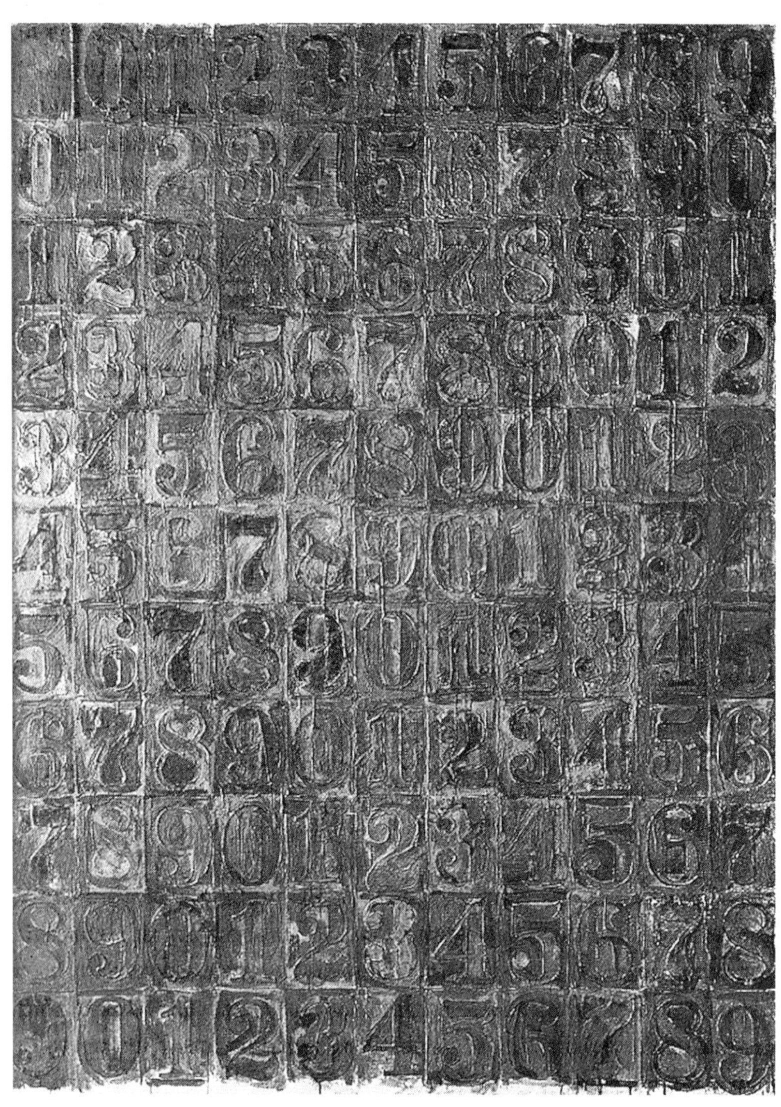

FIGURE 2.2 Jasper Johns, *Gray Numbers*, 1958.
Encaustic and newspaper on canvas, 67 × 49½ in.

ing based on the symbols he deploys (flags, targets, maps, numbers, and so forth), and further, when singular numbers are painted and titled as "Figures," they are read as human figures.[48] But his number grids emphasize the relationship between signs that then become abstract through repetition.

Conceiving of the grid as an excessive and queer technology of association, this organizational logic becomes an intimate contact site charged with sensuality. If the grid operates as a closed structure for sign systems, what we notice about this particular system is its emphatic materiality, a seemingly invariable pattern that is nevertheless inconsistent—while the numbers are repeated, they are each rendered differently. Difference might register in Johns's work in ways that are figural, but we can alternately imagine that the emphatic materiality of these grids constitutes a space that is more than enfleshed. The interaction between object and spectator is then not a contact between two bodies, but a collective, imaginative cruising ground for excessive flows of intimacies that refuses corporeal singularity.

Johns's gridded arrangement of numbers, painted using premade stencils, forms a highly depersonalized structure for painting that is nevertheless messy, tactile, and colorful even as it is rendered in shades of gray. While the gray might reiterate the newsprint surface upon which the numbers are painted, this is not entirely monochrome but glittering with shades of light blue and rosy browns, so that the surface appears to reflect bits of the world's color. The decorative pattern and tactility of its surface, the monochrome that is also not one, operate in a disruptive capacity to both render the sign and destabilize it at once. Indeed, color operates in particular ways through the grids I have discussed. Simpson's grids emphasize the black and white of the photograph, and precisely so: they are not merely devoid of color; instead, they bring our attention to this color contrast that carries associations with racial difference (I will return to the racial implications of color in the next chapter). The subdued palettes of Agnes Martin and this work by Jasper Johns are not neutralizing, but draw us into the materiality of their surfaces, the subtle shifts in tone and texture that become even more pronounced in hues of gray and white. Color inflects the grid with a decorative quality, rendering serial repetition as flamboyant pattern.

Contemporary artist Xylor Jane similarly uses number sequences to paint grids that are at once colorful spectrums and mathematical games. Jane's regular use of palindromes and prime numbers to determine both the colors and structure of paintings may be systems-driven, but the intensity of rainbow color configurations registers like the hypnotic perceptual illusionism of op art. The minuscule applied dots in Jane's paintings also retain the thickness of the oil medium so that they produce something akin to the texture of braille. They might then suggest alternative reading practices, making space for tactile engagement rather than purely visual—making space, that is, for the possibilities of crip as well as queer forms of spectatorship. Sometimes rendered in pure primary and secondary hues, sometimes sparkling metallic pigments that shimmer, these spots are not perfect pixels. They are singularly textured, even as their arrangement is emphatically systematic and seemingly rational. Jane's painting *Magic Square for SPSP 5385* (2015) (see plate 12) is a pattern of small painted dots arranged in a geometric grid pattern, but these dots also form numbers that create a magic square—a game where the numbers in each column, row, and diagonal must all add up to the same constant number. Jane's paintings often use complex mathematical coding systems, but the gridded number patterns both reference and disrupt the ostensible rationality of the semiotic square. This may appear to be a closed system, but it also yields a potentially endless sequence of possibilities, proliferating out beyond the picture plane in multiple ways: the thick texture of dots applied to the canvas creates both tactile and optical sensations, producing a colorful projection both material and illusory.

While Xylor Jane's practice is just as formulaic and meditative as Agnes Martin's, the surface pattern becomes somewhat random rather than adhering to a clear organizational logic, registering like the erratic gestural brushstrokes of Johns's stenciled numbers. These camped-up number grids render their seemingly generic and ordinary subject matter spectacular. At the same time, what seems like the subject matter of this work—the arrangement of numbers—determines the structure that also becomes decoration, *style*. I will also return to camp style in the following chapter, and the sensuality of Johns's tactile surfaces has already been discussed at length. At the same time, there is a tendency to view that tension between abstraction and representation as a closeting, and materiality becomes a way to reassert the body that has been elided—like that censored plaster cast of a penis so thoroughly analyzed in Johns's *Target with Plaster Casts*. This work is read as queer because the body is fragmented and unbounded, and because of the potential danger of the homoerotic gaze in the context of the fifties: "Fugitive, desubjugated, the body evades preordained signification, which is to say citation; the body is produced as a silent screen," according to Katz.[49] But I would argue that it is precisely the citation that makes it camp; the way in which body parts are held in their boxes points to the grid's function to categorize and contain while converting that order for its subversive potential. Certainly, the body is abstracted, and perhaps abjected or alienated, but this work's capacity to subvert signification lies not in a citational silence, but rather in an engagement with citation that wrests and torques the injurious charges targeted at those who might be seen to embody a queerness. That is, the casting and coloring of the bodily segments takes on the flaming colorful surface ascribed to the queer—and this is anything but a closeting.

Color and surface do not act as a silencing screen but project out as a flaming revelation. The following chapter expands on this capacity of color when it is deployed as a plastic medium, considering the ontological implications of colored surfaces that refuse to fix racial or sexual difference on the surface (where paint is so often read as skin). Taking the injurious charge of the flaming attached to vibrant surface decoration of color, these works again take up and transform the very terms of otherness, not disavowed, but to which they hold on, move through, and alter.

3 FLAMING COLOR

An enormous sheet of pure acrylic paint is suspended high above the viewer against a wall, its vertical stripes of bright colors descending like a giant taffy pull or a congealed plastic waterfall. This painting is freed from its canvas, buckling and folding in on itself where the wall meets the gallery floor, and rolling out at our feet. The striped pattern is dominated by lime green, with intermittent stripes of yellow, red, pink, blue, and darker green, creating a dynamic display of illusory movement. This is Linda Besemer's *Large Zip Fold #1* (2001) (see plate 13), and it demonstrates the artist's ongoing investment in abstraction as a strategy of queer and feminist critique. Beginning their practice in the 1980s when politics and painting seemed mutually exclusive, the artist has never given up on the possibilities for contemporary abstract painting to manifest cultural resistance. Besemer wrote about these critical politics of abstraction in relation to gender, race, and sexuality, years before the term *queer abstraction* emerged.[1] The artist creates undulating optical patterns and luminous color combinations in pure acrylic paint, sometimes peeled away from any surface so that paint and color both materialize in excess of a canvas. These playful engagements with the modernist legacies of abstract painting render it sensual and spectacular, prompting us to engage particularly with color as an affective, materializing force.

Linda Besemer's work exemplifies a tendency that I see as defining many of the practices associated with queer abstraction—an investment in color that is bright, synthetic, vibrant, and sometimes vibrating. These deployments of color in ways that I consider "flaming" also extend to the work of other queer, feminist, and nonbinary artists. We can see it in the pulsating paintings of Xylor Jane, the soft and taffy-colored paintings of Sadie Benning, the saturated hues and glitter in the paintings of Carrie Moyer, the brightly colored geometric textile work of Liz Collins, and the vibrant reflective cast objects of Carrie Yamaoka (discussed at the end of this chapter). This shared interest in color—and particularly the play between the surface of color as an optical or illusory encounter and the literal materiality and textures of painting; the use of light, figure-ground reversals and plays with perception; and the almost mechanical as well as meditative application of paints to create these tactile and emotive surface effects—all indicate that color already has, as Derek Jarman wrote, "a Queer bent!"[2]

"Flaming color" recalls *Flaming Creatures*, the 1963 experimental film by Jack Smith, to suggest the close affiliation of color to camp, drag, and glittering excess. Smith's "creatures" flame through their ambiguous nonnormative genders and sexualities, and that genderqueer glamour corresponds with the film's abstracting nonnarrative sequencing and disjunctive transitions. The film itself is black and white, but also colorful in more than one sense: controversial, scintillating, voracious. Another queer experimental filmmaker and artist cited above, Derek Jarman, became fascinated with color near the end of his life. His own particular history of color, *Chroma*, was published the year before his death from AIDS complications in 1994. Jarman's last film, *Blue*, consists of a saturated blue color filling the screen, suggestive of Yves Klein's monochrome paintings. Jarman's eyesight deteriorated near his death; the saturated blue field is a projection screen against which a queer crip vision is articulated even as it cannot be visually fixed. Chromatic abstraction can thus engage forms of spectatorship beyond the normative, not cohering a figure but producing more haptic encounters. While this chapter will focus on painting rather than film, the close affiliation between color and flaming excess in experimental cinema speaks to color's queer capacities as a tactic of abstraction that does not stagnate or settle.

Playing on the edges and in-between spaces of the normative and expected, color performs as a marginal substance with perverse capacities to exceed binaries of difference. David Batchelor has defined "chromophobia" as the attempts to devalue, diminish, and deny the significance of color in Western culture due to its association with "some 'foreign' body—usually the feminine, the oriental, the primitive, the infantile, the vulgar, the queer or the pathological." Color has historically been relegated to the cosmetic, the superficial; it is seen as trivial as much as it is dangerous and as merely a secondary quality of experience excluded from "higher concerns of the Mind."[3] This association extends into the twentieth century, as abstract expressionists such as Mark Rothko and Barnett Newman denied that color was the touchstone of their work, expressing the modernist fear of association with the decorative or superficial.[4] But it is precisely the marginal and even dangerous capacities of color that make it an animating medium for queer tactics.

Color's excessive capacities have been highlighted by theorists who understand color to operate at the limits of language and signification. Julia Kristeva puts forth a theory of color that challenges any easy analogy between painting and linguistic categories (signifier, signified, and referent), which, she argues, fail to account for the work of color in excess of meaning. For Kristeva, color evokes a triple register of Freudian drives (exterior drives, interior drives, and signifier) that frustrates both representation and language.[5] I will return to the drive later, but for now I want to point out the importance of this frustration that allows color, within an abstract formal language, to exceed a political regime of representation. Attributing the work of color to the modernist shift from figural realism to abstraction, Kristeva asserts that it is through color that "the subject escapes its alienation with a code (representational, ideological, symbolic, and so forth)" and that "Western painting began to escape the constraints of narrative and perspective norm ... as well as representation itself."[6] Operating in excess of language, color presents a crisis of naming;

for Thierry De Duve, if color appears to "speak" for matter, for the body, it nevertheless frustrates signification.[7] David Batchelor has also written that color can become "an embarrassment to language" because the difficulty of putting our experience of color into words constantly reminds us of the limits of linguistic expression.[8] Color is thus a crucial strategy for queering abstraction, refusing and exceeding the interpretive logic by which the surface of paint is read in terms of encoded bodily surface.

This chapter focuses on the work of Linda Besemer, in which color performs an emphatically material and synthetic drag—in the sense of both physical pull and the performative surface play of gendered camp. In a conversation with David Batchelor, Besemer also discusses color as a shamelessly excessive plastic element and explains that abstraction and color in particular offer potential freedom from representation and language.[9] Besemer's sculptural paintings have been likened to domestic objects (towels or curtains), where formalism meets the everyday through the particular behavior of their medium. This work is taken both as an extension of the midcentury modernist project of painting (extending from Jackson Pollock, Robert Ryman, and Frank Stella in one account) and from postminimal abstractionists like Eva Hesse who experimented with the elasticity of their synthetic mediums.[10] That is, Besemer's work achieves both formal and material innovation, intersecting with multiple generations that might seem to be at odds. Here, I am pursuing the queer potential of color in the artist's work as both a material and an optical element that performs affectively rather than representationally.

Comparing Besemer's folded paint sculptures to the 1970s postminimal work of Lynda Benglis, I consider how the removal of canvas support along with the use of unnatural color might challenge the binary divisions of surface and depth by which bodies are raced and gendered. While the medium of this work is plastic paint, the bright and sometimes fluorescent color both exists materially—it registers texturally as a tacky surface—and appears to vibrate or shine beyond itself. Besemer takes the materialization of color further through the use of optical illusion and surface pattern that I compare with the op art paintings of Bridget Riley, undermining modernist efforts to detach the surface of painting from illusion. Not only do these works produce an illusory sense of movement in space; they shake any sense of solid ground by deploying illusion as a playful force of affective encounter (rather than in the service of representation). These unruly physical and visual operations of dragging that destabilize spectatorship, prompting nonnormative ways of seeing, also resonate in multiple ways with genderqueer, crip, and antiracist potential. Turning to the cast sculptures of Carrie Yamaoka at the end of this chapter, I show how both Besemer's and Yamaoka's works activate color to undermine the logic that we could read the "truth" of a body on its surface.

Dragging Chroma

Deploying color as a medium, Linda Besemer's work drags on the loaded visual histories of color in ways that draw out its perverse possibilities. The folding and unfolding of Besemer's work might recall a thin skin for some viewers; but color registers as chemical, plastic, a false embellishment. This emphasis on the materiality of synthetic materials points back to the privileging of commercial paint, which characterizes the treatment of color in art since 1950.[11] The deployment of color as industrial "ready-made" is one way in which mid-twentieth-century artists would attempt to detach emotion from color, previously taken to be an expressive element of painting, even as so much desire and anxiety was still tied up in this abandonment of color as symbolic in favor of color as pure materiality.[12] But the use of unnaturally bright color might also work queerly to expose the affective resonance that is already there in the history of color since modernism. While it seems a straightforward or even apathetic aesthetic approach, the use of unmixed color and manufactured pigmented materials might actually produce mixed feelings in this work. It signals an ambivalent attachment to past aesthetic approaches that might seem to gloss over difference or specificity or feeling, but nevertheless hold out possibilities for affective encounters with difficult material—the laborious drag of something toxic and corrupting, slippery and ungrounding.

The fearful artifice of material color serves as a refusal of purity at the same time that it offers a sensual medium for queer encounters. The neo-avant-garde's disavowal of authenticity, originality, and the artist's singular subjectivity was served by color's status as industrial product. But plastic's associations and operations already exceed that of mere industrial substance; for Roland Barthes, plastic is "the stuff of alchemy," the miraculous "transmutation of matter" that embodies not form but infinite movement. Yet, plastic is also a disgraced material, unable to re-create natural colors, "retaining only the most chemical-looking ones. Of yellow, red and green, it keeps only the aggressive quality, and uses them as mere names, being able to display only the concepts of colours."[13] The artifice and toxicity of plastic color crucially points to the ways in which color exceeds language. The slippage between "mere names" and the colors to which they correspond, between signifier and signified, presses against the modernist project of abstract painting in which color was the ultimate semiotic element.[14]

Queer deployments of readymade color might similarly reject a focus on a singular body or perspective, while at the same time using color's surface effects in ways that draw out its sensual capacities. Linda Besemer's focus on the particular qualities of plastic color is not a move to reject expression as it was for some midcentury artists associated with strict formalist abstract painting. Instead, this work offers tactics for undermining direct representation—which was also useful for earlier post-expressionist painters as well as minimalist sculptors—while maintaining the affective work and stretching the elastic possibilities of color as folding surface. Rather than give us a signifier under which the signified is hidden, color's plasticity works in a perverse slippage and affective ambivalence, folding between oppositions of inside and outside, subject and object, nature and artifice.

Emphasizing the "pure materiality" of color over its symbolic associations was one important intervention of the monochrome. After painting *Pure Colors: Red, Yellow, Blue* in 1921, Rodchenko proclaimed, "This is the end of painting," and "There will be no more representation."[15] The end of representation would logically result in painting's "death," but in fact this move opened the practice of painting to the possibilities for tactile and material encounters that were traditionally associated with sculpture. Further, the material shift from artist's paints to household industrial paints in midcentury abstract art suggested a shift in the purpose and promise of painting: while artist's paints were developed for the primary purpose of representing bodies in space, industrial paints were made to cover larger surfaces in a flat layer of color, and, as David Batchelor suggests, "They form a skin, but they do not suggest flesh."[16] For Batchelor, the anxiety around this shift concerned the abandonment of an entire history of easel painting, now trading tradition for technology, but I want to consider the flesh. Queer deployments of color might reimagine this historic shift by dramatizing the ways in which this anxiety around representation and color in painting is also an anxiety about bodies and embodiment. Besemer's rendering of colorful matter in folding configurations, while retaining the artificial appearance of its elastic material surface, offers alternatives to notions of painted color reduced to the representation or sign of a body.

The monochrome is a modernist icon on par with the grid, positing a universal essence of painting and testing the limits of the medium. Ann Gibson offers a feminist account of the monochrome's potential as a site of difference, or where our perception is opened to difference. Looking to the work of Marcia Hafif in particular, Gibson views previous theories of the monochrome as problematically eliding the body and the specific and offers instead an understanding of the monochrome that speaks to embodiment even in its resistance to signification. She views the monochrome not as an escape from figuration, as modernists might have hoped, but as another sort of resistant otherness "that will not consent to being defined, hierarchized, placed. There is an aspect of monochrome that might be said to speak mainly from the body to the body. This aspect of monochrome, of color, qualifies a staple of postmodern thinking by making *words'* control of representation as contingent as the meanings of bodies *in* systems of representation." [17] While this reading might reduce the surface of paint to the body (though not reduced to the feminine), Gibson finds an insightful path through the thick modernist and postmodern discourses to read the surface of color as insisting on difference and variability rather than neutrality in terms of both surface facture and interpretive possibility. Lifting off from this space of possibility, I consider color's fugitive operations beyond physical containment not only to disrupt signification but to disrupt how we interpret substance on the surface.

The deployment of color as a singular material surface seems easy to interpret as a skin, and particularly skin as a site of difference in feminist analysis. But in *Thinking Through the Skin*, Sara Ahmed and Jackie Stacey point out that arguments that "the body" has been elided in masculinist thought can problematically fetishize the body as an object that is simply missing, assuming it contains these differences within a singular figure. Instead, they consider how social differences function to produce the boundaries—the skins—which appear to mark out the body. They ask how skin is given meaning and logic, how it is assumed to contain the body, identity, or value.[18] Similarly moving us toward a Black feminist analysis that troubles the spectator's desires to fix race on the surface of the body, Rizvana Bradley uses material metaphors of the stain and the (w)hole to theorize how Black women can both appear as marked violently by race and at the same time disrupt that signifying logic through an excessive and performative embodiment.[19] Here, I am investigating and challenging a skin fetishism—not that of bodies directly, but the bodily capacities attributed to the surface of painting, and particularly to color. For example, Briony Fer has discussed color as a fetishistic material, the site of fantastic bodily projection in the work of Italian colorists such as Alberto Burri, whose monochrome paintings have been read as wounds, cut and sutured. Fer is more interested in the painting surfaces sculpturally transformed through intense materiality in ways that are perverse and fetishistic.[20] I would like to extend this discussion of the perverse erotics of color, deployed beyond the signifying body, by considering how color works as a materializing force.

The artworks I discuss in this chapter activate color in two senses of the word: one of the etymologies of the term *color* (from Latin and Old French) derives from skin tone or complexion, that is, *colored*, and also originates in terms of appearance, as in a covering (from the Latin *colos*) that conceals or hides. On the one hand, color could be seen to drag out the truth of the matter on the surface—the truth of a body on its skin. On the other hand, rather than a cover that conceals, color's blush of exposure can also unfold as a flaming revelation, operating more like the psychoanalytic screen. Color registers perversely as the decorative surface of style, aligning with queer camp, and at the same time problematizes the opposition between synthetic surface and meaningful core. Rather than disregard color as decorative surface that covers over the real, I take color seriously as a substance with real ethical and ontological implications.

Reckoning with the racial implications of colored surface, this chapter considers the ontological trouble posed by the queer work of color deployed as a medium, undermining readings that would take its surface either as superficial or as an indicator of the "truth" of a raced, gendered, and sexed body. Flaming color resonates with the performative sense of drag as a play with gendered signifiers on the surface and deploys color excessively and evocatively in ways that seem so obviously campy and yet seriously undermine that surface-substance equivalence. Rather than a hardening or fixing of difference through material representation, these works open up a multiplicity of folding surfaces that do not adhere to singular or binary categorizations. Exceeding both representation and the language of its name, color's paradoxical role as both transcendent and particular can allow for an alternative understanding of painting's ontological implications.

Color Sense 1: Styles of the Flesh

Challenging the notion that surface is a direct index of substance, Linda Besemer's sculptures demonstrate the plasticity of paint as both surface and matter of the work. They challenge binary divisions of interior versus exterior that would imply that surface both is distinct from matter and, at the same time, reveals the truth of that matter. This paradox of color produces both a synthetic surface aesthetic as well as a materializing force. Returning to *Large Zip Fold #1*, the work's overwhelming size, towering above the viewer, as well as its malleable folding, gives it a certain weight despite its thinness. While the effects of alternating colors create a sense of illusion, depth, and movement, this work is all surface. Some of Besemer's "Fold" sculptures are draped over aluminum rods on the wall, so that both the front and back of the composition are visible, overlapping but distinct. Alternating colors and patterns emerge on either side to create a space that is both illusory and material, dramatizing the "flatness" of painting while defying its rejection of depth and insisting on its heft and physical complexity.

Besemer's paint sculptures recall the work of Lynda Benglis, who is known for pouring and peeling paint away from the canvas in the 1960s and '70s, a process that explicitly parodies the performative drip method associated with Jackson Pollock.[21] Rearticulating expressive abstract aesthetics of painting in sculptural form, Benglis pulled the medium of paint from its two-dimensional surface to take on a three-dimensional quality, severing it from the privileged canvas support, and this technique is clearly reiterated in Besemer's work. Rather than drip paint onto a flat canvas, Benglis poured layers of pigmented latex across gallery floors, where it dried to create plastic sheets that could then be peeled away from the ground and relocated. Benglis's sculptures are also composed of vibrant colors (they are not the moody color configurations of a Pollock). These latex pours and oozing sculptures have evoked associations with organic figurations while at the same time emphasizing their plasticity, their synthetic materiality.

Using artificial colors and materials to create organic forms, Lynda Benglis subverted the minimalist correlation between manufactured matter and industrial image, at a time when anti-illusion meant anticolor.[22] Rather, she used synthetic matter in ways that emphasize its unruliness and its sensual, visceral qualities that stress a process of potentiality over artistic intentionality. Benglis's *Contraband* (1969) (see plate 14) is a lengthy rainbow latex sheet that spans over thirty feet to enliven a cold gallery floor. Composed of red, orange, yellow, green, and blue pigmented latex that flows together in marbled patterns, it materializes bubbles and streams of color that are both uncontrolled and contained within the thin sheet of rubbery matter that, at its edges, appears to curl upward and lift off from the surface of the ground. Color figures itself in this work—rippling out, buckling and gathering at its edges, its plasticity allows it to take up an indeterminate space, where it moves and forms through its interaction with the environment and floor.

The feminist discourse around Lynda Benglis's work consistently relates her objects to nature, so that painterly matter also becomes bodily and distinctly feminine. Her sculptures have drawn associations with biomorphic and anthropomorphic gestures, a focus on the palpable "flesh" and erotic physicality of her work, and symbolic references to both male and female forms as well as natural phenomena.[23] Jack Halberstam has discussed Besemer's work in relation to the postminimal sculptures of Eva Hesse, positing that "the formal qualities of perverse and abject gendering" and "ambiguous states of being" are in alignment with qualities that Halberstam identifies as transgender.[24] I am similarly interested in the synthetic plasticity and colorful configurations of Besemer's paint sculptures and in reclaiming formalism and abstraction for a genderqueer art practice that undermines normative bodily inscription. Rather than take painted color as always being the representation or sign of a (gendered, sexed, raced) body or subject, however ambiguous, I consider the alternatives promised by the physicality, the depth, and the plasticity of color as it both inheres in matter and projects forth as optical sensation. As I will show, Besemer's work also brings something else to this discourse around Benglis—an ordered process and surface illusion that further destabilizes the ground of representation.

Concerns about the art object's relationship to the human body is central to debates on postwar abstraction; anthropomorphism is essential to Michael Fried's criticism of minimal art as "theatrical," while Donald Judd and Robert Morris explicitly rejected the anthropomorphic as having been exhausted by painting (they wanted to create independent objects, not human resemblance).[25] In the wake of postminimalism, Lucy Lippard framed the sculptures of Eva Hesse and Louise Bourgeois as "eccentric abstraction" that embraced the surreal, visceral identification from which male minimalists so urgently distanced their work.[26] Reconsidering Lippard's discussion of these organic, bulbous sculptural forms in work which would seem to deliberately evoke the body and the erotic, Briony Fer points to a different definition of anthropomorphism, one that might move beyond notions of bodily empathy. Utilizing Roger Caillois's model of mimicry—how an insect changes color in order to disappear and lose its distinctness, and where camouflage acts as a negative signifier and effaces rather than connotes—Fer notes that this desire for self-effacement corresponds to the spatial allure of these objects, running counter to bodily empathy and erotic identification. This sense of mimetic compulsion is not a matter of the art object's associations or resemblance, but rather has to do with the coming-into-being of the subject in the visual field which is inhabited from the inside rather than viewed from the outside.[27] Fer is getting at the ways in which the organic forms produced by these women sculptors, so often understood in terms of the feminine body as a kind of external resemblance, might instead offer an expression of what it means to inhabit that body, while refusing to contain its borders and exacerbating somatic affect. The materiality of the works I discuss here operates more as an affective, haptic flow between multiple bodies or forms rather than inhering within a singularity. At the same time, I want to press against the notion that a contemporary queer or feminist sculpture would necessarily reincorporate the body that minimalists rejected.[28]

While an organism uses color to "disappear" in Caillois's version of mimicry, the works of Besemer and Benglis announce their presence through alluring color that registers as both erotic and synthetic. Their plastic, rubbery materials and slippery latex sheets evoke the matter of sex toys—plastic, the great imitator, is the stuff of dildos. If these sheets of plastic paint evoke skins, they are more in the realm of skin-tight latex suits and BDSM gear: synthetic surfaces deployed for imaginative play rather than the accurate imitation of a different body (brightly colored strap-ons are obviously not made to mimic penises, or they do so in camp fashion). At the same time, the use of vivid and vibrant color might seem surprising as a queer tactic because surfaces that "blend in" might serve a survival function for nonnormative subjects. This camouflage might register in terms of passing in order to appear as a viable subject in the world or in particular spaces or communities. According to Butler, queering can operate as an exposure of passing that disrupts the repressive surface of language, which is exploded by sexuality and insistence on color.[29] Thinking about sexual and racial difference together, the insistence on bright colorful surface in these artworks might also insist on a flaming exposure of the subject who is raced, gendered, and sexed according to the appearance of that very surface. That is, synthetic coloring can reveal the potential violence of that abstraction. At the same time, the borders of this work refuse to contain its ooze and flow, and that which registers as bodily also resonates affectively and refuses to remain hidden.

Besemer's "Fold" sculptures, whether hanging directly from a wall or draped over a rod, make no distinction between interior and exterior. What we might perceive as the painting's exterior is another dimension of its interior, and vice versa. Besemer is an avowed Deleuzian, so it is not coincidental that this resonates with Gilles Deleuze's concept of the "fold," where matter is fluid and each fold or dimension is contingent upon its surroundings, constantly animated in motion, infinitely dividing but still cohering. The outside is nothing but a folding of the inside.[30] This spatial concept of matter is demonstrated by Besemer's folding sheets of pure acrylic, where back and front both constitute the painting's "surface," and both are contingent upon one another. While the matter of the work holds together, it does not cohere a figure (or subject) by reifying the boundary between inside and outside. Rather, its continuous surface insists on nothing hidden that could be revealed, no "truth" to be signified or indexed on the painting's surface. Further, this fetishizing of the surface—its brightness, its shininess—does not fetishize a surface or skin as container of a body. It fetishizes the decorative surface-as-surface, delighting in the camp of decoration that does not claim to be anything other than surface play.[31] The surface itself is matter, rather than the cover of material truth on a body. Further, the surface operates affectively as a field of interaction, allowing a dynamic relationship between interior and exterior that puts pressure on the binaries structuring subject formation.[32]

Considering how the surface of color works against or exceeds the stabilization of matter has important ethical implications for bodies or matter taken to be a fixed body. Asking "How does a body figure on its surface the very invisibility of its depth?" Judith Butler considers the interiority of the body as a function of social discourse and regulation on the body's surface. Gender, then, is a stylized corporeal surface with a history: "styles of the flesh" or a stylized repetition of acts that constitutes what we read as the body's interior signification on its surface.[33] The body cannot be taken as a coherent foundation on which gender is performed but is instead itself as malleable and marked as the surface that is taken to be its exterior. For Butler, the body is a medium, where the boundary of skin becomes the limit of the socially hegemonic, and notions of interiority and exteriority reify a binary used to stabilize a coherent subject. Rather than treat the materiality of gender or sex as given, Besemer's deployments of material color refuse to form a coherent whole. When paint is liberated and color is figured away from the canvas ground, it becomes a continuous surface that works not to conceal or reveal what's hidden "beneath," but to produce its own animate folding and unfolding.

This work also carries ontological implications, considering how color has been used to mark bodies as raced and othered through the reduction of a subject to the body's surface. This phenomenon has been described by Frantz Fanon as "epidermalization" and further elaborated by Paul Gilroy as "a historically specific system for making bodies meaningful by endowing them with qualities of 'color.' It suggests a perceptual regime in which the racialized body is bounded and protected by its enclosed skin." In Gilroy's notion of "epidermal thinking," the skin is conceived not as part of the body, but as its "faithful wrapping."[34] Gayatri Spivak's term for this is "chromatism," the reduction of race to skin color, or as Sara Ahmed describes it, a fetishism in which the surface of skin "becomes an object that tells the truth of a subject's racial origin."[35] If color is at the core of racial fetishism, projections that color bodies according to this epidermal thinking, then the queer work of color as an explosive, catachrestic, plastic surface potentially disrupts this logic. The refusal of Besemer's sculptures to act as a colorful surface *for* matter, instead insisting on color itself as plastic substance through a process that transforms the fluid paint to a slippery and stretchy sheet of folding and unfolding matter, also calls for an understanding of color as an unreliable and reductive indicator of the body's origins. That is, we might understand the transformative capacities of color deployed as a medium to refuse the fixity of chromatist stigma. Instead, the slippery and almost toxic appearance of surface in the works of Besemer and Benglis can reveal the processes of danger and difficulty implicit in visibility, or the appearance of a subject in the visual field.

Thinking of Freud's sexual drive with Frantz Fanon's *Black Skin, White Masks*, Teresa de Lauretis uses the trope of implantation, which links the drive at once to the ego and to the social, in order to discuss the model of psychic trauma as not only sexually but racially implicated. The projection and absorption of an unmetabolizable signifier is what Fanon describes in his experience of being interpellated as a feared Black man, when his self-image profoundly changed, "the corporeal schema crumbled, its place taken by a racial epidermal schema." This violent implantation of race on the skin, Fanon writes, "in the sense in which a chemical solution is fixed by a dye," invades the self with destructive, unassimilable presence. And it is precisely the materiality of the body that de Lauretis emphasizes as the site of exchange for the drive in its many forms.[36] Utilizing Jacques Derrida's notion of the Freudian impression that "draws a mask right on the skin," I think about color as something that both implants on the surface of matter and inheres within as depth.[37] These analogies between a chemical dye and the racialized surface of skin, and the impression that conceals the drive as a mask drawn on the skin, point to the violence of color that marks a body and attempts to conceal—in a process through which it makes visible—its own destructive force. I will investigate this idea of something the ego cannot metabolize—racial and sexual projections and interpellations—through two sculptures by Besemer and Benglis, respectively, that play in the space between surface and depth in ways that upset ontological certainty.

Linda Besemer's "Slab" sculptures are composed of multiple mono-chrome layers of pure acrylic paint applied in varying thicknesses and then carved down to create a colorful topography that rises and falls. These sculptures are carved not by hand but by an altered computer numerical control (CNC) machine, which cut the slabs of dried paint to Besemer's programmed specifications. Their patterns produce the effect of pulsating optical sensations that are at once illusory and material. *Red-Purple Slab* (see plate 15) layers flaming red and orange hues with yellow, green, purple, and blue—bright and unmixed pigments that then produce a ripple effect when carved in concentric circular waves. Moving between surface and depth, the eye is pulled between undulating layers of color, a thickness of monochrome surfaces that become topographical. In Benglis's *Untitled (vw)* (see plate 16), brightly colored polyurethane foam is poured out in layers against the corner of two walls, producing spills of red, pink, and orange that ripple out across and beneath one another, with a dark layer spilled over the top like a suspended avalanche of flowing black lava. Matter ripples across the surfaces of the forms, not layering external upon internal layers, but rolling out like waves where the substance swells and curls and envelopes itself in a fluid undulation. Rather than a homogenous substance that organizes into uniform movements, Benglis's brightly colored foam refuses to cohere into a whole; rather, it plays in and against a space that is both the grounds of its making and that it remakes and transforms through its emergence.

These deployments of flaming color act as excessive surfaces to produce a folding of interiority and exteriority. In both of these works, the stratification of surfaces to produce a depth speaks to a conception of matter that is both constituted on the surface and inheres within. While the suspended layers of Benglis's *Untitled (vw)* remember, holding on to the hand-poured process by which they were formed, Besemer's *Slab* is created through a subtractive process, forming a thickness through inscription. If this work demonstrates the psychic processes of epidermalization, it also speaks to the unmetabolizable foreign substance the ego cannot incorporate—the look of taffy and confection that appears sweet but also sticky and slimy, producing an uneasy material encounter. Consuming this work might make a viewer queasy: the synthetic matter suggests a processed sugary substance that might be difficult to chew and digest; Besemer's rippling color patterns provoke motion sickness; and Benglis's work threatens to melt and flow out to consume us. I also imagine this encounter in terms of a refusal or abjection, that which must be cast off or spit out in order to maintain the borders of the self, yet it sticks with us and threatens to submerge us.[38] This unmanageable, alien substance threatens the boundaries of bodies and of painting, calling attention to the materiality of color while refusing the encoded embodiment that some would ascribe to abstract painting. The difficulty of the encounter with these objects speaks to the danger of ascribing meaning to surface, symbolism to flesh.

Color Sense 2: "Perverse Perspectives"

Flaming colors are spectral in the dual sense that they are of the color spectrum and ghostly, producing waves and lingering impressions on the retina even after we look away. This energy is incorporeal, disembodied, and yet maintains a material presence that destabilizes through the work of perception. What Linda Besemer's work brings to our thinking about Benglis is an ordered technique and formulaic process; even as the work recalls Benglis's use of color-as-matter and the plasticity of paint, Besemer's work appears more precise and systematic. Besemer incorporates seriality and repetition in patterns that make color vibrate—as in the work of Benglis, the matter produces movement, but now, the color also moves in our vision. Perception and opticality return to the work of color. Depth is illusory as well as material and emphasizes a different kind of synthetic surface, a false sense of spatial depth that registers affectively rather than symbolically. Although the acrylic appears more controlled in Besemer's work due to its precise compositions, this work addresses a tension between the fantastic projections of optical perception and the literal materiality of plastic color.

Throughout modernist discourses on painting, there is a particular tension between the tactile materiality of the artwork as an object and the notion of a pure opticality that would transcend that work's specific matter and context.[39] Linda Besemer's work activates all of these potential qualities of painting and camps their definitions at the same time. This work literalizes and plays with notions of painting as pure and flat, while also insisting on the impurity of synthetic matter and the perversity of decorative surface qualities that Greenberg associated with a "crisis" in painting.[40] I trace Besemer's jarring optical surfaces back to op art exemplified by Bridget Riley's 1960s paintings in order to explore their dragging through a shifting of perception and imaginative projection. Riley experimented with the surface of painting as an illusory space that had been undermined in favor of an emphasis on its essential "flatness." She painted optical illusions of dizzying space on large canvases, immersing the viewer into this space through a hypnotic rhythm of mostly black-and-white patterns that appeared to ebb and flow beyond the canvas support. In 1967, Riley began using color to create her patterns with a series of "Cataract" paintings, producing waves with thin bands of red, blue, and white that might mimic a disabled vision. In *Cataract 3* (1967) (figure 3.1), blue and red lines ripple across the surface, undulating from thin to thick and back in a motion sickness–inducing pattern. The repetition of these waves is produced through a systematic structuring of the picture plane, and yet the overall effect is a space of constant flux, where the sensations of sight and its somatic manifestations are both pleasurable and agitating.

Disrupting the order or stability that pattern might otherwise produce, these paintings are even named for the disruption or blurring of vision, clouding what we normally presume to be clear. This is perhaps a cripping of painting's perspectival system in that it not only evokes vision loss but might actually disable the viewer—we feel dizzy or nauseous if we gaze at it for too long.[41] Both Riley and Besemer deploy the illusory capacities of painting, but they do so in a way that creates an instability that is felt and also has implications for how we perceive the surface of things. Nicole Archer has similarly shown how trans artists have manipulated the trope of the pattern in figural works in order to produce another way out of the ideology implied by pattern's oppressive regularity and repetition— a "dissonant and queer strategy of 'pattern-jamming.'"[42] But rather than a pattern used to jam up our gendering of the body's surface via figural representation, these queer abstractions play with pattern to insist on the distortions of colorful surface illusion and use that distortion in a performative painting drag.

Bridget Riley's work undermined modernist efforts to detach painting from illusion even before many feminist artists embraced the decorative and ornamental surfaces that were dismissed by modernist critics. But what might be the benefit or significance of returning illusionism to painting, and particularly through abstraction? Rather than an illusion of depth and recession into space, these paintings invert this dynamic and project out at us. This is what Lucy Lippard called "perverse perspectives," an illusionism emerging in the 1960s that does not abandon the modernist picture plane but "distorts and reconstructs that plane outside

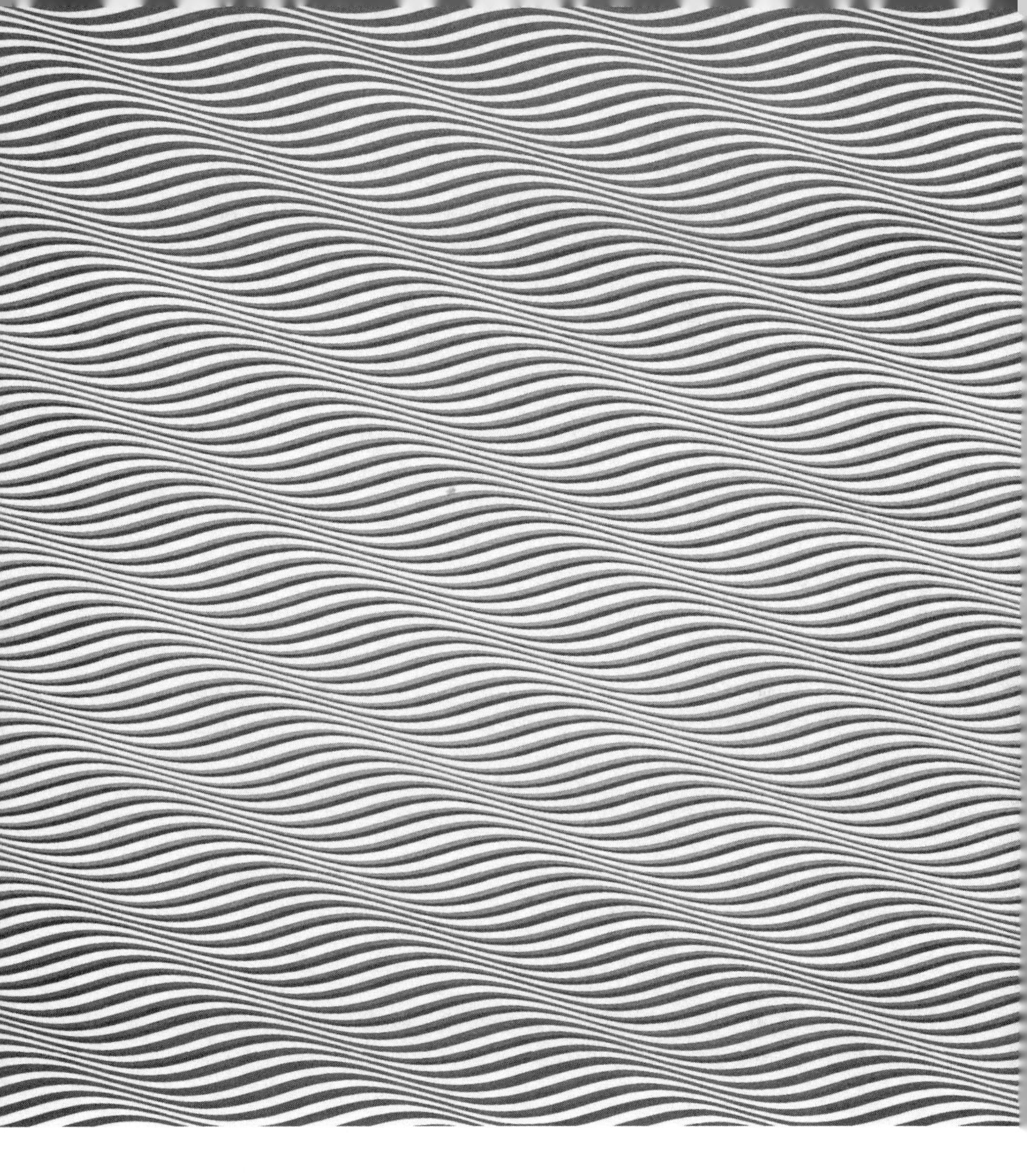

FIGURE 3.1 Bridget Riley, *Cataract 3*, 1967.
Oil on canvas, emulsion PVA on linen, 88 × 87 in.

of the conventions of depth simulation."[43] Op art such as Riley's denies the illusion of depth on a picture plane, but does so by utilizing illusionism directly "so that its falseness or trickery is apparent but necessary; persistent reversals of visual fact force the eye back to the plane."[44] And color is crucial to this formal dissonance; the visual vibration of surface is manipulated through both color and plasticity, which can both establish and destabilize our sense of volumes in space.[45] This opticality makes no effort to hide its construction of the spectatorial space of the canvas; rather, it makes perception visible or recognizable as illusion itself. While it is typically taken to be an act of deception, this term stems from the Latin *illusionem*, an ironic form of mockery, and *illudere*, "to play with." As a camp tactic of drag, this kind of illusion does not claim depth but delights in surface play.

Color is inherently unstable, plastic, and changeable. But Bridget Riley claimed that her medium is not color or paint itself, but perception, a matter of sensation evoked through colored light.[46] This emphasis on perception links her, not with minimalists working at the same time who were anti-illusionist and strove for a literal object in space, but with European artists such as Yves Klein who sought a dematerialization of the art object and believed in the transcendent power of color. While the dematerialization of color in Riley's painting might seem to adhere to the spiritual qualities associated with one history of abstract painting, Besemer returns its material plastic status, confronting the ethics of transcendence at play in this history by dragging us back to the surface. We do not just take in these paintings visually; they vibrate in ways that alter the spaces between us, shaking the very ground from which we view the work.

Investigating the construction of spectatorial space in painting, Peggy Phelan also identifies something perverse at work in the theatrical technology of perspective. The structure of the vanishing point becomes a structure of disavowal, some form of looking away: "we know it is a flat canvas, but we want it to have depth enough to hold the interiority of the bodies it displays."[47] In this "theatre of perversions," perspective draws us in, but it also casts us out; we turn away from the image—somehow, the painting looks back, causing us to doubt our own boundaries and limits. Through the transformation of the flat surface into deep space, our perspective elicits our desire for precisely what skin cannot offer us—the depth to contain our subjectivity.[48] For Phelan, it is Caravaggio's painting that allows us to witness this radical disembodiment of subjectivity, this frustrating formlessness. But I would like to think with this conception of perverse perspective through the kinds of optical illusions that we encounter in Linda Besemer's work. These sculptural paintings draw us in—they are bright, shiny, colorful, and lively—but those same qualities make them repulsive, their surfaces thrust us out. This takes Lippard's "perverse perspectives" further, as the falseness of surface not only is made apparent, the depth perception inverted, but prompts a different understanding of skin and bodily surface which never really contains us.

Besemer's *Fold #8, Baroqueasy* (1999) (see plate 17) is a flat sheet of acrylic paint folded over a metal rod. Vertical and horizontal bands of color appear to be woven over and under one another, creating a pattern that both resembles woven fabric and begins to vibrate in our vision as dominant shades of yellow, blue, black, and white interact in their close proximity. Folded over, one side of the acrylic sheet hangs down below the other so that both sides of the fold are visible and interact as a continuous surface. It produces both harmony and dissonance through chromatic vibration that, taking its title seriously, references Baroque decoration and culture of excess—and so excessive in this case as to produce a queasy effect. Here, perceptual projection is made literal and material; not pure or unified, but unruly, unpredictable, and uncontrollable. These interactions between colors and spatial illusionism might also speak to difference—the way in which two colors interact in close proximity also produces something else, a third nonbinary dimension or possibility that we can perceive even as it does not exist materially. Besemer's work makes human perspective material in this way, creating a push and pull between illusion and matter that makes things move. Our bodies and the space around us, or between ourselves and the object, the floors and wall, all become surfaces upon surfaces—nothing inheres within.

Op art has this potential not only for exploring human perception in relation to the illusory space of painting, but also for the ethics of perception, and the politics of how surfaces are read and represented. Discussing the transformation of the object in relation to the subject in *The Fold*, Deleuze defines *perspectivism*, or point of view, as not a "dependence in respect to a pregiven or defined subject" and "not what varies with the subject," but "the condition in which the truth of a variation appears to the subject. This is the very idea of Baroque perspective."[49] So while we commonly understand the relativism and the variability of points of view based on subject positions or identities, this concept of perspective is based not on a fixed subject but on the very recognition of a transformation, so that we *come to* the point of view. Besemer's work speaks to the impermanence not only of ontology and surface structure, but also of perception—how color changes and moves and is not dependent on our position in the world but brings us to the object (or Deleuze's *objectile*) without ever really arriving at a stable condition or orientation.

Carrie Yamaoka's Deep Blue

The material drag of transformation and volatile alchemy of flaming color takes on further resonance in the work of Carrie Yamaoka, who addresses the political present by making visible and material that which usually goes unseen. Yamaoka is one of the founding members of the queer art collective fierce pussy, circulating images and texts that speak directly against social and political violence while gesturing toward possible future transformations. At the same time, she utilizes abstract processes in various mediums to investigate the exposures and perceptions that govern our views of subjectivity and the violence that results from those views. Yamaoka creates iridescent objects that refuse to be fixed. Using reflective polyester film as the ground for these objects, Yamaoka pours layers of urethane resin to cast a luminous thickness that becomes a mirror-like surface, as seen in *72 by 45 (deep blue #3)* (see plate 18), which is colored a rich lapis blue. I am drawn into this large panel—its hard candy hue produces a sumptuous deep space that is actually the rippling reflection of the space around me. The object is impossible to photograph without also capturing its context. Any head-on photograph of Yamaoka's objects will also contain the distorted reflection of the photographer (or the apparatus of camera and tripod). But the indeterminate chemical reactions of the curing process produce ruptures beneath the surface—bubbles, ripples, and folds in the polyester disrupt the transparency of this screen. I see myself in the object as it engulfs me and distorts my image, the surface of my body becomes as materially indeterminate as the work itself. At the same time, the work implicates me in my own gaze, destabilizing any sense of clear perception. In their ongoing transformative drag via a queer corruption of matter, these works also undermine the power of the gaze to fix a subject according to predetermined codes. All of our bodies are colored by the object.

While some of Yamaoka's objects are vibrant glowing colors, the majority of these works are metallic silver or black. Indeed, I would not say that the artist's practice is focused on color in the way that Besemer's is—Yamaoka's work has a more compelling relationship to photography than to painting due to the alchemical processing that creates the final work, which never stops developing. While Linda Besemer's work is more methodical, Yamaoka embraces chance processes and unruly materials, allowing more precarity in terms of materializing the object itself. Similar to Besemer's work, these objects evoke tensions between painting and sculpture, the fluid and the still, surface and depth. They embrace plastic materiality and artificial surface. But Yamaoka's objects behave differently in their relation to their spectators and environments, in that they both reflect and interrupt that same reflection of their surroundings, oscillating between reflection and absorption. Taking the outside in, they transform and render strange that which they seem to incorporate. Even as the topography of these objects suggests that color is the cover for that reflective substrata of polyester film, the thick substance of color renders that reflection as volatile as its own chemical elements.

Yamaoka's work is profoundly disorienting in ways that suggest something like a queer optics, a sensation of seeing that also materializes the lens itself, the way in which some difficult affect might "color" one's vision. For example, Wayne Koestenbaum writes that humiliation resembles a fold—the moment when something interior and private and shameful is thrust to the outside, a sudden visibility in the wrong place: "My skin has been turned inside out. This fold (the self become a seam) is the structure of revulsion."[50] There is also the shrinking into oneself, the inward-folding and hunching of shoulders and downward gaze in response to that eruption. In this way, the terrain of the body can be visualized both materially and psychically, and color is not a cover that conceals but, like the bright red blush of shame, unfolds in a flaming revelation on the surface. Bodies are colored not only in the racialization of skin but, just as involuntarily, through the affective power of shame, the heat of lust, or the chalky blue blush of death.[51] This external manifestation of affect gives way to a disintegration of inside and outside, corporeal surface and ontological core. We color the world and are colored by it.

Rather than a cover that glosses over the things we might most want to push aside or negate—the problematic histories and toxic sludge of the past that continue to pollute our present environments and experiences—the materializing work of flaming color is a covering that does not conceal but reveals something altered on its surface. Thinking about the surface of color with Freud's "screen memories," the screen might function to suppress as well as provide a surface for projection, where memories are formed when their traces are aroused by fantasy, yet this surface is also a defense used to screen out unacceptable content.[52] An in-between surface for repressed elements to take shape and for their suppression, the screen might allow us to think exterior surface with interiority, a folding where something new takes shape even as some elements never appear. Yamaoka's work might drag up the surface of the screen, even as it holds on and incorporates from the outside. The material layering of colored matter does not stagnate into a smooth and passive surface of form but instead does the ambivalent work of subjectivity to both conceal and reveal, ebb and flow, hold and emit. Recognizing our intimate bonds to things we most want to keep separate—ties between internal and external, nature and artifice, the image and the real—also allows for the productive and transformative use of the negations, of the toxic or unnatural mixtures of matter and feeling. These are the very perverse affects that project out with the promise of unforeseen alternatives.

These objects attend to our perverse desire for the flat surface of color to also have depth enough to hold us. But at the same time that Yamaoka's work gives us a certain depth, the material thickness of fluid resin, it also registers the difficulty and impossibility of fully appearing in the visual field. The image of a self is returned to us, but the appearance that might otherwise be identified—raced, gendered, othered—is rendered as yet one more surface and one that is contingent on the alchemy of the medium through which our image develops. Absorbing our surface into its depth, the object thrusts us out again with the denial of a transparent representation. But rather than merely abject what it reflects, the surface of color here is also a medium of transformation and revelation. These objects beckon us and seem to invite attachment with their sumptuous hues and textures, but they refuse to simply give us an easy representation to consume or to hold. Instead, they challenge any certainty that surface appearance operates as a transparent index of substance while simultaneously insisting on the transformative capacity of that seemingly shallow surface. Color might seem to externalize difference, but that appearance is made difficult by a flaming eruption of material and visual excess that refuses to be categorically contained.

4 TRANSFORMING EVERYDAY MATTER

Sheila Pepe's fiber installations are knotted, twisted environments, where intersecting threaded nets span entire rooms from floor to ceiling. In *Mind the Gap* (2005) (see plate 19), monumental braided ropes of bright blue nautical towline pull viewers into the gallery, running along the walls in piles, coupling and diverging as they meander around the floor. These huge ropes anchor the bright red crocheted nets made of shoelaces and pulled upward to the ceiling. Looking across the room, we see a tangled proliferation of lines of various thicknesses that intersect in warped grids. Excess materializes in the endlessly twisting blue rope, thick enough to anchor a ship, and in the bright web of linear forms that frame a multiplicity of apertures and gaps. *Hot Mess Formalism* was the apt title for a 2018–19 survey of Pepe's work, including this piece.[1] The artist is known for these large-scale crocheted installations and sculptures made of everyday materials. Working since the 1980s and utilizing mediums that are often ephemeral and crafty, Pepe has pursued experimental processes of abstraction that contribute to feminist and queer craft traditions. Her work exemplifies an approach to queer abstraction that drags and deforms the art object itself—the canvas or sculpture—to produce whole environments that materially alter their spaces. In Pepe's case, these environments are spectacular and chaotic, transient and expansive, signaling the importance of particular spatial and material dynamics to the queering work of dragging away.

Queer abstraction may be considered a recent movement, but it is indebted to a previous generation of postminimal sculptors in the 1960s and '70s who boldly experimented with form and materials in order to forge new paths away from hetero-male norms of art making, such as Lynda Benglis, Eva Hesse, Harmony Hammond, Yayoi Kusama, or Senga Nengudi. This chapter focuses on the particular strain of queer abstraction that continues this legacy through the use of soft and ephemeral materials and readymade industrial objects. These works are often not singular sculptures, but more expansive space-making installations that transform everyday matter. I trace this tendency that we see in Sheila Pepe's work back to the sculptural installations of Harmony Hammond, an influential figure of the feminist art movement in the 1970s. In 1977, Hammond wrote about the feminist possibilities of abstract art in the first issue of the feminist art journal *Heresies*, which she also cofounded.[2] Hammond's sustained commitment to a lesbian feminist politics of abstraction has contributed to ongoing conversations about how forms, materials, and processes speak to gender and sexual politics. I compare her sculptures of accumulated everyday materials to the more recent work of Shinique Smith, who has been working for the past twenty years to construct monumental abstract works that combine painted calligraphy, textiles, and collage. Smith's transformation of readymade materials and objects speaks to experiences of race, gender, and citizenship while also producing new affective interconnections among the seemingly disparate things we encounter every day. I conclude the chapter with an installation by Tiona Nekkia McClodden, whose films, time-based work, and readymade objects explore shared ideas and perspectives of Black and queer communities. Considering all of these practices that are dimensional and environmental in scale, I elaborate the importance of spatial materiality for how abstraction works queerly. These artists' focus on process and uses of ephemeral and debased media actively form and deform things to illustrate the spatial and material tactics of dragging away.

The works in this chapter queer abstraction by making it material and felt and not at all divorced from the real. These abstractions are substantial, countering perceptions that form would somehow stand in opposition to matter; they also challenge notions of abstraction as immaterial or as a kind of outer shell that obscures substance.[3] These works are emphatically material, like all of the work in this book, but these are also distinctly three-dimensional and architectural in scale and orientation. The works' materializing is not about hardening or fixing difference in figural form, but is an active ongoing process and an excessive multiplicity; they manifest in ways that are materially voluminous and expansive rather than severely self-contained. While there is something distinctly queer about the small and the minor, these artists assert minoritized materials (craft media and mass-produced matter) in formations that take over their spaces. Their works overflow excessively and refuse the abstraction of containment in favor of abstraction as a catachrestic spatial and material process that resonates affectively rather than cohering around a physical representation.

Dragging and Deforming the Object

The works that are the focus of this chapter by Pepe, Hammond, Smith, and McClodden take on the contingencies of their materials to emphasize precarity, ephemerality, and the volume of matter worked, wrapped, and knotted in ways that also evoke their opposite—unraveling and coming undone. These active processes demonstrate the spatial tactics of dragging away in terms of their material deforming: the tearing, shredding, and cutting that transforms everyday matter with close attention to form along with the power of that matter to unmake or harm.[4] Their spatial movements and material activities encompass their destruction while asserting their aesthetic and political potential for transformations. Embracing the risk of uncertainty, they *do* things with the disregarded processes and shamed associations carried by their formal approaches and materials. Some of these works also exemplify the tendency for practices of queer abstraction to reckon with the exclusive modernist forms and objects that would seem to actively jettison difference, pointing to institutions and discourses that have excluded queer work. In all of their unmaking and remaking, they also make something new from the refuse and the refused, the discarded materials that carry their particular burdens of association with the readymade and with craft. These queer perversions drag by deforming the conventions of high art and sculpture right along with the compulsory feminine and domestic sanctions of textiles.

These works drag through their physical material processes of deforming, transforming the shape of something in ways that seem out of shape, disfigured, twisted. These deformations suggest a crip approach to form, as "deformed" carries the implications of physical disability, a body out of shape from the norm. I consider the deforming material processes of this work while also acknowledging the lived experience of disability that the term implies. While I am focused here on elaborating a queer approach that drags away from bodily legibility, there is much at stake in nonnormative deployments of form and matter that intersect with crip theoretical concerns about the radical potentials of material precarity.[5] Deformity powerfully undermines ideal form with defamiliarizing crip excess.[6] Here, I am concerned with material *processes* of deformation (rather than a fixed sign of deformity) that drag on certain formal ideals, modernist as well as postmodern or antimodernist concepts, to activate their queer and crip potentials.

These deforming distortions might be the queer crip answer to the tendency of "anti-form," Robert Morris's term for postminimal sculptural practices that refuse total control and embrace ephemeral mediums and more intuitively guided or chance-based processes that show up as part of the final work.[7] The queer abstractions in this chapter might drag on the anti-form approach by allowing the inherent qualities of their raw materials to dictate the final work (also an extension of modernist medium specificity), embracing the mess and sag of their soft materials. These works also recall Bataille's *informe* (*formless*), and Yve-Alain Bois and Rosalind Krauss's redeployment of the formless as a tendency in twentieth-century art that embraces a base materialism, destabilizes, and resists definition paradoxically through its performative material manifestations.[8] Many sculptural practices of queer abstraction create a strange interplay between material forms and the visible processes of their undoing, and these processes speak to ways of being and doing that nevertheless defy certainty or categorization.

Many of these abstract spatial and material processes also perform their drag in a manner of *distraction*, implying their more physical processes of pulling apart and drawing out in different directions. Revaluing the negative implications of a mental frenzy or madness, distracted abstractions might divert our attention away from the subjects and histories that have been centralized norms, out toward the margins and to the wildness of unimagined possibilities for being together in difference. The artworks I focus on here demonstrate a distracted spatial and material disorder along with a reimagining or refocusing on multiple and even opposing possibilities and perspectives. The work prompts movements in multiple directions to pull away from monolithic unity, performing a material ambivalence. The deforming materials and distracted processes of this work open up their formations to unpredictability, embracing the contingencies of unbinding, sprawling, and dispersed form.

The works in this chapter further undermine the representational function of form by igniting the affective and relational resonance of material tactics that also exceed the body. Sculpture in particular is considered to always carry some figural or corporeal signification, to behave according to an implicit anthropomorphism, even when the work is abstract.[9] But the works I am highlighting here offer spatial and material dynamics that drag on such assumptions and conventions of sculpture (as well as painting), often deploying readymade objects and materials that pervert their common uses.[10] Exploding out from singular form, they also drag on feminized, raced, and classed materials to bring out their substantive and world-making potential. These works demonstrate how queer abstraction can both engage spectators in a very real and present physical encounter while at the same time exceeding representational forms to suggest new possible formations. These queer world-making tactics do not foreclose possibility by cohering around a singular figural or bodily form, but produce haptic formations, sometimes a sprawling chaos, that are as materially present and "real" as they are transcendently excessive. This work drags on modernist notions of abstraction's spiritual transcendence of the everyday, not to transcend the realities of politics or social relations, but to distract away from the normative perceptions restricting our ability to imagine new possible lifeworlds—those that might not wear us down with phobic formations. Moving us beyond the realm of normative perception, these abstract spatial tactics shift our entire physical orientation, shaking up our sense of the space around us.

In what follows, I will outline three spatial and material tactics of dragging away that are demonstrated in works by Pepe, Hammond, Smith, and McClodden. The visual and material strategies of these works intersect and diverge in various ways. All have particular ties to familiar things and media that have been disregarded and have also historically challenged the very bounds of the art object, such as the readymade and craft tactics. Sometimes their deforming occurs through the artist's intuitive and experimental processes. And sometimes this contingency is more about the processes by which an object might be presumed to create meaning, yet that process is disrupted and those associations become precarious. The suggestive power of the familiar is often deployed and undermined at once, shifting our perspective toward what seems to be given, reckoning with the harmful misrecognitions and misidentifications that result from the surveilling demand to appear. These works often perform a material and affective undoing through their precarity, their ephemerality, their unraveling, or other damage. They might not always immediately signal a utopian transformation of the everyday but take on the power of their chosen objects and materials that also suggest harmful histories.

Negative Spaces

Sheila Pepe's approach to abstraction, "hot mess formalism," engages and directly challenges the traditional modernist formalism of Clement Greenberg, who understood abstraction as not material but purely visual, even when it came to sculpture.[11] This challenge to opticality can be traced to minimalism's assertion of abstract form as material presence, as form that engages the embodied viewer, and even more explicitly to the postminimal sculpture that rejected the cold aesthetics and industrial materials of minimalism in favor of more ephemeral, softer, "lower" media. Pepe continues to drag on this loaded term, *formalism*, to bring it into contact with readymade industrial matter (shoelaces, industrial rubber bands), crafting processes (crocheting), and postminimal ephemerality and the tendency to allow materials to dictate their own form. That is, Pepe brings formalism into contact with all the ways it has also historically been undermined, continuing to corrupt it by queerly insisting on formalist tactics that also deform.

Sheila Pepe's work is often discussed in relation to its engagement with a legacy of feminist crafting, which in turn lends itself to an affective interpretive lens.[12] Pepe's work is not typically discussed in terms of post-minimalism, however, or the work she does to deconstruct the privileged art object by unraveling the canvas and exploding sculpture. While Pepe may be utilizing craft material and processes, she also doesn't do doilies; if she does, they are enormous, beyond the realm of the everyday even as she uses everyday materials. Refusing medium categories of painting or sculpture, detaching from the canvas or the pedestal, her work undermines the representational function of form. Due to the environmental scale and dispersed forms of Pepe's installations especially, it is much harder for viewers to reduce this work to some representation of a body, and thus perhaps more clearly reinforces my insistence that being with the work is itself a queer experience.[13] This work transforms the viewer's space of encounter, and I want to consider how the dragging and deforming of the work is particularly generative for queering abstraction.

Pepe's approach to formalism is ephemeral, messy, and contingent. But she also methodically pursues a formal strategy that persists across her work over two decades—the deployment of lengthy threads to produce expansive installations that also materialize *negative space*. That is, they highlight the spaces between and around forms in ways that take up space while still insisting on the gaps and openings between. These negative spaces are deforming in the sense that they emphasize not just a making or forming, but also their opposite—an unraveling that opens up to queer possibilities beyond the representational. As in many of her fiber thread installations, *Mind the Gap* demonstrates how the webbing of intersecting strands highlights the space around and between the lines and chains of shoelaces, meeting and departing in crisscrossing formations. Rather than producing a mass composite, they focus us on moments of connection, nodes of contact where forms and threads meet. Line is mobilized but is never linear, materializing somewhat randomly and also projected onto the walls to create webbed shadows. The openings produced by Pepe's intuitive and distracted formal process actually take up more space than the material itself; our attention gets caught up in the shifting spaces between and among the pulled and draped lines.

If we attempted to physically navigate through the space, the materials would present something of an obstacle course, so the openings are potential but still complex and challenging. "Minding the gap" might propose attentiveness to the spaces around and between what we assume to be the subject or object of a work, creating a push and pull of formation and deformation.

When abstraction actively refuses categorical visibility, it also makes space for something else. Pepe's installations materialize substantively and expansively, and they also materialize these negative spaces that are not "empty" but actively opened. They assert the material agency to shape and alter their spaces while also insisting on opening it up. This work makes space for movement, for flows of feeling and desire. Pepe's negative spaces are not necessarily affectively pessimistic in the sense of materializing the worst, but rather open to what may materialize or happen, making space for the "not yet." These openings are not merely vacant space, but an aperture for a different vision, a space for manifestation, or an opportunity for something new to begin. Apertures allow us to see through and beyond and also create the possibility for a refusal to materialize the expected, or to materialize difference as expected. The material apertures in Pepe's work are also intermediaries through which something passes, haptic carriers of affect.

Sheila Pepe's formations of negative space also do their distracted, deforming work by undermining the normative position of those foundations of formalism—the canvas and pedestal—in order to make us feel the contingency and precarity around us. These installations never materialize the same way twice, changing according to their site of display and altering that site to drag on the white gallery walls or the cold minimalist architecture of many museum spaces, contaminating these sites with their visceral mess. Pepe's installations refuse to solidify a form and insist on substantive materiality at the same time, moving us instead through a haptic framework of indeterminacy. Her work emphasizes a shared space, mutual interdependency both of the form of the work (strands multiplying and intersecting, meeting in space) and of spectatorship (those who interact with the work in real time and space). Some of her installations are also communal art projects, embracing queer feminist community-building tactics and DIY (do-it-yourself) processes that are both exceptional and everyday. Pepe's practice uses processes of abstraction as forms of queer world-making based more on chance and ephemerality rather than predetermined coherence. In *Put Me Down Gently* (2014), for example, installed at the Institute of Contemporary Art in Boston—where shades of blue and green yarn, laces, and parachute chords were crocheted and knotted together at various points, suspended from the atrium and attached to the elevator—the work's shape-shifting movements were determined by the actions of visitors. This work is viscerally abstract in its intuitive processes and material presence that both drags away from representation and still engages the senses tangibly.

The negative spaces materialized by Sheila Pepe perform their precarity through an intuitive process that mobilizes contingency rather than certain intention. Pepe's refusal of a particular kind of mastery that may typically be associated with crafting (expertly making a perfect object by hand) also resonates as a deforming and distracting tendency. I've been calling the artist's process intuitive because for the most part, her site-specific installations are not preplanned but made through her physical engagement with the environment, trial-and-error, and sometimes relies on community members to help create the work. In this sense the work is open-ended and never installed the same way twice. Allowing the work to be guided by the contingencies of the material conditions and moment in which it is created, Pepe makes space for what may come—a formalist approach that does not preemptively represent but comes into being and visually and materially holds onto that process of becoming. That is, the work holds on to the look of how it was formed, creating something in the risky space of uncontrolled difficulty or unknowing.

This work visually and materially suggests unraveling, strands extracted from their usual function (shoelaces, nautical towline, unraveled textiles) to be redeployed and deformed. Their making also suggests unmaking. They pervert both the coherence of usable craft objects and the pristine gallery spaces that they occupy to transform. They embrace the mess and the risk of precarity to make something new from disregarded matter. To some extent this work acknowledges the trapping formations materialized by such craft mediums; even as the web-like environments are expansive and utopian in their world-making gesture, they might also suggest the ways minoritized subjects are bound by a relation to the "low" decorative and domestic practices deemed nonart. And the work suggests that it is far more generative to work from within to alter such spaces than to pretend we are not conditioned by them.

Accumulations

While Sheila Pepe's installations are generated through deforming processes of entangling and unraveling, the sculptures of Harmony Hammond are formed through processes of thick accumulation and tight wrapping. The central relevance of excessive materiality to queer abstraction, which I have highlighted throughout this book, arguably began with the tradition of lesbian feminist artmaking tactics exemplified by Hammond's work. Her thick sculptural abstractions of the 1970s typically deploy the salvaged material of cloth rags, sometimes worked together using craft approaches such as crocheting and braiding, and she often painted the rags in whatever form they took. Sculptures such as *Hunkertime* (1979–80) (figure 4.1) are bulky ladder forms leaning against a wall, all densely bound in painted fabric. Hammond wrapped rags around these scaffolds in thick layers, painting them with gesso, latex rubber, and acrylic resin. This particular group of nine sculptures are arranged in close proximity, six of them leaning together in the center and flanked by a single black form on the left and a pair of forms on the right. They suggest a functional everyday ladder, but their volume and the occasional frills at their edges also exceed this functional potential to delight in the visceral qualities of decorative painted acrylic and rubbery matter that coats them. The physical intimacies of this work demonstrate what, beyond suggesting a metaphorical figure, Hammond's formal tactics do to queer the art object itself and drag away from their presumed anthropomorphism.

Hammond's crucial role in theorizing the political potential of abstraction in the 1970s, asserting queer difference into the masculine sites of abstract form, cannot be overstated as foundational to the contemporary field of queer abstraction. Her ongoing refusal to take for granted the hetero-male established forms of art, forging the creative processes and formal experimentation that she defined as distinctly feminist and queer, have dragged the art object itself by defying categorical conventions and incorporating the mess of everyday matter and feeling. Refusing to depict any transparent lesbian content, Hammond's artwork and writing insisted on the revolutionary political potential of abstraction,

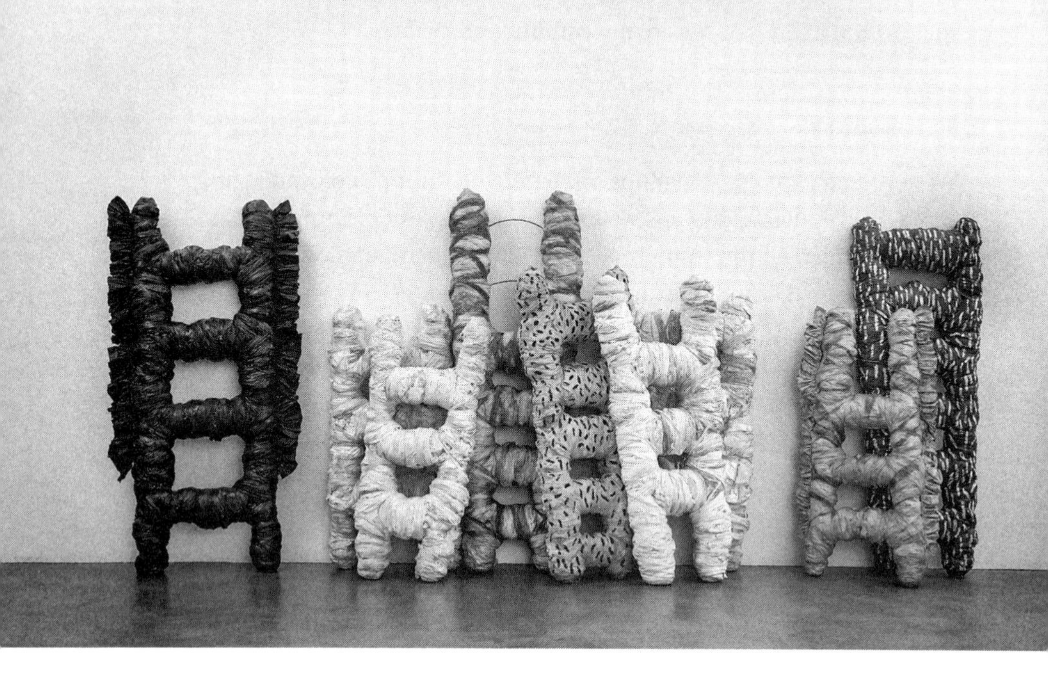

FIGURE 4.1 Harmony Hammond, *Hunkertime*, 1979–80. Cloth, wood, acrylic, metal, Rhoplex, and latex rubber, dimensions variable.

claiming formal tactics for refusing the "abstraction of the oppressor" to transform it in feminist terms.[14] Her work is situated in relation to legacies of postminimalism as well as queer and feminist crafting. And readings of her work never stray far from the body.[15] Julia Bryan-Wilson has positioned Hammond's work, particularly the rag rug *Floorpieces*, as combining "feminist politics, avant-garde abstraction, queer sensuality, and 'middlebrow' hobbyist crafting," while also troubling the application of singular or binary categories that her work queerly resists—high art versus low craft, masculine versus feminine, and so forth. Bryan-Wilson argues that Hammond's braided rag rugs invoke "a radical queer 'third space'—an orientation beyond the heteronormative binary."[16] Bryan-Wilson importantly describes this work in terms of camp ("rugs in drag") and understands these objects themselves as operating queerly. I want to lift off particularly from readings of the work's indeterminacy to expand on the queering of form that Hammond's work might incite. Even as the 1970s context in which this work emerged demanded that issues of identity or the personal be coded beneath layers of formalism—and much the same has been said of the postminimalist generation of women artists such as Eva Hesse and Lynda Benglis—I want to consider how this work also offers queer material tactics for new possible formations.

Even as I imagine what Hammond's work can do beyond stand in for bodies, I want to acknowledge there was much at stake for women artists working in the 1960s and '70s who were invested in reasserting bodily eroticism and expressivity in abstract sculpture in the wake of minimalism. Minimalism is commonly taken to be antisubjective, utilizing aesthetics that would distance the work from affect. Postminimalism is then thought to reassert a body that had been elided by masculinist practices of postmodern sculpture. The discourse around how the body might appear (or not) in the work of women artists is especially complex, and scholars have complicated definitions of the anthropomorphic. At times these readings essentialize and reduce the work to mere body surrogates or a direct human mimicry, while some feminist scholars have offered more complex readings of sculpture's relationship to anthropomorphism. For example, Susan Best understands minimalist antihumanism and the eclipse of authorship to intensify the affective resonance of the work of women artists such as Eva Hesse and Lygia Clark, where the subject who engages with their work is rendered destabilized rather than fixed.[17] Briony Fer troubles a language of anthropomorphism that implies bodily projection and empathy, challenging accounts where "organic forms seemed deliberately to inscribe an 'erotics' of the body" in abstract work by an artist such as Louise Bourgeois.[18] I touched on the issue of anthropomorphism in the previous chapter, but I want to continue to trouble the notion that in order for an abstract visual language to operate queerly or in ways that are useful for minoritarian politics, it must necessarily evoke bodily associations. Scholars have problematized this interpretive logic, and yet it maintains in current scholarship and art criticism. I am interested in continuing the valuable work that feminist scholars (Ann Wagner, Anna Chave, Lucy Lippard, and others) have done in elaborating the importance of materiality and affect in the work of a generation of women artists responding to minimalism.[19] Moving beyond the work's possible bodily association or encoded gender or sexuality, I want to delve into its material capacities for catachrestic excess and queer refusal to signify.

Hammond's approach to formalism is often to accumulate and transform everyday materials, undoing the categorical conventions and material structures of painting and sculpture. Her particular sculptural approach to canvas, and painterly approach to sculpture, not only deforms the conventional art object but insists that those objects operate as sites for negotiating everyday relations and feeling. In *Hunkertime*, Hammond deploys everyday matter to produce an affective situation of closeness and care as well as a restrictive binding. This work materially unravels the canvas or painted fabric, which is then applied to the wooden armatures, minimalist grid sculptures built up with the messy thickness of accumulated rags. The particular tactic of accumulation performs a gathering, an amassing of matter that builds up and proliferates across multiple forms that are repetitive yet distinct from one another. Hammond's accumulations are excessive in multiple senses: deployments of those often discarded, leftover materials that also perversely decorate the sanctioned minimalist object. The particular use of fabrics to create swelling thickness also implies an affective buildup, as cloth in particular holds onto its material history in many ways—the wear and tear and stains it gathers over time. Wrapping so tightly might provide a kind of comfort, and applied across multiple objects, an amassing of structures for support that also lean uneasily together. But then, those bindings also suggest harm or an anxious twisting, ambivalently evoking a relational closeness along with a tight physical repression. *Hunkertime* might then produce an affective situation rather than an embodied presence; a queer and potentially crip experience of relational precarity where our material proximity to the work prompts a sense of instability, of something having come undone and needing to be scaffolded and reassembled.

In transforming everyday materials along with conventions of painting and sculpture, Hammond's works also navigate art objects as sites of damage. Common terms used to describe her paintings in particular include "wounds" and "sutures," such that a language of physical damage and repair circulates around the objects but typically treats those surfaces as skins.[20] I have argued in chapter 2 that Hammond's queering of modernist forms such as the grid need not depend on reinscribing the figural content it historically rejected. Rather, her refusal of the neutralizing ges-

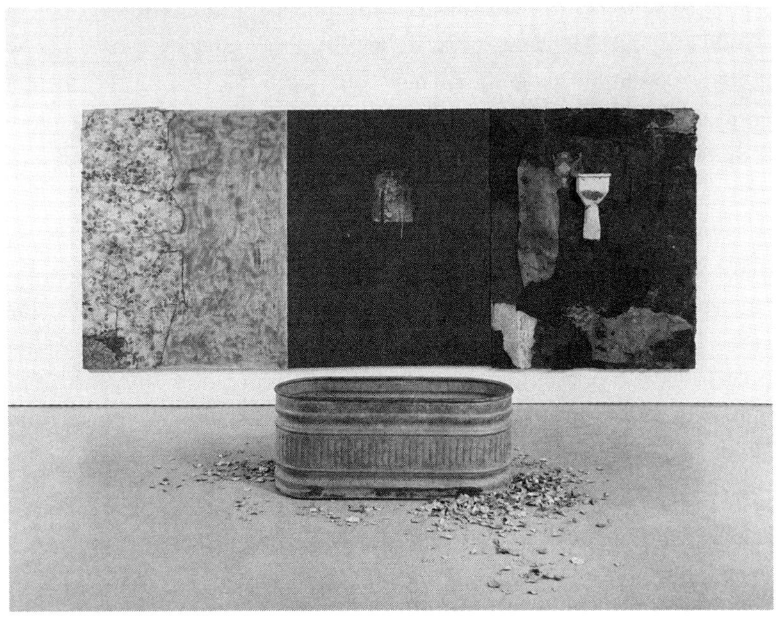

FIGURE 4.2 Harmony Hammond, *Inappropriate Longings*, 1992. Oil, acrylic, canvas, linoleum, latex rubber, metal gutter and water trough, and dry leaves, triptych, dimensions variable.

tures of modernism depends on material refusal of purity and asserting excessive sensual material presence in space. I am compelled to explore their surfaces physically, and those unruly haptic qualities also work on me emotionally—surface damage can suggest harm and its remainders without representing a skin.[21] Hammond's triptych painting installation, *Inappropriate Longings* (1992) (figure 4.2) demonstrates how this material surface damage can also deform to transform everyday sites of harm. These three monumental panels assemble the readymade stuff of a rural domestic space, objects salvaged from deserted farmsteads. A field of cracked and torn floral linoleum meets fields of amber latex rubber and thick burnt sienna pigment; one panel is covered in an accumulation of the dirty gray and brown undersides of torn linoleum shards, topped with a single gutter downspout. A large rusty metal trough sits on the floor in front of the triptych, partially filled and surrounded by dead leaves.

The suggested scene of violence is compounded by the subtle carving of "Goddamn dyke" into the latex rubber. Ripping and tearing readymade matter to assemble it together in new configurations, Hammond's formal approach may speak to harmful processes of oppression that take many forms. But the accumulative formation in particular here salvages and drags the color field or perhaps more closely what Leo Steinberg called the "flatbed picture plane" in order to refuse the transcendence of culture, playing the dirty field of relational harm so often abjected onto low-class and rural life.[22] The work reckons not only with the homophobic violence associated with domesticity and rural regions, but also the violence of that very projection or assumption that rural spaces are inherently hostile to queer lives. The deforming of this work emphasizes the contingency of its presumed context, opening its accumulated objects to unpredictability.

Bales and Bundles

The accumulative approach to abstract sculpture seen in Hammond's work is similarly demonstrated by the work of Shinique Smith. Putting their work in contact also helps to rethink the assumed anthropomorphism of Hammond's work, shifting to consider how their materials and forms perform the ambivalent drag of holding on to, even as they transform, everyday sites of damage. Shinique Smith's practice (since the early 2000s) often involves accumulating, bundling, and wrapping fabrics into bulging forms—these have taken the form of "bales," towering columns of bundled fabrics in a spectacular variety of patterns and textures. *Bale Variant No. 0024 (Everything)* (2017) (figure 4.3) is over eight feet tall, composed of colorful patterned fabrics that burst out from their tight wrapping as thick strands of denim and tie-dyed fabric pour down from the top. The tall, bundled mass is gathered atop a fabric-wrapped plinth, appearing bulky and somewhat precarious, like a monumental minimalist object that has been lovingly built up with decorative cultural outgrowths. Smith's accumulations form something from the discarded matter that

FIGURE 4.3 (*opposite*) Shinique Smith, *Bale Variant No. 0024 (Everything)*, 2017. Clothing and other fabric, ribbon, rope, acrylic mirror, acrylic, fabric dye, wood, metal, and pigments, 103 × 29 × 26 in. Courtesy of the artist.

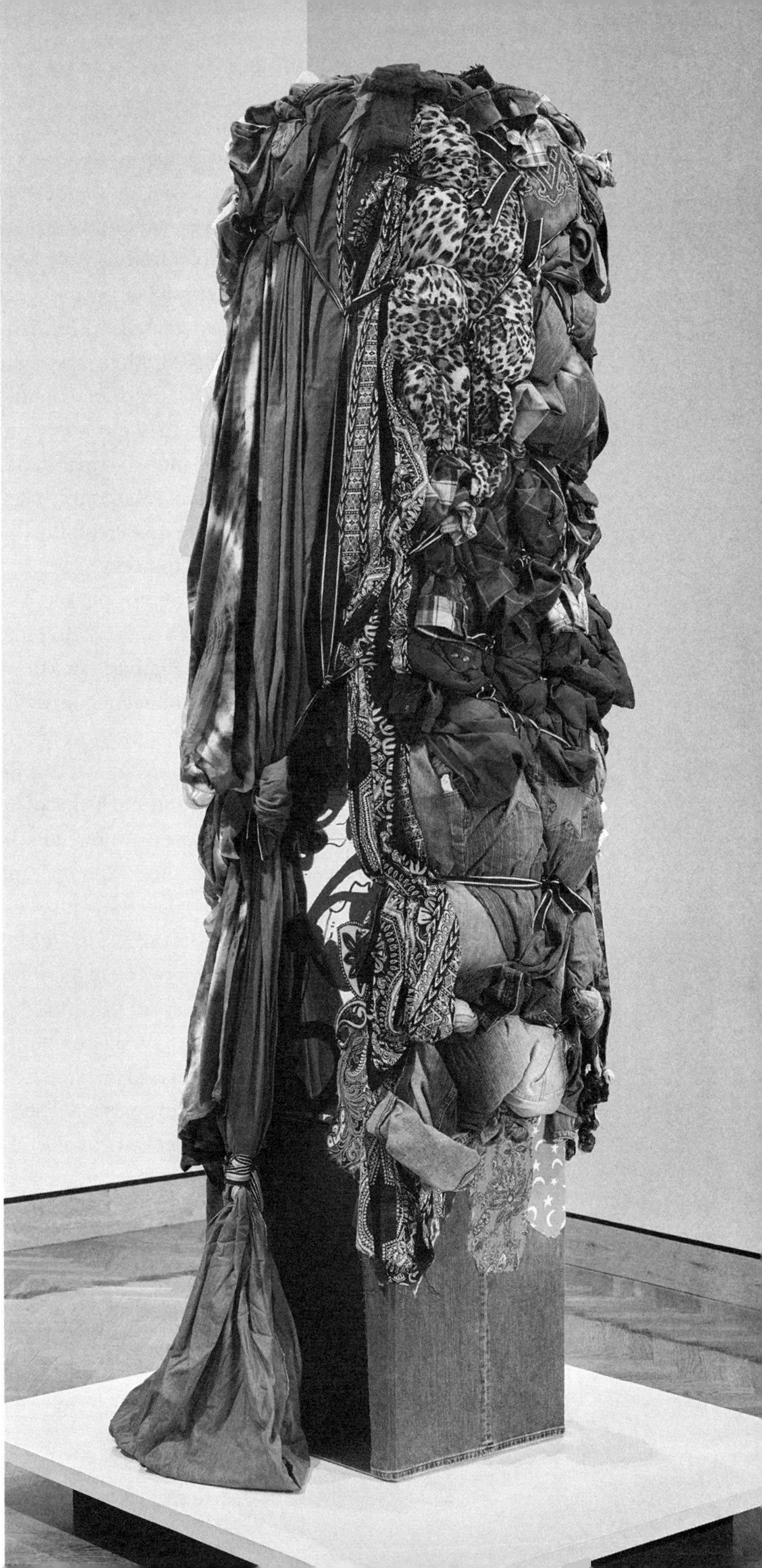

also carries with it a complex history of harmful labor practices as well as labors of shared community. These accumulations drag by creating something new from the refuse—a transformational, utopian gesture—without covering over those ambivalent and even shameful associations.

Smith's primary material, clothing, holds onto its history of production and circulation in a postcolonial, global capitalist economy. These are the everyday materials we consume and cast off, and the form these second-hand clothes take in Smith's work suggests both intimate gathering and wrapping, as well as the forms of labor that produced them. The form of the bale made primarily of accumulated cotton, curator Jaime DeSimone has noted, cannot be removed from its relationship to the cotton industry and specifically Black labor.[23] The formation of the cotton bale evokes both the history of the slave trade that fueled the modern cotton industry and, at the same time, our contemporary global industry driven by outsourced labor. Smith's process of collecting, gathering, and wrapping these fabrics also suggests our consumerist practices of accumulation that keep such exploitative global industries turning (exploitative in that they rely heavily on underpaid labor by those within the global economy who have little other choice—primarily women of the global majority).[24] Smith's use of the bale form also suggests trash bales, the compacted cubes designed to keep our waste in a manageable form. But the forms of Smith's bales appear less manageable. These are not neat accumulations; instead, they overflow and threaten to exceed their wrappings. They do imply discarded materials, everyday stuff, but the form that the matter takes does not keep it controlled—Smith's process promotes its precarious self-forming, and the sculpture is seemingly ready to fall apart if a single ribbon were cut. Smith's wrapped bales and bundles transform the everyday discarded matter in a way that formally suggests they exceed our control, allowing her materials to hold onto shameful histories and material realities of their production and circulation. Rather than picture particular bodies performing these kinds of labor, the work instead gives us the objects themselves as sites for possibility, for doing otherwise under precarious conditions.

The dragging and deforming operations of Smith's work also rely on cultural recognition while at the same time undermining the certainty of our identification. Our familiarity with the articles of clothing and fabrics in Smith's work prompts associative ties with formations of our everyday lives, while at the same time tying us in with the everyday violence of those global industries and persistent colonialist practices in which we are all implicated. That is, if we are captivated by immediate recognition in the work, perhaps something that represents "us" through a particular attachment to something like flannel or leopard print, we are also wrapped up in the form these materials take—the bale itself and all of the histories and unstable processes it implies. As I have already shown, one of the major useful possibilities of abstraction is its ability to gesture out in uncontrolled ways and proliferate multiple meanings from a single form (Smith's bales are also numbered "Bale Variants"). The title of Smith's bale discussed here claims to encompass *Everything*, as the accumulation of patterns registers according to different cultural readings; as a whole, this is a conglomeration of differences in a single form. Fabrics and patterns including dashiki, kente, plaid, paisley, and denim are accumulated together in a form that suggests not merely a united global multiplicity or a neutralized sameness, but the messy mechanisms of globalization that bring those differences into contact in sometimes violent and harmful ways. Rather than use these articles of clothing to identify a subject or create an anthropomorphic form, Smith's deployment of clothing drags it away from a singular representation of identity and points us toward the mechanisms that produce some of our external expressions and (mis) recognitions of cultural difference.[25] Heaped up together, they suggest an excessive remainder of globalization, discarded matter transformed into a monumental sculpture that draws us in with signifying promise and in turn refuses singular meaning.

Like Hammond's sculptures of the 1970s, Smith's bales embrace the formal qualities associated with postminimal sculpture and undermine the pure minimal structures that it subsumes with accumulations of fabric. Considered together, Hammond's and Smith's accumulations build up everyday fabrics and objects in ways that hold on to their potential as sites for harm, while also transforming them to produce precarious formations that speak more generatively to lived conditions than a figural content. They also formally exceed their minimalist sculptural foundations, defined by what Anna Chave considered the aggressive industrial "rhetoric of power," to pile on the soft stuff of everyday feeling and relational expression.[26] The messy physicality of postminimal work like Hammond's might lend itself to anthropomorphic readings; however, these works also produce destabilizing experiences for the viewer. Deploying unconventional materials that are unstable and ephemeral, their work speaks to possibilities for the redeployment of materials to undermine their presumed signification. In turn, they might suggest that we enact a structure and ethics for mutual care even as we are burdened by the damage of systemic violence that manifests in the everyday.

Polishing and Piercing the Readymade

Tiona Nekkia McClodden's *Sort of Nice to Not See You but to Feel You Again* (2019) (figure 4.4) is a Marcel Breuer club chair, its black surface worked with leather dye, Angelus shoe polish, and Florida Water—a type of cologne that is also used for spiritual practices, for cleansing.[27] A razor blade is stuck directly into the center of the seat bottom, its corner gently piercing the surface, standing on edge. This old icon of modernist design is polished up and reconstituted in the context of an installation filled with queer BDSM cultural objects. McClodden's 2019 exhibition at Company Gallery, *Hold on, let me take the safety off,* deploys the materials of Bootblacking and queer BDSM culture, using readymade objects such as leather boots and jackets, and this B3 chair faces an enormous black cattle squeeze chute. The installation puts these seemingly disparate objects into contact: clothing associated with queer butches and Bootblack culture along with objects of industrial design and icons of modernism, such as this Breuer chair and large monochrome black leather canvases. McClodden's particular use of everyday materials and the devoted craft of queer BDSM communities—lovingly working the surfaces of leather until they are soft and shining and renewed—operates to make contingency and precarity materially felt around us. McClodden's deformation of the readymade, particularly some icons of modernism that function as readymades, also negotiates these everyday sites to help us feel the push and pull of harm and repair.

Readymade objects may not readily signal abstraction or formalism, as they are typically recognizable objects made from mass-produced materials. The readymade is most associated with Marcel Duchamp (particularly the 1917 *Fountain*), but we could also look to the radical assemblage and readymade sculptures made at the same time by the often-overlooked Dadaist Baroness Elsa von Freytag-Loringhoven. The readymade itself is a kind of modernist perversion, not a handcrafted object but something

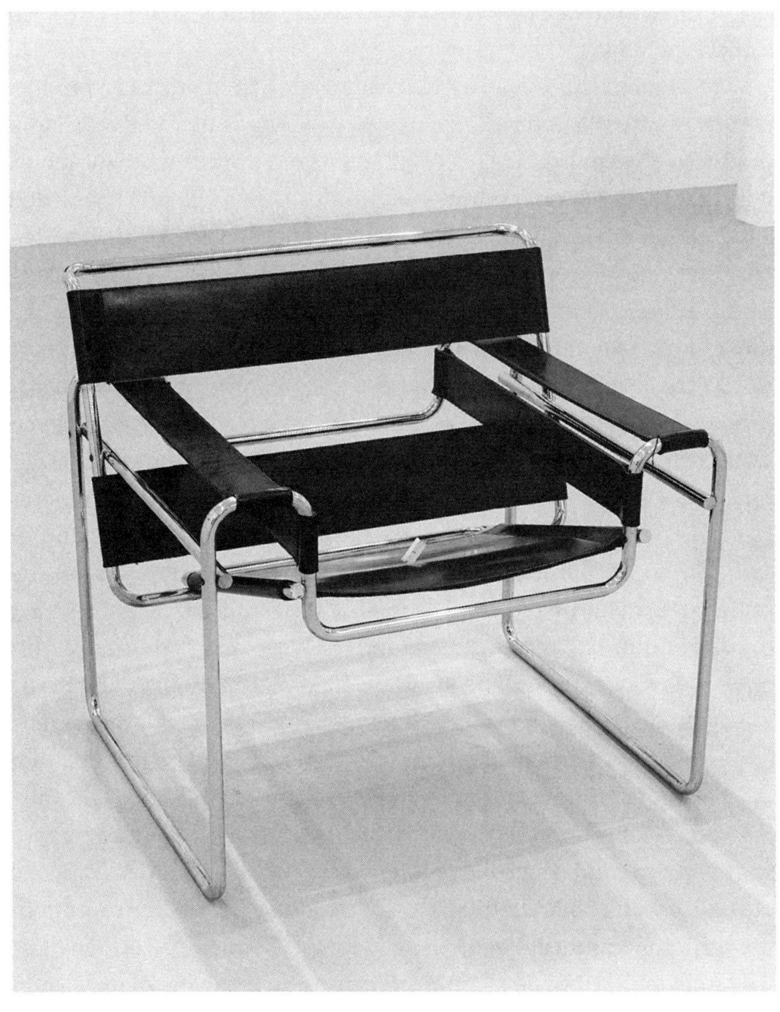

FIGURE 4.4 Tiona Nekkia McClodden, *Sort of Nice to Not See You but to Feel You Again*, 2019. Model B3 chair, leather dye, Angelus shoe polish, Florida Water, and razor blade. Installation image, Company Gallery, New York, 2019. Courtesy of Tiona Nekkia McClodden.

already existing in culture that is reconstituted by its changed context—the museum or gallery that renders it a work of art. The readymade was aimed at challenging authorship and institutional power, putting the responsibility of meaning on the spectator and the contingencies of its context and circulation. The readymade may be a transformation of an object from "low" culture into something potentially more significant, but it also works in more complex ways by holding on to some of its original associations while at the same time abstracting or distracting from settled meaning. McClodden drags on the familiar modernist form of the readymade to demonstrate this contingency, suggesting that objects that might seem to signify very clearly or function literally do not have such settled operations.

The Breuer chair is now itself a readymade of modernism, a product of early twentieth-century Bauhaus abstract design translated into mass-produced objects. In an art gallery, the chair is a work of art; in the lobby, it is utilitarian, but not entirely comfortable (Breuer clearly prioritized streamlined modernist aesthetics over physical comfort). McClodden creates further discomfort by placing a razor blade into the seat, making the object itself vulnerable while making us feel it too—we cringe at the thought of accidentally sitting down on it. While this pain and harm is evoked, the leather surface of the object is also lovingly treated according to Bootblack ritual and care. This cold, hard readymade is rendered softer, made to resonate affectively, and even endowed with spiritual significance through the use of Florida Water. Even as some of the process is unseen, McClodden works over the European design with a mixture of Afro-Caribbean spiritual and queer BDSM ritual. These tactics work the boundaries of harm and care, reckoning with while also transforming the object's normative associations and histories. McClodden makes this universal modern design affectively personal, specific, queer, and Black. We might not notice this object's literal blackness if not for the context of this exhibition, a pristine white gallery space filled with black leather objects. The large monochrome leather hides are texturally rich—in proximity, everything becomes a kind of black monochrome contrasting with stark white ground. There is a proliferation of blackness and multiplicity of surface texture across the space, from matte to shiny, hard to soft. In the exhibition and catalogue, *Blackness in Abstraction*, Adrienne Edwards characterizes one tactic of "thickness" in the material realization

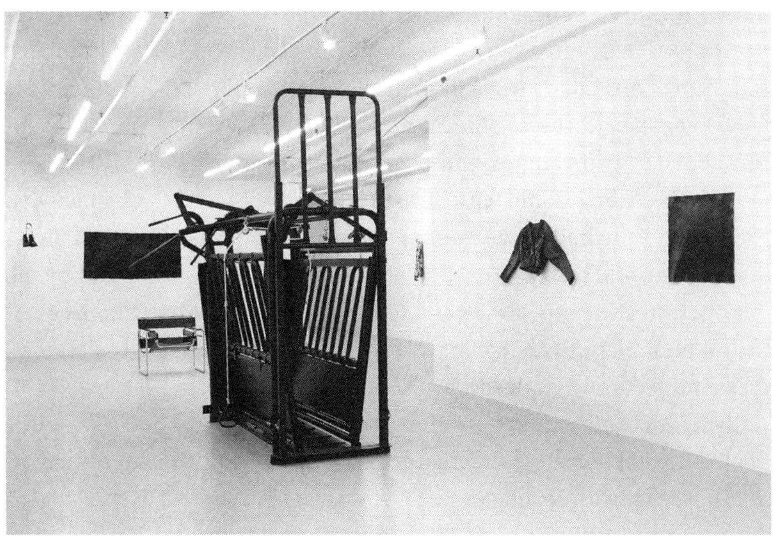

of black art objects: "These dynamically textured objects disrupt an easy gaze. As much as they act as screens/scenes for the projection of desire, they express a desire of their own."[28] Like Edwards's characterization of thick black works, McClodden's works speak of the "real world" through their tactility and use of everyday matter. But they do not merely resist the formal preoccupations of minimalism; rather, they work with and through those qualities to open them to unpredictable, everyday relational possibilities.

McClodden's queer crip Black abstraction speaks to minoritarian communities and prompts visceral engagement without giving us access to bodies or direct representations of difference. Not only are bodies not represented but their absence is palpably felt—objects that would normally be worn such as leather boots and jackets, belts and harnesses hang on the walls more like devotional objects. These are objects that hold or support bodies, but they also suggest potential violence. In the center of the room, the Breuer chair faces *The Full Severity of Compassion* (2019) (figure 4.5), a monumental black manual cattle squeeze chute, suggesting both physical comfort and violence. The large rectangular form and vertical bars of this industrially produced geometric form signal minimalist sculpture, particularly in relation to all the other objects. The squeeze is used to calm cattle before they are slaughtered; it was also famously appropriated in an invention by autism activist and animal scientist Temple Grandin to calm people with autism who experience hypersensitivity. Projection is invited as we might imagine a body pressed into that cattle squeeze, and not just the violence done to animals exploited by the livestock industry, but also the violence of normative expectations of affective and relational behavior. These social readymades we call norms that render people on the autism spectrum disabled also suppress neurodivergence and other possible ways of being in the world. From this perspective, deforming and distracting resonates again with disability. McClodden's work negotiates this site of damage to suggest that structures of support might also always carry the potential for material violence or that the severity of a hulking minimalist structure can also potentially enact something like compassion or care.

These deployments of the readymade trouble stable representations of difference, or of communities, while also making difference felt texturally.[29] The sensory sensitivities implied by McClodden's installation refuse a monolithic reference to blackness or queerness or crip modes of being in favor of vulnerable engagement with everyday violence, along with the privileged forms of modernist abstraction that would normally exclude the everyday. The works may at first seem too utilitarian to be transformed via abstraction, but they also cannot be used in the everyday sense; rather, they evoke something new imagined from what we think we know. The seemingly familiar objects that become uncannily abstracted in this space work to unfix meaning and undermine the representational function of form. These formations might signal some of the identities we would attach to bodies, but here these signals are more about feeling and sensation. McClodden transforms seemingly universal modernist designs, from the monochrome to the minimalist structure, rendering them as particular and as vulnerable as we are.

I first wrote the conclusion to this book during "gay pride month," June 2020. It was a year when many pride events were not celebratory parades but protests in solidarity with the Black Lives Matter movement. Nationwide protests were sparked by the recent police murders of yet more Black people, most visibly Breonna Taylor and George Floyd, and all in the midst of the deadly COVID-19 pandemic. Even as I mark this moment as past, we continue living in its wake.[1] These events fueled the still surging conversations about the persistence of antiblackness, and a sudden urgency toward "diversity and inclusion" efforts on the part of many institutions—highly visible but often empty, symbolic moves.[2] Issues of symbolic representation are indeed central to these conversations, due in part to the ways in which news images travel globally through virtual channels of social media. Confederate memorials that have long been subjects of controversy are falling; Confederate flags are coming down; Black Lives Matter has been painted in enormous murals on our roads. These material moves to dismantle representations of white supremacy and Black oppression, long protected as if they were neutral remainders of history, and to assert visible signs of protest for racial justice also point to the shifts in our national culture that are marked by representation. At the same time, every June, rainbow pride flags are hoisted onto state flag poles across the country to signal support for the LGBTQ community—or, they are not—as ongoing battles for LGBTQ rights to employment and health care under state and federal laws wage on. While the rainbow flag has circulated as a clear symbol of gay and lesbian identity since the late 1970s, many additional flags have been made to represent particular communities under the rainbow, and recent redesigns in 2017 and 2018 have incorporated black and brown stripes to include Black and Brown people in this vision of queer unity. The ongoing development and proliferation of the pride flag and images of the rainbow indicate that its symbolism is under continual investigation and questioning.

Writing about the political potential of abstraction in this moment when symbolic gestures and images seem at once crucial and yet not enough, I want to test the limits of queer abstraction's drag against the rainbow flag—arguably the most public, recognizable form of queer abstraction in the world. This work of geometric textile design is an abstract object that resonates as queer, or at least "gay," to a larger global public. The rainbow flag circulates transnationally through virtual and commercial vehicles, graphed onto all manner of products (stickers, mugs, tee-shirts) to signal solidarity and pride in queer identity. The concept of pride is now wrapped up in "rainbow capitalism," which banks on the purchasing power of mostly middle and upper-class Western gays and the trends of queer cultural capital (drag bars, *Queer Eye*, and so forth). Still, when those of us who identify as queer see the rainbow in a shop window, waving over a bar, or on someone's office door, the symbol communicates that we are welcome in that space; we belong there. Or at least that safety is symbolically sold to us. But given my insistence on the limitations of abstraction functioning as a straightforward sign of difference and the political stance against transparent symbolism that I have mounted in this book, what can I make of the possibilities and limitations of this particular form of queer abstraction? The rainbow flag has circulated internationally as firmly coded "gay," if not queer; can it also be dragged away, abstracted from limiting representationalism? What other complicated significations do the flag and the rainbow carry? Aside from merely signaling a queer identity politics, what else might they do or make visible?

The design and creation of the rainbow pride flag is attributed to Gilbert Baker, a white drag queen and activist in San Francisco in the 1970s. As the story goes, Baker was asked by Harvey Milk to design a new symbol of gay freedom to replace the pink triangle, which seemed to carry too much stigma and trauma as a Nazi symbol of oppression.[3] Baker worked with a team of artists including Lynn Segerblom and James McNamara to design, sew, and dye the first rainbow flags that were unfurled during the Gay Freedom Festival at the United Nations Plaza on June 25, 1978. In this context, the new symbol of pride also worked to mark gay and lesbian liberation as a global human rights issue. The rainbow design has multiple possible inspirations—gay icon Judy Garland's "Over the Rainbow" from *The Wizard of Oz* (calling all "friends of Dorothy"—a code for gay men), the popularity of the rainbow in hippie subculture, the "Flag of Races" used to demonstrate for world peace in the 1960s, or the ubiquity of the rainbow in mythology and as a symbol of hope across cultures. The two original pride flags had eight stripes and a complex symbolism: pink for sex, red for life, orange for healing, yellow for sunlight, green for nature, turquoise for magic, indigo for serenity, and violet for spirit (the hot pink and turquoise soon dropped out). One of the original flags included tie-dyed stars to mimic the United States flag, a strategy to signal to the public that this was, in fact, a flag. According to Baker, the ubiquity of Americana and the United States flag, "from Jasper Johns paintings to trashy jeans at the Gap," also inspired the need for a symbol that could claim both visibility and power.[4]

Queer cultures have long deployed tactics of flagging to signal identification and desire. The gay cruising semiotics of the colored bandanna "hanky code" is another late twentieth-century example in a long history of queer codes, many operating as a covert language when queer affection was criminalized.[5] Now there are a multiplicity of pride flags to represent different communities under the rainbow umbrella: transgender, bisexual, intersex, asexual, leather, and so on, each with their own symbolic color combinations. Flagging has shifted from a closeted code language to a means of vibrant visibility politics. This proliferation of flag designs also signals a desire for more inclusive forms of representation—an insistence on multiplying differences rather than conflating them. In 2017, Philadelphia began to incorporate the colors black and brown into the rainbow flag; this is now increasingly embraced as a move for more queer causes to include BIPOC communities and perspectives. Queer communities are also becoming aware of the Black and Brown trans women, namely the activists Marsha P. Johnson and Sylvia Rivera, who were central to the gay rights movement and Stonewall riots, but who were pushed aside in favor of white, straight-passing leadership. In this moment when Black and Brown trans women are disproportionately targets of violent hate crimes—this has always been the case, but their murders are more visible now—the limits of representation are acutely felt, and the promise of inclusive movements for justice is all the more urgent.[6]

Considering the potential for the pride flag to operate as a queer abstraction, I am particularly interested in the recent redesign of the flag by Daniel Quasar in 2018, the "Progress Pride Flag." This new design adds to the horizontal rainbow stripes an intervening chevron of white, pink, and blue (the colors of the trans pride flag), as well as the brown and black stripes of the Philadelphia flag. The chevron of stripes on the hoist of the flag also creates an arrow pointing out in new directions (the promise of progress as mentioned in its title). This design opens the flag up to the potential for dragging by raising some questions: Is it possible to gender-queer the rainbow flag? To pervert it? To color it more? The "progress" flag performs a visual intervention, the colors that have come to signal trans are additions to the rainbow—not just added below but charging into the traditional flag. The black stripe has also come to symbolize the losses of the AIDS crisis, insisting on the death that cuts into our communities—and now in the throes of yet another pandemic, COVID-19 disproportionately affects BIPOC communities. It is no mistake that the black stripe functions to symbolize both Black people and people lost to AIDS, acknowledging those who are already most marked for death. The chevron of Quasar's flag performs a visual drag through the rainbow to insist on the intersections of a queer sign with stripes that represent issues of gender and race. This is an attempt to make the flag more inclusive, more universal, by accounting for difference within the queer community. At the same time, it insists, there is more work to be done. It signals the importance of continually interrogating our symbols.

The rainbow flag operates differently from the other forms of queer abstraction I have discussed in this book. On the one hand, it would be difficult to claim that this flag drags away entirely from representation or that it interrupts processes of signification—it seems to solidify according to a globally recognized LGBTQ iconography. This rainbow sign attaches firmly to queer identities and communities. Rather than offer an alternative to visibility politics, the pride flag seems central to those politics. On the other hand, taking abstraction seriously as a process and tactic rather than merely an appearance can show the expansive performative operations of this abstraction to exceed the taken-for-granted meanings of its form. In relation to queer identity, the rainbow flag offers both a vibrant visibility and a freedom from representation at the same time (this sign does not attach to a particular person or body, but floats and multiplies). And in its many redesigns, the pride flag begins to resonate with an ethics of relationality that I have proposed throughout this book as essential to queer abstraction—refusing essentializing unification in favor of relational models for being together in difference. Quasar's redesign shows that the flag can still be dragged: the use of the hard edge begins to account for important lines of distinction between various forms of identification, not conflating the trans with the queer, for example. The historical evolution and cultural proliferation of the pride flag also suggests it is not merely a fixed sign. While the rainbow of pride may seem to represent (and attempt to represent all members of) an identity and community formation, it also functions excessively and catachrestically across multiple different contexts. Like the other abstractions in this book, it deploys an overloaded, overburdened sign—the form of the flag itself—in multiple and ambivalent ways.

Flagging Citizenship

Following the Supreme Court decision that made gay marriage legal in all fifty states on June 26, 2015, the White House was illuminated in the colors of the rainbow flag. The proximity of the rainbow pride flag to the United States flag on state flagpoles across the country in the month of June suggests that this nation may also be for queer people (sometimes).

The form of the flag itself brings queerness in contact with citizenship, as flags are otherwise used to claim national belonging and patriotic pride. The original pride flag's incorporation of the stars along with its rainbow stripes, and similar iterations of this unified United States and rainbow flag seen at pride parades, also points to the underlying homonationalism of flagging. Jasbir Puar coined the term *homonationalism* to describe a national US homosexuality and homonormativity corresponding with a particular set of racial and national norms, hinging on white hegemony. The national belonging granted to particular queers is thus contingent on disqualifying populations of racial and sexual others (particularly the Orientalized terrorist) from this national imaginary of citizenship. Writing in the wake of September 11, 2001, Puar also points to the proliferation of the United States flag in gay spaces, like gay bars and pride parades, as symbolic gestures of patriotism to enfold gays and lesbians into a vision of national unity. Homonationalism also works strategically to uphold the opposition of a progressive, democratic, and "gay-friendly" United States against an oppressive Middle East.[7] As gays and lesbians are no longer totally excluded from the possibility of national belonging, producing and upholding a particular kind of gay subject has become necessary to protect the sanctioned boundaries of citizenship. The rainbow flag might thus be tied to a national assimilation and heteronormative productivity such as marriage and reproductive kinship. The flagging of patriotism also points to the fact that queer and trans citizens cannot opt to refuse national belonging—our very lives require state support and suffer when protections are removed, when our sexualities and genders are policed against the national norm. But as Puar shows, our national belonging (in the US context) comes at the cost of preserving a dominant whiteness at the core of homonormativity. Might the rainbow flag be redeployed in ways that do not immediately enact homonationalism or a gay version of colonialism?

The form of the flag—the rainbow or the stars and stripes—already signals camp due to its iconicity and deployments in so many different contexts. The flag is serious business, as much as it is also printed on socks and bikinis. In their 1992 essay on "Queer Nationality," Lauren Berlant and Elizabeth Freeman demonstrate the camp aesthetics of early nineties America, and central to the spectacle of Camp USA is the flag. Testing the limits of parody and nationalist camp to forge queer possibilities of citizenship, Berlant and Freeman assert that "it is not enough to 'include' women, lesbians, racial minorities, etc. in an ongoing machine of mass counternationality. Achieving the utopian promise of a queer symbolic will involve more than a story of a multicultural sewing circle sewing the scraps of a pink triangle onto the American flag, or turning that flag, with its fifty times five potential small pink triangles, into a new desecrated emblem."[8] In their view, redeployments, camping, and parodies of nationalist symbols such as the flag (and queer occupations of hegemonic public spaces in general) will fail to mobilize alternatives to oppressive national norms.

It may be that the rainbow flag merely operates according to hegemonic norms of the state—certainly if we interpret it as a parody of the US flag or another stand-in for this nationalist symbol of unity. A critical reading of the rainbow flag might be that it cannot accomplish real change, that it might be a signal of support for a certain identitarian politics but does not produce actions or result in true freedom without necessarily excluding some people and communities. The rainbow flag may seem to be merely about optics rather than real politics. At the same time, it would be difficult to imagine our queer counterpublics or ongoing movements for justice without the rainbow. Flags generally operate by visually staking a claim, marking territory and borders, and thus might necessarily signal a colonial project. The rainbow flag has been deployed literally in this way: gay rights activists in Australia established a micronation under the rainbow flag to claim the Coral Sea Islands as a gay and lesbian "kingdom" (it was declared dissolved after Australia legalized gay marriage in 2017). In this context, even as the action was focused on the homonormative goal of securing marriage rights, the rainbow flag was used to claim not only a separate nation by and for gays, but a "hostile nation" that symbolically declared war on Australia.[9] This demonstrates that the rainbow flag is not always merely unfurled over gay bars to signal a safe space to spend our money, but is also more radically used in opposition to the state.

Even as the proximity or conflation of national and pride flags suggests we are in bed with the state (whether we like it or not), I have also shown throughout this book that putting two objects in proximity can trouble them both. Pressed close to the US flag, might the rainbow trouble normative regimes of nationhood and the state? The bright vibrancy of the pride flag projects its colors onto our national flag to put pressure on its failed promises of liberty and justice for all. It visually produces a perverse excess running off from a vision of unified "America," and deployments of the rainbow in different global contexts also point to its queer contingency.

Moving beyond the United States context demonstrates that the rainbow flag is not tied to a singular state or national "home" but crosses national borders and allows an imagined, projected home that is fleeting and contingent. Considering the transnational trajectories of the rainbow flag, Christine Klapeer and Pia Laskar show that this flag functions as a "boundary object" and a floating signifier of queer communities that expresses a connection across borders. They demonstrate the complex negotiations of a precarious home or homeland via everyday uses of the rainbow flag and rainbow objects (circulating via local events, through hyperspace and the global channels of capitalism) that also negotiate local and transnational ways of queer being and belonging that are also never equal.[10] The symbolic power of the flag to connect us does not work without the exclusions and processes of (homo)nationalism, capitalist formations of "global queering," and the displacements of migration and colonial formations that it also puts in play.[11] In related work, Laskar, Anna Johansson, and Diana Mulinari attempt to decolonize the rainbow flag by exploring its deployment in peripheral locations of the Global North and South. Challenging the Eurocentricity and colonial models of the flag, their case studies demonstrate the crucial role of place in the creation and conflict of the flag's meaning. When a Palestinian artist painted the rainbow on Israel's apartheid wall, for example, the flag encompassed the struggle for justice against military occupation.[12] In the global framework, the rainbow pride flag is not presumed to belong solely to white Westerners, nor is it only about politicized sexuality. While in the United States our continual redesigns of the flag are made to signal other identity intersections, in other contexts the rainbow already encompasses struggles against racism and imperialism and for national belonging and trans rights. Even as the rainbow flag traffics in a symbolic economy, it puts into play the contingencies of its context and modes of belonging to suggest this is not a stable sign, but a global abstraction open to queering complications of its presumed meanings.

The globalization of the rainbow also depends on capitalism's mainstreaming of LGBTQ rights movements. The "pride" seemingly embodied by the flag has been countered by the Gay Shame movement, a radical protest against the commercialization of gay pride events, state-sanctioned marriage and gays in the military, and other forms of homonormative assimilation. In emphasizing shame as opposed to pride, this movement, along with queer theory's preoccupation with shame and the political value of negativity, points to the affective politics of the pride flag.[13] In this light, the rainbow seems too positive, too optimistically gay (as in "happy"), and not nearly radical enough to be queer (as in "fuck you"). While the flag might seem to reinforce the status quo of acceptance and assimilation, it operates more ambivalently across borders and categorical boundaries. The rainbow can be deployed to gloss over difference and subsume us all beneath a promise of unity; it also points to the no place of utopia, the as-yet-unachieved promise of rights along with a freedom from national norms that determine those rights. Negotiating all of these complex layers of sexual and gender identity, nationalism, and global migrations that exceed a singular symbolism, the rainbow may yet be dragged away from representational legibility to perform other affective and relational maneuvers.

Dragging the Rainbow

The many manifestations of what seems to be the most secure sign of queerness, the rainbow in its material forms (the flag or otherwise) also demonstrates the contingency and precarity of our symbolism as it attaches to identity and politics. If our flagging refers to a literal thing in the world, that thing is not a physical object at all, or an identity that attaches securely to a body, but a fleeting phenomenon. The rainbow is already catachrestic, excessive, and need not be queered. Its visibility depends on the right conditions, on being in just the right place at the right time, and it is impossible to reach. It is composed of many additional colors that the human eye cannot perceive, its projected spectrum produced from the light that it also colors.[14] The rainbow's contingency and impossibility might also impose a distance between the sign and its meaning or function—a freedom that has yet to be realized under the ubiquitous rainbow. There is far more at stake in this seemingly transparent sign than what is within the limits of representational politics. The endlessly generative operations of queer abstraction have to do with its multiplicity, as seen in the rainbow; it can move across contexts and objects, not in a universal gesture, but proliferating difference in so many unexpected ways.

One final example demonstrates this precarious and difficult drag. Angela Hennessy's *Black Rainbow* (2017) (see plate 20) is an enormous arch of crocheted hair towering at ten feet tall. A spectrum of black, brown, and blonde synthetic and human hair cascades down in arcs to re-create the colored bands of the rainbow. Tangled threads and puffballs hang loose at either end of the arc and gather on the floor, producing a physical drag that also implies its affective weight. The tallest blonde band is illuminated from behind, creating a glowing portal to the void of the black wall behind it—a black hole of all that is unknowable to us. This work drags on two loaded signs of identity and difference, the rainbow and Black hair, to abstract them from representational transparency.

Black hair is not a neutral material but a fetishized sign of racial Blackness. It is burdened by projections of racial inferiority, abject white horror and fascination, along with its important role in Black cultural pride, kinship, ritual, and community belonging.[15] Hair is taken to be a transparent signifier of racial difference and otherness in our white supremacist culture, but Hennessy abstracts it by removing it from a specific body. The result is not to remove hair from its ambivalent social and political meanings or disavow the many manifestations of its significance, but rather an investigation of this material signifier when it is detached from the racialized body to which it is assumed to refer. Black hair is literally objectified here. We have to reckon with the stark distinctions between colors—platinum blonde and brown-black hair is woven together yet quite different in cultural value, as blonde hair is linked with white ideals of beauty and purity set in opposition to Blackness. Yet the texture and thickness of the "white" hair is the same as the rest, materially undermining the visual cues of racial coloring that also other.[16] That is, however we assume color to materialize on the surface of bodily matter in terms of race, those assumptions are undermined via the *Black Rainbow*'s materializing of difference in excess of these categories.

Rematerializing this fraught site of projection in the form of a crocheted textile and a glowing rainbow, Hennessy renders these comfort objects somewhat discomfiting. This is not a gay-as-in-happy rainbow of multiculturalism that unifies via a celebration of diversity, but a labor of reckoning with the color and matter of hair as a specific site of projection or identification that attaches to both shame and pride simultaneously. Perhaps this also maps the affect of shame onto the rainbow itself as a site of pride. The eroticism and sexual fetishism attached to Black racialized hair also intersects with the rainbow's politics of sexuality, pointing to the complex ways in which Blackness both is already queered via racism (or at least considered nonnormative in terms of sexuality) and is also rendered invisible in many whitened queer spaces. But while the symbolism of the rainbow's visible colors is thought to also make queerness visible right up front, *Black Rainbow* obstructs easy transparency. It plays on our assumption that the color black will obscure or obstruct vision in order to refuse binary representation. At the same time, it materializes a more complex netted thickness of racialized color to insist the rainbow of our pride flags is not at all universal or all-encompassing. Hennessy's rainbow acknowledges the burden of representation while it also shifts the grounds of this projection, using abstraction to activate a different relationship between representation and subjectivity.

Considered in relation to the redesigns of the rainbow flag that have incorporated brown and black stripes, *Black Rainbow* not just insists on including yet another band of color in an additive model of diversity, but recolors the rainbow itself in shades of black, brown, and white. As Gilbert Baker's initial pride rainbow symbolism attached to universalizing terms of "sex," "health," "spirit," and so on, Hennessy's rainbow demonstrates our arbitrary symbolic attachments to racialized color. Shades of black and brown are not just additions but encapsulate the full spectrum. Hennessy refracts our perception of the rainbow through the prism of blackness, rather than bright whiteness. Even as the blonde band at the top of the rainbow is lit from behind, further dramatizing its contrast with the black wall, this is not the illumination of a surveilling exposure. Deforming and reforming the rainbow that also begins to come undone, this work also materializes a negative space to create an opening of utopian possibility through that black hole. Hennessy's rainbow is also accompanied by a statement:

1   To say that blackness is a rainbow is to speak of a spectrum of visible
    and invisible color.

2   To say that blackness is a rainbow is to reveal the limitations of a
    black and white binary.

3   To say that blackness is a rainbow is to recognize the complexities of
    identity.

4   To say that blackness is a rainbow is to see in the sun.

5   To say that blackness is a rainbow is to speak of luminosity.

6   To say that blackness is a rainbow is to see light through rain.

7   To say that blackness is a rainbow is to speak of refraction.

8   To say that blackness is a rainbow is to say black is beautiful.

9   To say that blackness is a rainbow is to know black joy.

10 To say that blackness is a rainbow is to love the black hole.[17]

The idea of a black rainbow seems impossible—we believe blackness will swallow the light. To materialize blackness as a rainbow is perhaps to show that blackness can be freed from its representational burden while still illuminating, revealing, complicating, and pleasuring. Blackness is not lost to obscurity in Hennessy's work but is intricately material and substantial; the glowing black rainbow does not merely produce a traumatic end point but leads us to new possible futures yet to be formed, even as we drag that psychic weight along with us. As a model for imagining possible modes of relating in and through difference, *Black Rainbow* not only refuses to fix racial categories onto a corporeal schema, but it suggests that exceeding binaries and categorical preoccupations of our politics can manifest a different world.

And yet, the physical heft of this rainbow cannot lift off from the floor; it is not some transcendent gesture of abstraction, and thus manifests the difficulty of queer abstraction's drag. I have shown how the artworks in this book have the power to alter perspectives, to make problematic past aesthetics viable for the present and future even as we feel their harm, to generate abstract tactics for political engagement in excess of a fixed sign. And I have taken up these same acts of abstraction precisely because they are risky and burdened and hard. Part of my intervention in this thought experiment is to insist that we do not take such objects as fixed, that even the rainbow flag of queer visibility might also function via a queering that performs dynamic movement and deforms in unruly directions. Because even as I have made some world-making projections for what queer abstraction might do, these processes never transcend the difficulty they are working with. They drag that difficulty with them in physical and affective manifestations that we feel and negotiate when we witness these processes, dragging us on and away toward something else—to reckon with the burdens of harm that come in many forms, and yet never settle.

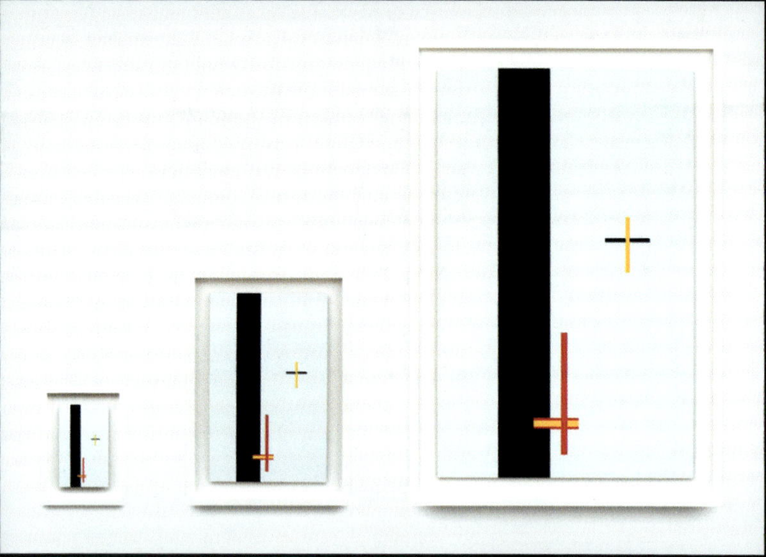

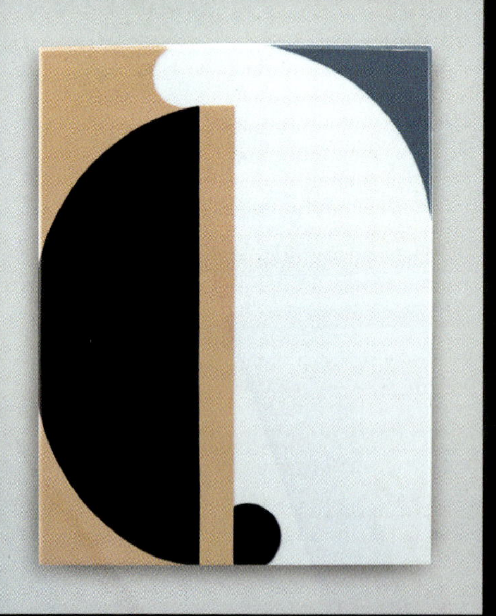

PLATE 2 (*above*) László Moholy-Nagy, *Construction in Enamel 1, 2, and 3* (also known as *EM 1–3*), 1923. Porcelain enamel on steel. EM 1: 37 × 23⅝ in.; EM 2: 18¾ × 11⅞ in.; EM 3: 9½ × 6 in.

PLATE 3 (*left*) Ulrike Müller, *Curls*, 2017. Vitreous enamel on

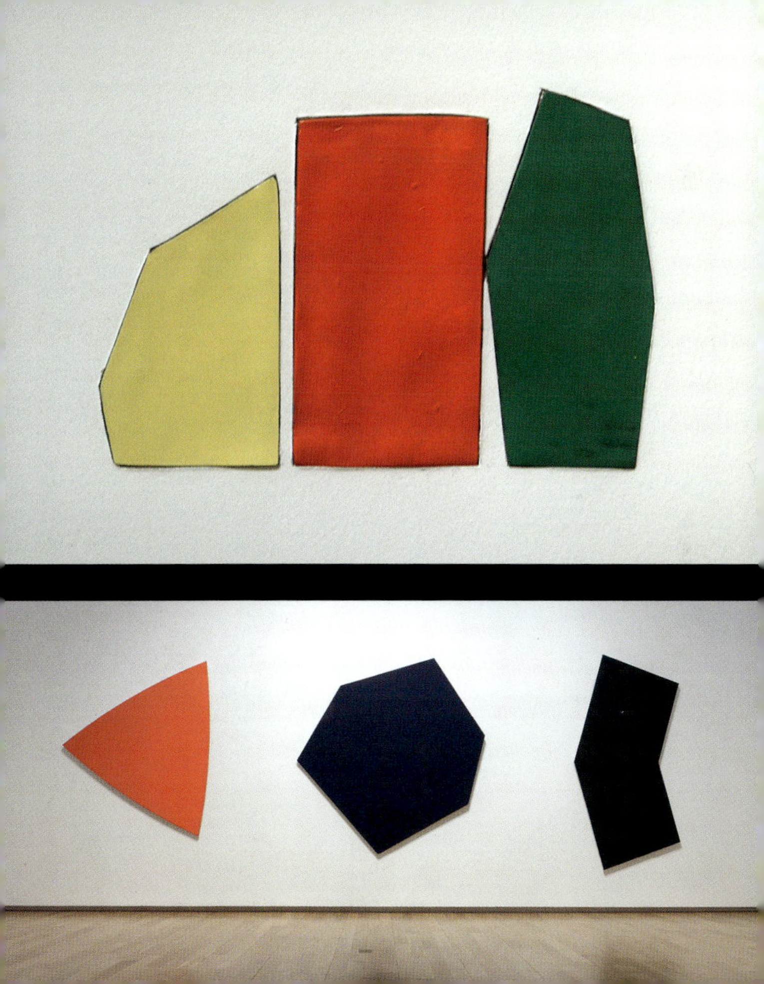

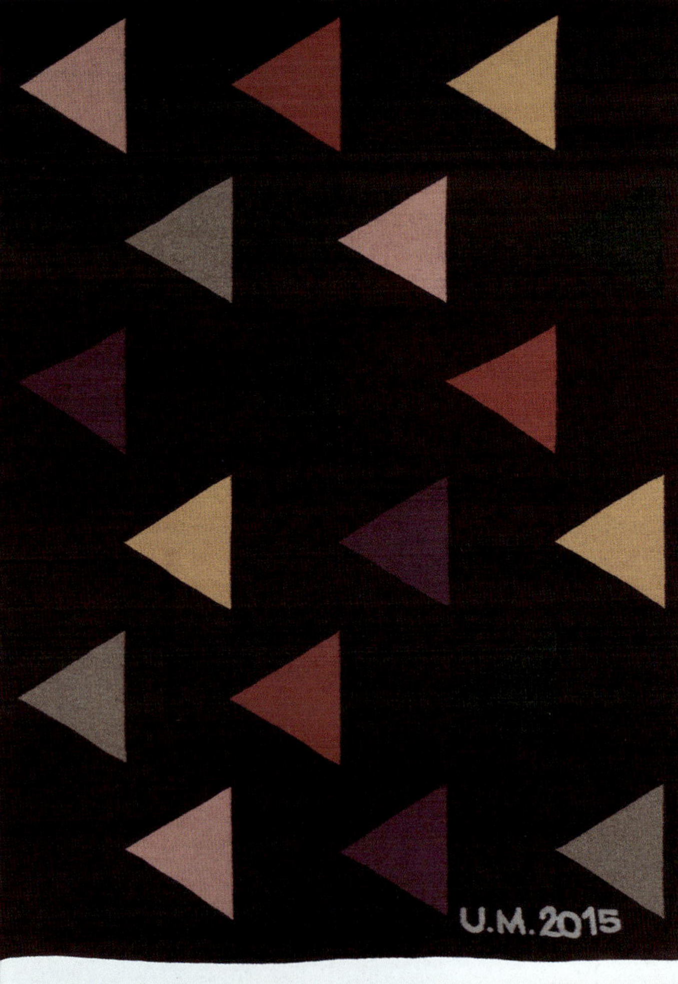
U.M. 2015

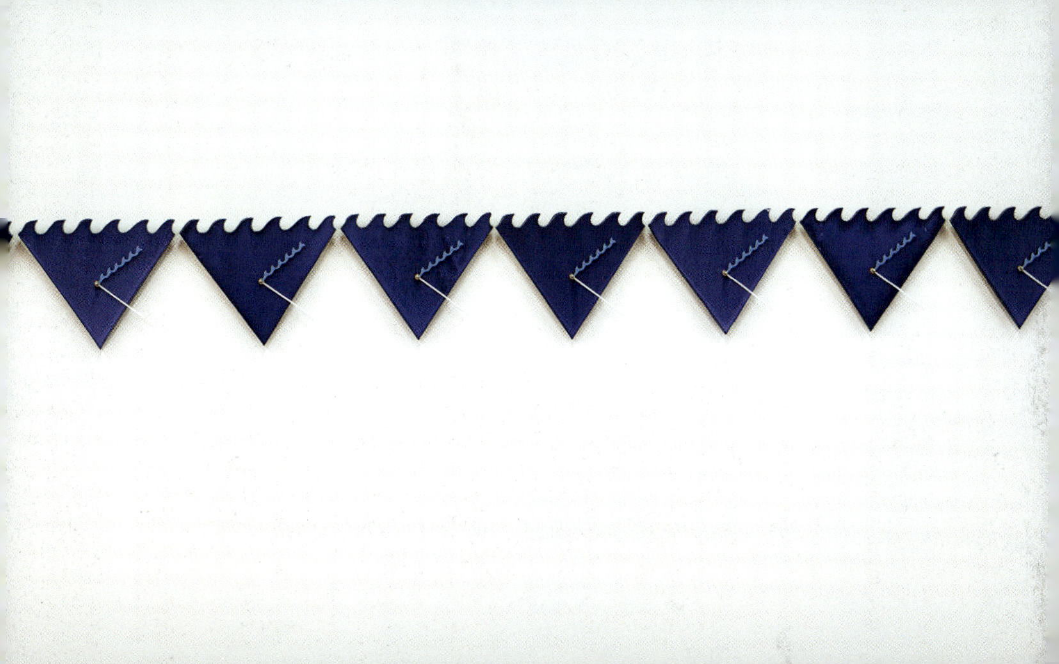

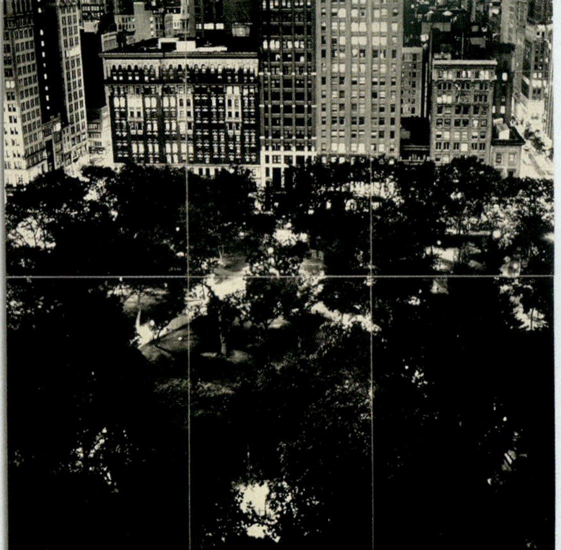

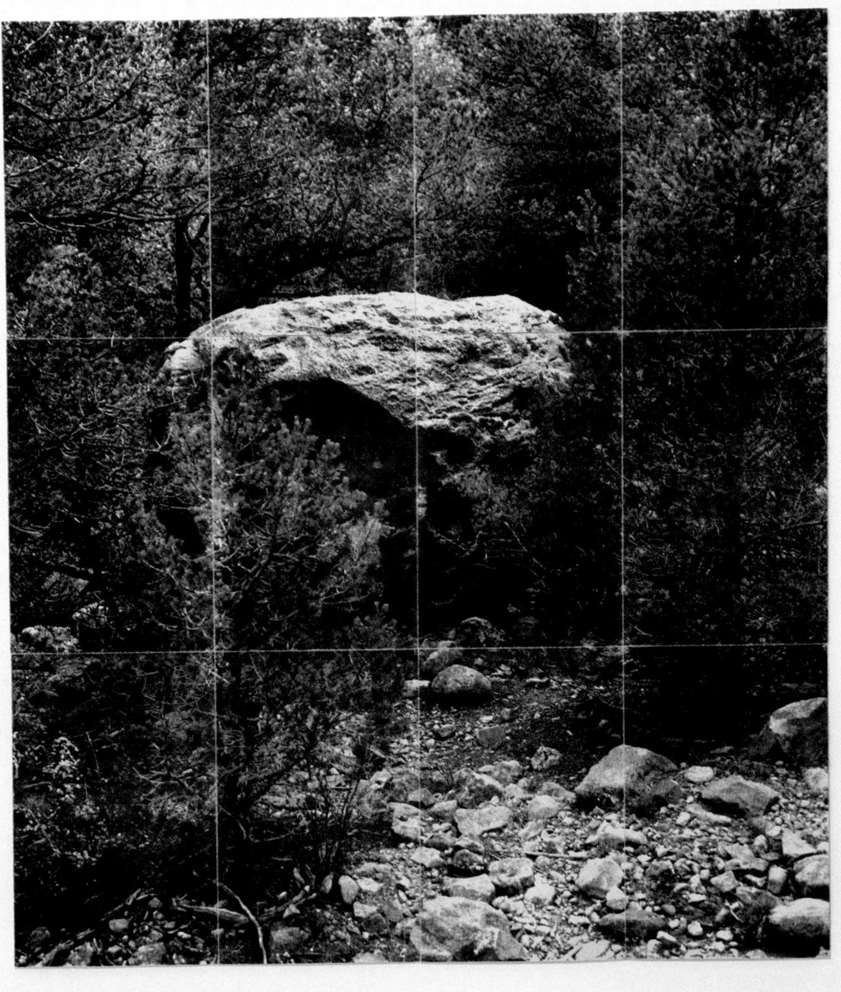

PLATE 10 (*below*) Agnes Martin, *Friendship*, 1963.
Gold leaf and oil on canvas, 75 × 75 in.

PLATE 11 (*opposite*) Lorna Simpson, *Curtain*, 2011.
Serigraph on 8 felt panels. Edition of 3 with 2 APs,
overall: 68 × 100 in., each panel: 34 × 25 in. © Lorna
Simpson. Courtesy the artist and Hauser & Wirth.

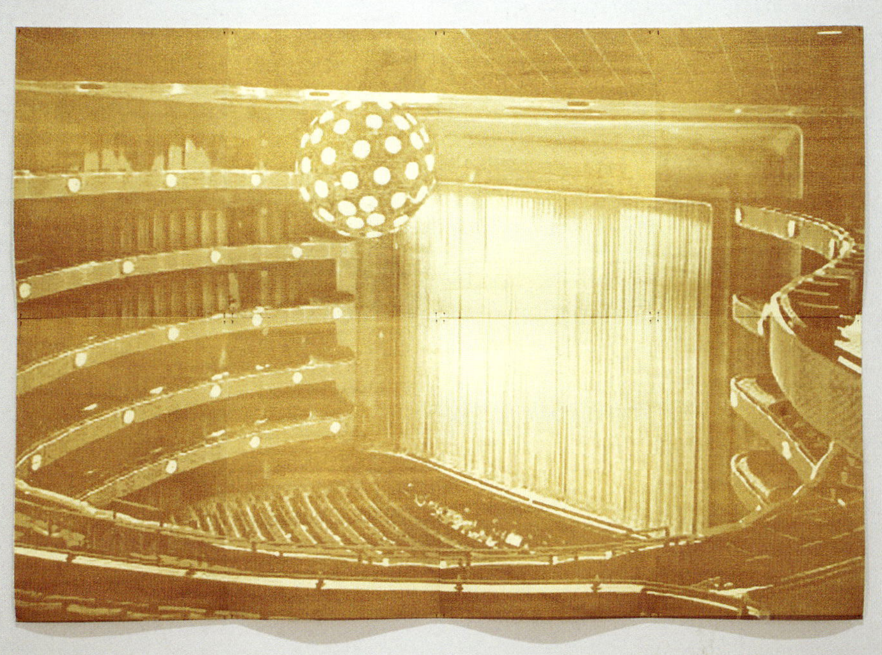

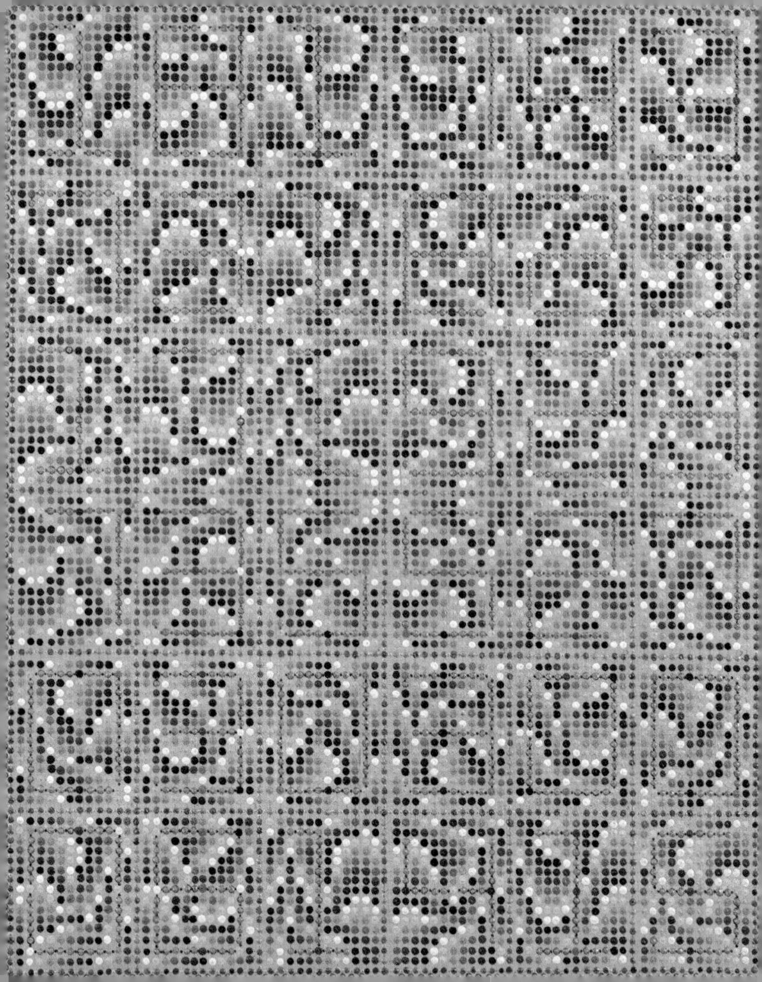

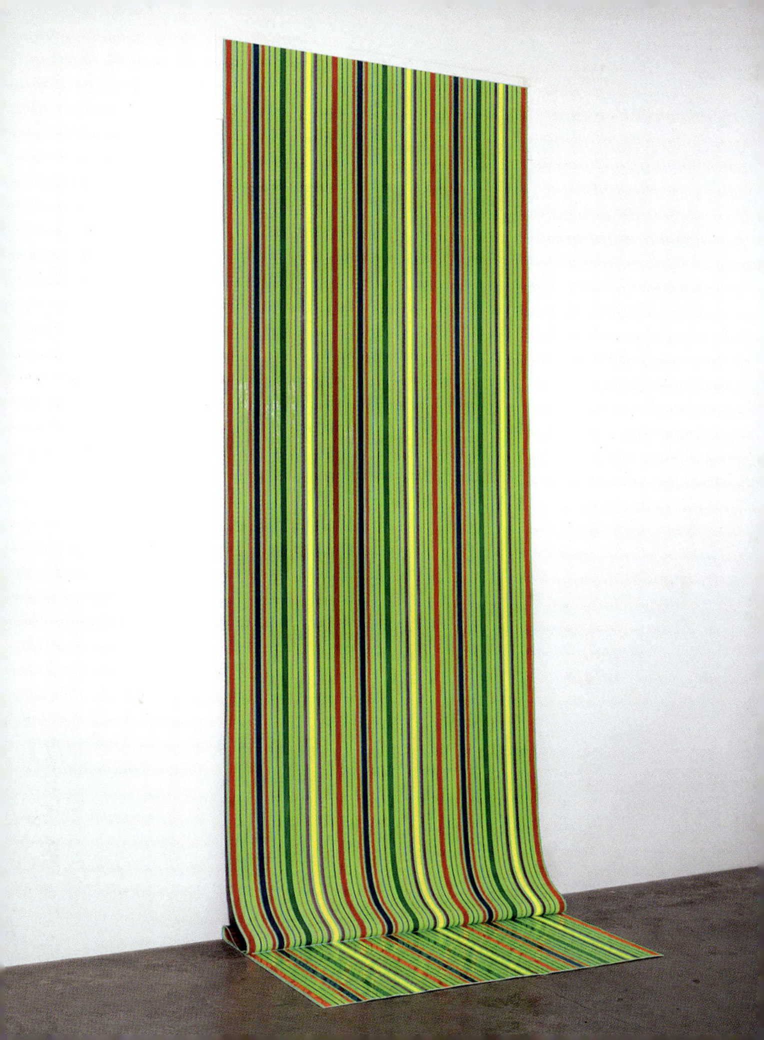

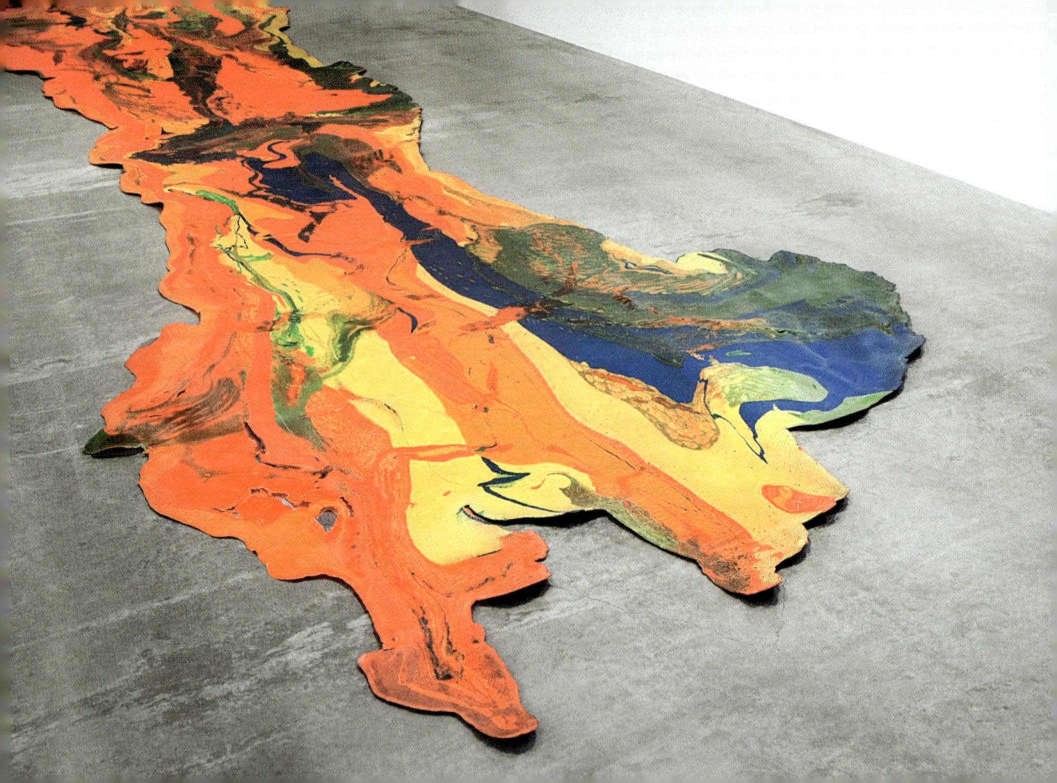

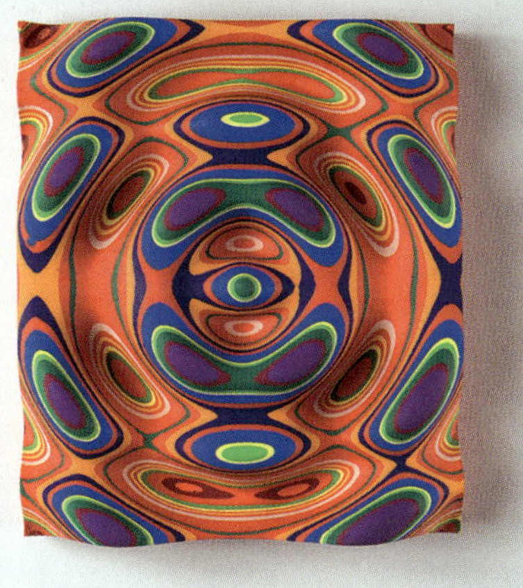
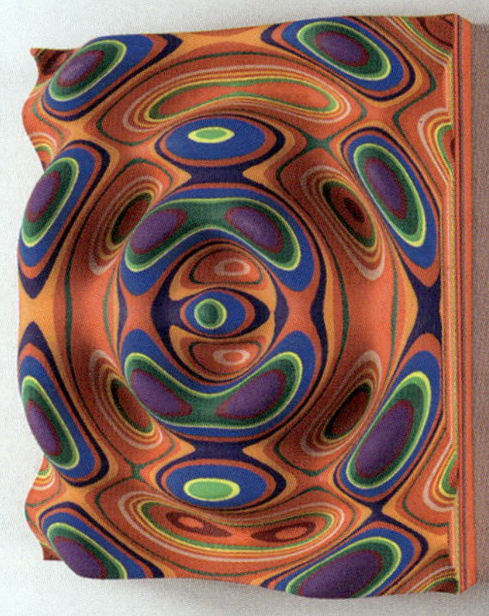

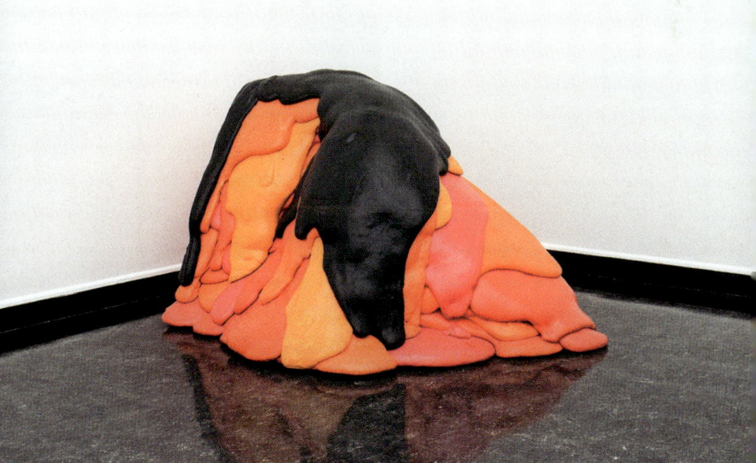

PLATE 15 (*top*) Linda Besemer, *Red-Purple Slab*, 2009. Acrylic paint, 10 × 8½ in. Courtesy of the artist and Jean Luc and Takako Richard, Paris, France.

PLATE 16 (*bottom*) Lynda Benglis, *Untitled (VW)*, 1970. Dayglo and iron oxide black pigmented polyurethane foam, 48 × 69½ × 41¾ in. Installation view: *Lynda Benglis: Adhesive Products* PRAXES at Bergen Assembly, Bergen Kunsthall, Norway, September 2–October 9, 2016. Photo: Thor Brødreskift.

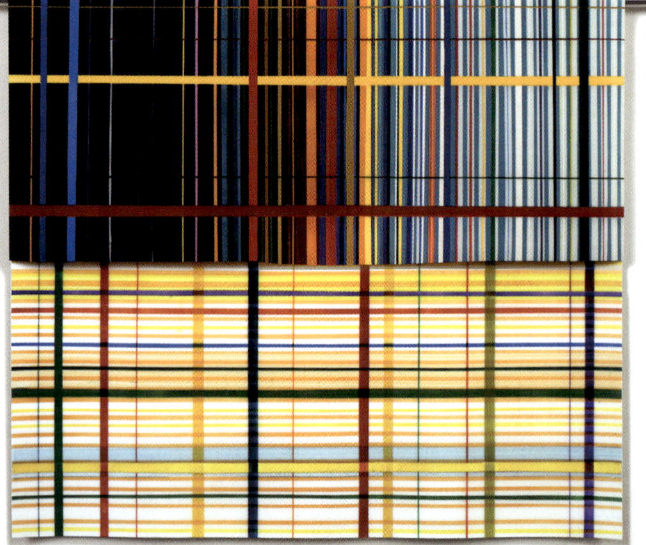

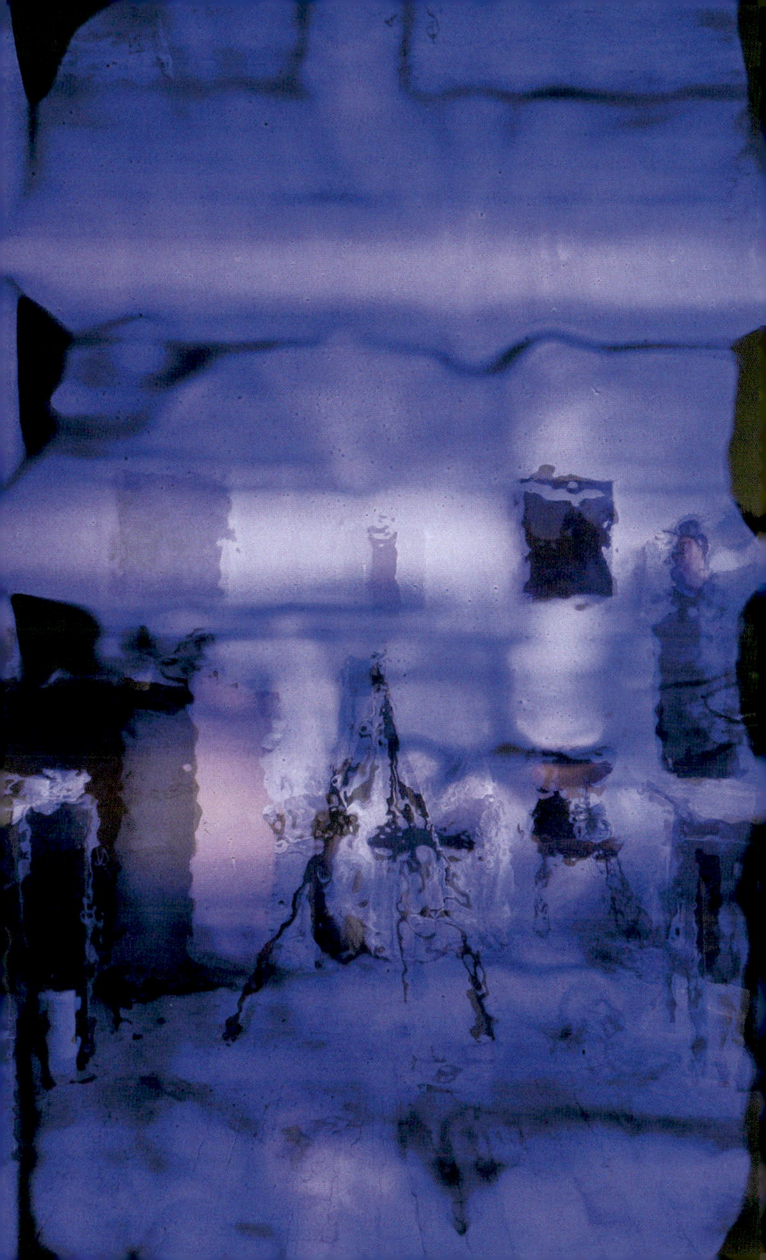

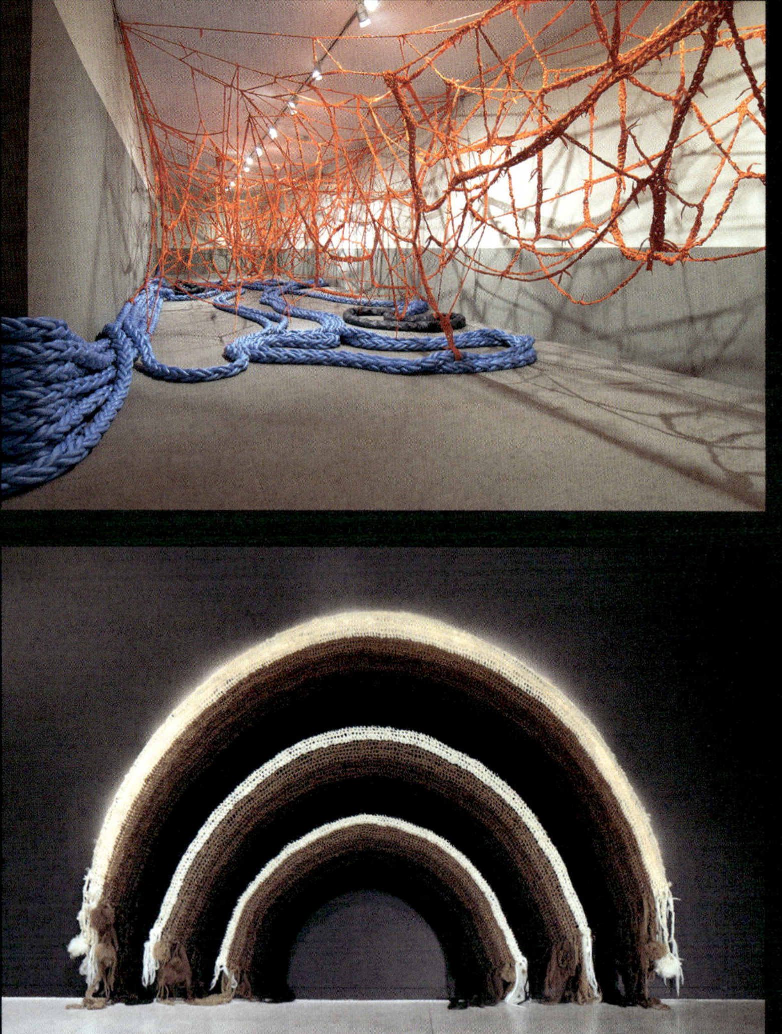

PLATE 19 (*top*) Sheila Pepe, *Mind the Gap*, 2005. Shoelaces,
nautical towline, paint, and hardware, 96 × 120 × 720 in.
Installation view at the University Gallery, University of
Massachusetts, Amherst. Photo: Thom Kendall.

PLATE 20 (*bottom*) Angela Hennessy, *Black Rainbow*,
2017. Crocheted synthetic hair, artist's hair, LED lighting,

Introduction

1   A fifth chapter also appeared at the Institute of Contemporary Art, University of Philadelphia, September 13–December 22, 2019.

2   On Episalla's *foldtogram* practice, see Casid, "Thanatography."

3   These four artists talk about fierce pussy as the fifth artist. Jill H. Casid discusses their work in relation to queer abstraction, in conversation with my work, in a lecture at the Beeler Gallery: Columbus College of Art & Design, "Beeler Gallery—Conversation: Nancy Brooks Brody, Joy Episalla, Carrie Yamaoka, and Jill Casid," YouTube, February 5, 2019, https://www.youtube.com/watch?v=TiVdeTwGHG8.

4   Freeman, *Time Binds*, 62.

5   For a discussion of fierce pussy's ongoing practice, then and now, and particularly their performative use of language, see O'Neill-Butler, "Labor of Love."

6 See Smith, "At the Whitney"; Saltz, "Jerry Saltz on '93 in Art"; Saltz and Corbett, "How Identity Politics Conquered the Art World."

7 Lancaster, "The Wipe."

8 Yve-Alain Bois and Rosalind Krauss use Bataille's *formless* as a third term to displace "form" and "content" in favor of a performative operation of matter, splitting off from modernism's opposition of formalism and iconology. Bois and Krauss, *Formless: A User's Guide*, 15. This interest in excessive deployments of matter that collapse this distinction between the work's form and content intersects with some of my thinking here.

9 Getsy, "Ten Queer Theses on Abstraction," in Ledesma, *Queer Abstraction*, 65–66.

10 "Queer Abstraction: Harmony Hammond and Tirza Latimer in Conversation with Julia Bryan-Wilson," quoted in McBane, "Queer Abstraction," 11.

11 A spate of gallery exhibitions in recent years have addressed this broader shift in both contemporary art practice and understandings of what constitutes a queer aesthetic. For some curators and critics, this "new" queer aesthetic has less to do with the artist's identity or overt sexuality and more to do with the artist's deployment of materials in nonnormative or excessive ways, embracing the devalued or craft-based mediums and processes. This approach might describe two parallel Chicago-area exhibitions, *The Great Refusal: Taking on New Queer Aesthetics*, curated by Oli Rodriguez (Sullivan Galleries at School of the Art Institute of Chicago, September 14–November 10, 2012), and *All Good Things Become Wild and Free*, curated by Danny Orendorff (Carthage College in Kenosha, Wisconsin, September 11–November 17, 2012). See Eler, "Queer Art's Not Just about Gender." *Surface of Color*, curated by Paul Pescador (The Pit, October 2015), challenges the notion that identity and issues of cultural difference be depicted explicitly through figuration or performance. See Ahn, "Forging Queer Identity with Abstraction." For others, concerns with form and content overlap in that the work may not be explicitly sexual, but still either pictures bodies or is read according to bodily reference enacted through suggestive form even as it does so in an expansive and indeterminate sense. Examples of this approach include *Harmony Hammond: Becoming/Unbecoming Monochrome* (curated by Tirza Latimer, Red Line, 2014); *Eyes, Lilacs, and Spunk: Queer Aesthetic from Suggestion into Abstraction* (curated by Aaron Tilford, Visual AIDS, 2014); *Read My Lips* and the attendant roundtable on "Queer Abstraction" at Knockdown Center (2016).

12 Writing about mid-twentieth-century abstract art by Robert Rauschenberg, Jasper Johns, and Agnes Martin, Jonathan D. Katz understands abstraction to constitute a "queer code," a means by which gay artists could express desire and sexuality through a veiled formal language. See Jonathan D. Katz, "Agnes Martin and the Sexuality of Abstraction," in Cooke and Kelly, *Agnes Martin*, 170–96; Katz, "Dismemberment."

13 This treatment of abstract form understood as a coded reference is a broader

tendency that David Batchelor has traced as a method of bringing modernist abstract art into the realm of social art history. He uses the example of Anna Chave's readings of Rothko, Flavin, Andre, Noland, and others as "highly schematized *depictions*" that have "reduced abstract art to the condition of resemblance-based representation by treating it as cryptically iconic." See Batchelor, "Abstraction, Modernism, Representation," 49.

14 Phelan, *Unmarked*, see particularly chapter 1, 1–33.

15 Glissant, *Poetics of Relation*, 189–94. Zach Blas also understands this ethical stance as fundamentally aesthetic and useful for feminist and queer politics: "Opacity, therefore, exposes the limits of schemas of visibility, representation, and identity that prevent sufficient understanding of multiple perspectives of the world and its peoples." See Blas, "Opacities: An Introduction," 149.

16 Eng, Halberstam, and Muñoz, "What's Queer about Queer Studies Now," 3–7.

17 Gayatri Spivak proposes that the political use of words, and perhaps all language in the deconstructive view, is catachrestic. In *Outside in the Teaching Machine*, she highlights the term "woman" as a catachresis, a metaphor without a literal referent (141), while also asserting that the task of feminist political philosophy is to "accept the risk of catachresis," to use it strategically rather than ignore it in an attempt to establish "truth" (182). David L. Eng has defined "historical catachresis" as a problem of naming that works to dislodge a reified version of history by denying the possibility of any singular historical context. Eng, *The Feeling of Kinship*, 59.

18 Ngai, "Visceral Abstractions," 33–63. See also Rizvana Bradley's special issue "The Haptic: Textures of Performance," which, as Bradley explains in "Introduction: Other Sensualities," aims to consider "the haptic as an explicitly minoritarian aesthetic and political formation," 129.

19 Hammond, "Feminist Abstract Art," 70.

20 Hammer, "The Politics of Abstraction," 70.

21 See Cowan, "Texturing Abstraction."

22 Lorenz, *Queer Art*, 53–56.

23 See Chave, "Minimalism and the Rhetoric of Power"; Chave, "Minimalism and Biography"; and Gibson, *Abstract Expressionism*.

24 Teresa de Lauretis's foundational edited volume on queer theory, for instance, offered the queer as precisely a way to connect feminist and gay and lesbian studies (while at the same time maintaining the distinctions and the difficulty in connecting these terms). De Lauretis, "Queer Theory," iii–xviii.

25 Jack Halberstam's *In a Queer Time and Place* offers a reading of abstraction as a strategy for destabilizing representation in ways that speak to difficult transgendered embodiments which paves the way for my study of the resonance of modernist aesthetics in contemporary art practice. David Getsy's *Abstract Bodies* considers how artists and viewers of 1960s abstract sculpture

"mapped bodily or personifying metaphors onto patently un-figurative, non-representational sculptural objects" (9).

26 Getsy and Simmons, "Appearing Differently."

27 Hall, "Object Lessons."

28 See Steinbock, *Shimmering Images*; and Vaccaro, "Felt Matters."

29 See Namaste, "Tragic Misreadings"; Stryker, "Transgender Studies"; and Keegan, "Against Queer Theory." Gayle Salamon also gives a useful overview of the vexed relationship between transgender studies and feminist and queer studies in part 2 of *Assuming a Body*.

30 Getsy insists that we differentiate between a queer abstraction that has to do with relations (love, desire, kinship) and abstraction that thematizes trans experience and politics, which has more to do with combating normative gender ascriptions. Getsy, "Ten Queer Theses on Abstraction," in Ledesma, *Queer Abstraction*, 67.

31 On the term *genderqueer*, see Love, "Queer," 173; and Honkasalo, "Genderqueer."

32 *Trap Door*, edited by Reina Gossett, Eric A. Stanely, and Johanna Burton, does important work to tackle the issue of visibility as a trap rather than a path to liberation for trans people, though the focus is still largely on how trans people can claim agency over representation rather than refusing it or undermining it through abstraction.

33 See English, *How to See a Work of Art*; and Mercer, *Discrepant Abstraction*. Phillip Brian Harper, in *Abstractionist Aesthetics*, argues against current norms of aesthetic reception that insist that Blackness be represented and he asserts the critical need for abstractionism to displace realism as a primary stake in Black cultural engagement.

34 See Simpson, *Blues for Smoke*; and Sheets, "Black Abstraction." Thelma Golden has done much work in this regard at the Studio Museum in Harlem, including *Freestyle* (2001) and *Energy/Experimentation: Black Artists and Abstraction 1964–1980* (2006). The Contemporary Art Museum Houston's two-part *Black in the Abstract* exhibition explored the contributions of Black artists to abstract movements since the 1960s (2013–14).

35 Edwards, *Blackness in Abstraction*, 10.

36 Harper champions abstractionist artwork (though privileging narrative over visual art) because its emphatic distance from an easy referent in reality "invites us to question the 'naturalness' not only of the aesthetic representation but also of the social facts to which it alludes, thereby opening them to active and potentially salutary revision." Harper, *Abstractionist Aesthetics*, 3.

37 See McRuer, "Crip"; and Sandahl, "Queering the Crip or Cripping the Queer?"

38 See McRuer, *Crip Theory*.

39 Kafer, *Feminist, Queer, Crip,* 5–7.

40 Cooley, "Crip Materiality."

41 Butler, *Gender Trouble,* 34; and Butler, *Bodies That Matter,* xxiii.

42 For Sedgwick, *queer* points to excesses of meaning. Sedgwick, *Tendencies,* 8.

43 Lorenz, *Queer Art,* 21.

44 Freeman, *Time Binds,* 62.

45 Said's work has encouraged my insistence that the past is alive and useful for us in the present. The longer quote is: "Thus later history reopens and challenges what seems to have been the finality of an earlier figure of thought, bringing it into contact with cultural, political and epistemological formations undreamed of by … its author. Every writer is, of course, a reader of her or his predecessors as well, but what I want to underline is that the often surprising dynamics of human history can—as Borges' fable of *Pierre Menard and the Quixote* so wittily argues—dramatize the latencies in a prior figure or form that suddenly illuminate the present." Said, *Freud and the Non-European,* 25.

46 Barthes, "Style and Its Image," 92–93.

47 Sontag, "Notes on 'Camp,'" in *Against Interpretation,* 277–81.

48 Doyle and Getsy also discuss queer formalism in terms of camp in "Queer Formalisms," 62–63.

49 Cleto, *Camp,* 4.

50 For a campy account of abstract expressionism's queer potential through its various revisions, see Sillman, "AbEx and Disco Balls."

51 Sedgwick, *Touching Feeling,* 8–9.

52 Amin, Musser, and Pérez, "Queer Form," 230.

53 For examples of these readings, see Gibson, "Color and Difference"; Latimer, *Harmony Hammond*; and Betterton, *Intimate Distance.*

54 Puar, *Terrorist Assemblages.*

55 While Halberstam argues that forms of abstraction offer representations of unstable embodiment that produce transgender aesthetics, I am exploring the postmodern pastiche practice of these recitations in order to show that their instability and mutational capacities actually exceed bodily signification. Halberstam, *In a Queer Time and Place,* 122.

56 Muñoz, *Cruising Utopia,* 138.

57 Muñoz, *Disidentifications,* 12.

58 I am not alone in this endeavor. A similar claim is made for the political potential of "queer form" by Kadji Amin, Amber Jamilla Musser, and Roy Pérez in "Queer Form."

59 Doyle and Getsy, "Queer Formalisms." In "Notes on Queer Formalism," William J. Simmons understands queer formalism (he credits painter Amy Sill-

man with the phrase) as a paradox: "It advocates for a 'queer subject' while attacking the notion of 'subjecthood.'" See Simmons's book expanding on this essay: *Queer Formalism: The Return.* See also Getsy's expansion on queer formalism: "Queer Relations."

60   See, for example, Nizan Shaked's outline of this debate within the art history journal *October,* "Is Identity a Method?," in Jones and Silver, *Otherwise,* 204–24.

61   Lauren Berlant and Michael Warner popularized the term for queer theory in their influential essay "Sex in Public," where they write of queer culture as "a world-making project": "The queer world is a space of entrances, exits, unsystematized lines of acquaintance, projected horizons, typifying examples, alternate routes, blockages, incommensurate geographies." This is a utopian concept, "by definition *unrealizable* as community or identity" (558). It is worth repeating from "Queer Form" by Amin, Musser, and Pérez: "The world-making ethos of contemporary queer studies is vulnerable to critique, because when it is perceived as unmoored from history it appears idealistic and facile. The essays in this volume demonstrate our view that scholarly and artistic world-making need not be a historically unmoored interpretive act, however, but can be a creative orchestration of historical objects to create assemblages that expose archival ties, making critical perspectives on the past intelligible, and summon possibilities that unseat political stagnation" (229). They go on to discuss the particular queer analytical strategies that are also in alignment with mine, drawing from Sedgwick, where "established categories often take a back seat to affect, feel, style, or disruption" (230).

62   See Coole and Frost, *New Materialisms*: "For materiality is always something more than 'mere' matter: an excess, force, vitality, relationality, or difference that renders matter active, self-creative, productive, unpredictable" (9).

63   Sedgwick, *Touching Feeling,* 17. The connection between texture and affect, Sedgwick asserts, is due to the fact that "both are irreducibly phenomenological" (21).

64   Karen Barad, interview in Dolphijn and van der Tuin, *New Materialism,* 59.

1. Edging Geometry

1   "Temporal drag" is Elizabeth Freeman's term; see Freeman, *Time Binds,* 62.

2   For a discussion of postexpressionist geometric abstraction, see Falconer, *Painting beyond Pollock.* Iwona Blazwick traces a history of early utopian ambitions to postmodern critiques of geometric abstraction in *Adventures of the Black Square,* 15–19.

3   Brandon Taylor's *After Constructivism* traces the long-reaching effects of constructivism, even after the collapse of its ideals, *through* modern and contemporary art.

4   See Lancaster, "The Wipe."

5   See Joseph, "Ulrike Müller," 220. For more on the collective *LTTR* (including Müller), see Bryan-Wilson, "Repetition and Difference." Müller also resists the impulse to view this work through the lens of biography, answering the interview question "Who are you?" with this response: "I'm much more challenged by figuring out ways to refute rather than answer this question. With its implications of self-sameness and stability it directly points toward some of the things that I try to undo in my work. Rather than assuming meaning or identity as given, I strive to activate seeing and knowing as processes." "Ulrike Müller: Why I Paint," *Phaidon*, accessed June 10, 2021, https://www.phaidon.com/agenda/art/articles/2016/october/17/ulrike -muller-why-i-paint/.

6   For more on fierce pussy's work (including Brody), see O'Neill-Butler, "Labor of Love."

7   Aruna D'Souza writes of Müller's work, "The body is evoked in the most maddeningly formalist, modernist terms, which constantly slip and become indeterminate." D'Souza, "Feminist Forms," 41.

8   Press release for *Figurative Geometry* at Collezione Maramotti, October 16, 2016–April 2, 2017, on Artsy, accessed June 13, 2021, https://www.artsy.net /show/collezione-maramotti-figurative-geometry/info.

9   See Corinne Fitzpatrick's review of "Reflecting Abstraction" at Johannes Vogt Gallery, April 14–May 14, 2011: Artforum, accessed June 13, 2021, https://www .artforum.com/picks/reflecting-abstraction-28096.

10   Lochner, "Ulrike Müller."

11   Getsy and Simmons, "Appearing Differently," 54.

12   See Muñoz, *Disidentifications*, 12.

13   Here, I am building on José Muñoz's concept of a queer utopian aesthetic praxis in *Cruising Utopia*, 138.

14   Langsner, "Four Abstract Classicists," 7.

15   Alloway quotes Langsner in order to make this argument in "Classicism or Hard-Edge," 60.

16   Alloway, "Classicism or Hard-Edge," 60.

17   Alloway, "Systematic Painting."

18   Barad writes of the constraints of a Euclidean logic for feminist understandings of positionality, social location, and embodiment, where issues of positionality are figured in geometric terms, and "intersectionality" is still considered "in Euclidean geometrical terms as mutually perpendicular set of axes of identification within which marked bodies can be positioned." For Barad, this topological model is problematic because it presumes that race, gender, sex, and other identity categories are separate characteristics of human beings, whereas intersectionality is much more topologically complex.

Barad draws from their own theory of agential realism and offers the dynamics of "iterative intra-activity" as an alternative to this geometrical metaphor. Barad, "Re(con)figuring Space, Time, and Matter," 98.

19 Moholy-Nagy, quoted in Doherty, "Constructions in Enamel, 1933," 130.

20 Doherty, "Constructions in Enamel, 1933," 132.

21 Ahmed, *Queer Phenomenology*.

22 Lorenz is specifically discussing the abstract candy installations of Felix Gonzalez-Torres, in "Bodies without Bodies," 160.

23 D'Alessandro, "Through the Eye and Hand," 62.

24 Langsner also used the term *colorform* to describe the hard-edged painting of "Abstract Classicists," where "color and shape are one and the same entity." Langsner, "Four Abstract Classicists," 7.

25 On Kelly's process of "emancipating" shapes from their ground, see Gottfried Boehm, "In-Between Spaces," 27.

26 Boehm, "In-Between Spaces," 23.

27 Bois, *Ellsworth Kelly*, 22.

28 Brody described this process to me in an initial studio visit, and later in a phone conversation, January 12, 2021.

29 Sigmund Freud, "Beyond the Pleasure Principle," in Gay, *Freud Reader*, 602.

30 Briony Fer discusses the "radical impurity" of the originary project of abstract art since Malevich, stating that the resilience of abstraction lies in its ability to adapt, transfer, and translate across time, space, and media. Fer, "Abstraction at War with Itself," in Blazwick, *Adventures of the Black Square*, 227.

31 Bersani and Phillips, *Intimacies*, 90.

32 Kelly, "Notes of 1969."

33 Butler, *Gender Trouble*, 178.

34 The ambivalence of queer attachments has been discussed by José Esteban Muñoz as one aspect of an aesthetic practice that does not simply refuse that which is overloaded but works with and through those charged elements. Muñoz, *Cruising Utopia*, 138.

35 See "Classification System in Nazi Concentration Camps," United States Holocaust Memorial Museum, Washington, DC, accessed December 24, 2021, https://encyclopedia.ushmm.org/content/en/article/classification -system-in-nazi-concentration-camps.

36 Every Ocean Hughes, *Uncounted*, text on poster designed with Carl Williamson for *If Only a Wave* (Participant, Inc., January 11–February 22, 2015).

2. Feeling the Grid

A version of this chapter appeared in the article "Feeling the Grid: Lorna Simpson's Concrete Abstraction," *ASAP/Journal* 2, no. 1 (2017): 135–59.

1   Simpson discusses this shift in "Representing the Black Body: Lorna Simpson in Conversation with Thelma Golden," Artspace, March 17, 2017, https://www.artspace.com/magazine/art_101/book_report/representing-the-black-body-lorna-simpson-in-conversation-with-thelma-golden-54624.

2   Krauss, "Grids," 50.

3   For Krauss, the grid "compels our acknowledgement of a world beyond the frame." Krauss, "Grids," 60. For Meyer Schapiro, Mondrian's paintings "take us beyond the concreteness of the elements and suggest relationships to a space and forms outside the tangible painted surface." Meyer Schapiro, *Mondrian*, 33. For Jack Williamson, the modern grid suggests the window of the canvas beyond which the grid extends to infinity. Williamson, "The Grid," 21.

4   McNamara, "Between Flux and Certitude," 70.

5   Bois, *Painting as Model*, 102–3.

6   McNamara, "Between Flux and Certitude," 66–67.

7   Mark C. Taylor asserts, "When the ideal of universality is put into practice uncritically, it can quickly lead to a uniformity that excludes or represses everything and everyone deemed different." Taylor, *Moment of Complexity*, 31.

8   See Higgins, *Grid Book*; and Taylor, "From Grid to Network," in *Moment of Complexity*, 19–46.

9   Meltzer, *Systems We Have Loved*, 9.

10 Halley, "Crisis in Geometry," 56.

11 Williamson, "The Grid," 25–29.

12 Kaira M. Cabañas points to the work of Latin American artists who used the grid in ways that both addressed political concerns and rejected the notion that Latin American art should always appear realistic and overtly political. Cabañas, "If the Grid Is the New Palm Tree of Latin American Art," 367.

13 On Hammond's "soft grids," see Goldsmith, "The Soft Grid."

14 Haynes, "Queering Abstract Art."

15 Simmons, "Betty Tomkins," 45.

16 Rosemary Betterton in *An Intimate Distance* considers nonrepresentational painting as a reclamation of female authorship, where abstraction functions as a representation of the gendered body; see particularly chapter 4, "Bodies in the Work: The Aesthetics and Politics of Women's Nonrepresentational Painting," 79–105.

17 Sheila Pepe's installation "Hot Lesbian Formalism" (2005) was exhibited at Sesnon Gallery, University of California, Santa Cruz. A. K. Burns's performance work *PICA TBA: Leave No Trace* (2016) utilized grid projections, and

the grid appears across their sculpture and installation work such as *Survivor's Remorse*, 2018.

18 Fake, *Memory Palaces*.

19 See Jill H. Casid's formulation of "intimate distance" in "Handle with Care," 126.

20 Brooke Belisle argues that the felt works are not a departure, but a continuation of Simpson's previous work, even in the absence of the body. Belisle, "Felt Surface, Visible Image," 158.

21 See Sekula, "The Body and the Archive." Kellie Jones also points out Simpson's engagement with this history of photography used to classify and control Black subjects. Jones, "(Un)Seen & Overheard," in *Lorna Simpson*, 32. Okwui Enwezor discusses Simpson's ongoing redeployment of minimalist tropes in ways that point to this history (though he does not investigate the grid). Enwezor, "Social Grace," 50.

22 Butler, *Gender Trouble*, 178.

23 Butler, "Endangered/Endangering," 18; Wallace, *Constructing the Black Masculine*, 135. Both are quoted in Simone Browne's *Dark Matters*, 20.

24 Elderfield, "Grids," 53.

25 Briony Fer views repetition as the essential ground of all representation, even as it often gives way to difference. Fer, *The Infinite Line*, 33. Krauss describes the grid as a system of reproductions without an original, much like processes of signification, and this creates one myth of originality for Krauss in *Originality of the Avant-Garde*, 161–62.

26 See Butler, *Gender Trouble*, 34; and further, Butler, *Bodies That Matter*, xxiii.

27 "Thus, as a series *woman* is the name of a structural relation to material objects as they have been produced and organized by a prior history." Young is drawing on Sartre's concept of serial collectivity. Young, "Gender as Seriality," 728.

28 I am thinking here with Alison Kafer's political/relational model of disability in *Feminist, Queer, Crip*, 6.

29 Muñoz, "Race, Sex, and the Incommensurate," 112–13.

30 Fer, *Infinite Line*, 58.

31 Fer, *Infinite Line*, 53.

32 Brandon Taylor says this of Mondrian in *After Constructivism*, 164.

33 See Fer, "Decoration and Necessity: Mondrian's Excess," in *On Abstract Art*, 33–54; Krauss, "Grids," 59; and Schapiro, *Mondrian*.

34 Krauss, *Originality of the Avant-Garde*, 162.

35 Deleuze and Guattari, *A Thousand Plateaus*, 475–76.

36 For Vaccaro, this allows for alternative theories of transgender becoming, for a "trans-corporeography" that can imagine material processes of em-

bodiment that are not stagnant topological points. Vaccaro, "Felt Matters,"
253.

37 Christina Bryan Rosenberger, "Sophisticated Economy of Means," in Cooke
and Kelly, *Agnes Martin*, 104–5. According to Krauss, as the grid came to co-
incide more closely with its material support, the supposed "'logic of vision'
became infected by the tactile." Krauss, "Agnes Martin," 89.

38 The tensions between various readings of Martin's work in relation to her titles are discussed by Suzanne Hudson, "On a Clear Day," in Cooke and Kelly,
Agnes Martin, 121–22.

39 Krauss, "Agnes Martin: The /Cloud/," 75–90.

40 Jonathan D. Katz, "Agnes Martin and the Sexuality of Abstraction," in Cooke
and Kelly, *Agnes Martin*, 190–91.

41 Kellie Jones has also discussed the sensuality of the felt surfaces in Simpson's
"Public Sex" series; Jones, "(Un)Seen & Overheard," 68.

42 Casid, *Scenes of Projection*, 41.

43 For Muñoz, the connotations of the mirrored orb might be that of "an aerial
perspective of a great glittering landscape. It can appear to be something like
a demographic or population-density map of a queer utopia." Muñoz, *Cruising Utopia*, 142.

44 Casid, "Epilogue," 101.

45 I am thinking with Roland Barthes, who formulates aesthetic surface *as* substance in "Style and Its Image."

46 Krauss, "Grids," 63.

47 Fer, "Color Manual," in Temkin and Fer, *Color Chart*, 34.

48 For a detailed discussion of Johns's paintings of numbers, see Roberta Bernstein, "Numbers."

49 Katz, "Dismemberment," 180. See also Butt, "Bodies of Evidence."

3. Flaming Color

1 Besemer, "Abstraction."

2 Jarman, *Chroma*, 58.

3 Batchelor, *Chromophobia*, 22–23. A long history of color as a philosophical
problem is due, in part, to its association with matter and its threat to the
mimetic order, as Jacqueline Lichtenstein explains: "Being material, color
has always been seen as belonging to the ontologically deficient categories
of the ephemeral and the random." Lichtenstein, *Eloquence of Color*, 63.
The Renaissance-era debate in painting between *disegno e colore* (design/
drawing or color) stemmed from the notion that color was inferior to form;
color seemed dangerous and volatile as a spontaneous painterly medium,
while drawing was the orderly and objective measure of artist's skill. Martin

Jay provides a summary of this debate in "Chromophilia," 3–4. See a chapter on this theme in Gage, *Color and Culture*, 117–38.

4   Anfam, *Masters of the Gesture*, 5.

5   Kristeva, "Giotto's Joy," 218.

6   Kristeva, "Giotto's Joy," 221.

7   In "Colour and Its Name," Thierry de Duve writes, "The name of a color risks losing its designated referent, even though it vouches for that to which it corresponds." De Duve, *Pictorial Nominalism*, 124.

8   Batchelor, *Luminous and Grey*, 14. Batchelor also usefully discusses the experience of color as ambivalent, attending to the impulses of chromophobia and chromophilia that can coexist in tension in our experience of color. In *Colour*, Batchelor noted this tense relationship between color and language and included a cluster of texts that reflect on this, including Kristeva and de Duve.

9   Linda Besemer and David Batchelor, "Too Colorful," in Besemer, Yau, and Batchelor, *Linda Besemer*, 20–22.

10 See John Yau, "Something New under the Sun," in Besemer, Yau, and Batchelor, *Linda Besemer*, 10–11.

11 This shift is the basis for the exhibition *Color Chart: Reinventing Color 1950 to Today*, curated by Ann Temkin and Briony Fer (MoMA, 2008), which traces a genealogy of commercially produced color "after the palette," divorced from subjectivity and belonging to the realm of consumer and industrial life rather than a transcendent medium.

12 Benjamin Buchloh discusses this shift with the monochrome in "The Primary Colors for the Second Time," 44. Fer shows how the color chart came to operate as a space of desire in the midfifties, caught between historical avant-gardism and the possibilities of serial models already in formation. Temkin and Fer, *Color Chart*, 34–35.

13 Barthes, "Plastic," 98. It is easy to see why Barthes's writing on plastic has been a popular citation in writing on both Linda Besemer (Batchelor, "Too Colorful," 20) and Lynda Benglis (Richmond, *Lynda Benglis*, 28), but the queering capacities of plastic color remain unexplored.

14 De Duve argues that it was Duchamp who drew out the possibilities for "short-circuiting" when these arbitrary names lose their designated referents. De Duve, *Pictorial Nominalism*, 135.

15 Rodchenko, quoted in Buchloh, "The Primary Colors," 44.

16 Batchelor, *Chromophobia*, 99.

17 Gibson, "Color and Difference," 199–200.

18 Ahmed and Stacey, *Thinking Through the Skin*, 3.

19 Bradley, "Living in the Absence of a Body," n.p. Bradley also reckons with is-

sues of Black embodiment in the abstract work of Senga Nengudi. See Bradley, "Transferred Flesh," 161–66.

20 Fer, "Color-in-Pieces," 52.

21 *Life* magazine's 1970 article "Fling Dribble and Drip" solidified abstract expressionism, and specifically Pollock, as the ultimate source of her work. Susan Richmond discusses this legacy in *Lynda Benglis*, 23–24, as does Amelia Jones in *Body Art*, 96–97.

22 For a contextual account of Benglis's controversial rebellion against black and white, see Dave Hickey, "A House Built in a Body," in Marshall, *Lynda Benglis*, 17–21.

23 See Richmond, *Lynda Benglis*; Marshall, *Lynda Benglis*; and the essays "Lynda Benglis: All That Matters" by Elizabeth Lebovici and "Lynda Benglis: Clandestine Performer" by Judith Tannenbaum in Gautherot, Hancock, and Kim, *Lynda Benglis*. The tension between nature and artifice in Benglis's work is discussed by all of these authors.

24 Halberstam, "Technotopias," in *In a Queer Time and Place*, 110–20.

25 Fried, *Art and Objecthood*, 150; this debate is discussed at length by Bernstein in "Aporia of the Sensible—Art, Objecthood, and Anthropomorphism," in *Against Voluptuous Bodies*, 117–43.

26 Lippard, "Eccentric Abstraction," in *Changing*, 98–111.

27 Fer, *Infinite Line*, 108.

28 For example, James Meyer writes, "A latent anthropocentrism would seem to inhabit *any* sculpture, including those works that we take to most strenuously undermine such associations. Some of the most compelling sculptural endeavors since the 1990s have attempted to do exactly this by means of an uncanny or queer figuration, making explicit the anthropomorphism that Minimalist artists sought to repress." Meyer, "Anthropomorphism," 25.

29 Butler, *Bodies That Matter*, 176–77.

30 Deleuze, *The Fold*. On Besemer's engagement with Deleuze's theories, see Besemer, "Abstraction."

31 Color's surface effects in this work link it to the particular formal and aesthetic properties of style, drag, camp, artifice, and excess, resonating with a queer disruption of a binary logic by which we come to understand an image-as-surface. The importance of color as a surface—taken to be at once marginal and excessive, disregarded and dangerous—is tied up with the ethical implications of aesthetic style. Roland Barthes problematizes the division between form and content, the aesthetic and the substantive, which governs our understanding of style: "Form is reputed to be the appearance or garment of Content, which is its truth or body; the metaphors attached to Form (to style) are therefore of a decorative order: *figures, colors, nuances*"; Barthes, "Style and Its Image," 91. Much like color, style is believed to func-

tion as a disguise: a signifier under which the signified is hidden. Exposing the ethical implications of this binary logic, Barthes also lays out how style came to be seen as exception (deviance) to the rule (norm), casting aesthetics as anomalous and superfluous, beyond the margins of the natural and normal. With Barthes, I take the colorful surface image not as a layering of skin over the body of content, but as proliferating layers whose volume contains no secret truth. And the surface of color does not name an identity or subject, but its function *as* surface, with no "truth" beneath its decadent layers.

32 On the Deleuzian tradition of affect theory and this understanding of surface, see Muñoz, "Introduction," 123–29.

33 Butler, *Gender Trouble*, 183–90.

34 Gilroy, *Against Race*, 46. Fanon put forth this theory of a racial epidermal schema in *Black Skin, White Masks*; see especially 109–12.

35 Spivak, "Imperialism and Sexual Difference," 237; Ahmed, "Animated Borders," 52.

36 De Lauretis, *Freud's Drive*, 53–57.

37 In *Archive Fever*, Derrida posits a death drive which is "archive-destroying." Although this drive eludes perception, there are exceptions to its silent destruction according to Freud: "except if it disguises itself, except if it tints itself, makes itself up or paints itself in some erotic color. This impression of erogenous color draws a mask right on the skin." The archiviolithic drive does not appear and leave no traces, "it leaves only its erotic simulacrum, its pseudonym in painting, its sexual idols, its mask of seduction: lovely impressions," 11. Derrida allows me to think of a queerly volatile archival impulse that not only works against itself, but with the function of painted color as the external impression of something like erotic seduction, "lovely impressions" which mask the destructive force of the archiviolithic impulse while they also render it visible.

38 On abjection, see Kristeva, *Powers of Horror*.

39 We can see this in Fried's oppositional understanding of "art" vs. "objecthood," in *Art and Objecthood*. Modernist theories that privileged the materiality of paint are also caught up in a rhetoric of purity: for Greenberg, the essential two-dimensional "flatness" by which modernist painting distinguished itself as "pure" and self-contained medium was also a turn away from representational illusionism, though "it does and must permit optical illusion"; Greenberg, "Modernist Painting," 6. As Hope Mauzerall has argued in "What's the Matter with Matter," Greenberg's apparent commitment to medium can be deceptive, as he privileged form over matter, where to achieve "pure form" art must transcend matter, the stuff of the world. And Mauzerall traces this tradition through Krauss's "optical unconscious," where a push toward transcendence is achieved through the effacement of matter.

40 See Greenberg, "Crisis of the Easel Picture," 1948, in *Clement Greenberg*, 221–25.

41 Jessica A. Cooley similarly considers how viewing disability in art might render a viewer disabled, in "An Inartistic Interest."

42 Nicole Archer, "Dynamic Status," in Gossett, Stanly, and Burton, *Trap Door*, 293–319.

43 Lippard, *Changing*, 169.

44 Lippard, *Changing*, 171.

45 Lippard, *Changing*, 173.

46 Shiff, "The Unaccountable," 21.

47 Phelan, *Mourning Sex*, 39.

48 Phelan, *Mourning Sex*, 41–42.

49 Deleuze, *The Fold*, 19–20.

50 Koestenbaum, *Humiliation*, 15–16.

51 For this consideration of blush on the surface of skin as parallel to the surface of a photograph, see McClure, "Prima Facie," 116.

52 Freud's concept of a "screen memory" is "one which owes its value as a memory not to its own content but to the relation existing between that content and some other, that has been suppressed." In Gay, *Freud Reader*, 126.

4. Transforming Everyday Matter

1 *Sheila Pepe: Hot Mess Formalism* was organized by Phoenix Art Museum and curated by Gilbert Vicario, October 19, 2018–March 10, 2019.

2 Hammond, "Feminist Abstract Art," 66–70.

3 Sianne Ngai considers abstraction as something actively withdrawn, refusing this notion of abstraction as a hidden truth or immaterial and somehow less real. Ngai, "Visceral Abstractions," 52.

4 I am also thinking with the "deformative," which Jill H. Casid formulates as a particular set of tactics drawn from that other side of performativity haunting the origins of queer theory in the work of Eve Sedgwick and Judith Butler: "The performative holds within it not merely the negative, undoing power of regulatory and restrictive—even deadly—norms, which render some ways of existence viable and others unlivable, but also the potential of doing otherwise." Casid, "Queer Deformativity," 222. For Casid, the deformative is not merely a direct refusal or a not doing, but "ways of negotiating and even transforming everyday sites of damage for livable life that refuses the demands and codes of the normative." Casid, "Doing Things with Being Undone," 31. Casid also theorizes a "queer expressivity" in terms of this performative and deformative tension, in "Queer Expressivity."

5   I would like to acknowledge here the work that Jessica Cooley is doing to theorize what she calls "crip materiality" in contemporary art: Cooley, "Crip Materiality."

6   See Deutch, "Deformity."

7   Morris, "Anti-form."

8   Bois and Krauss, *Formless.*

9   David Getsy, in *Abstract Bodies,* 8–19, provides an overview of the discourse around anthropomorphism in 1960s sculpture, particularly the criticism that established a latent anthropomorphism in minimalist sculpture that so staunchly refused to picture it.

10   Jennifer Doyle and David Getsy, in "Queer Formalisms," 61, consider how queer formal approaches flip common uses for objects, and how even minimalism can evoke a "bitchy" queer sensibility.

11   Richard Meyer has cited Clement Greenberg's "The New Sculpture" (1958) to explain his preference for the work of Anne Truitt due to its optical appeal: "The human body is no longer postulated as the agent of space in either pictorial or sculptural art; now it is eyesight alone, and eyesight has more freedom of movement and invention within three dimensions than two." Meyer, *Minimalism,* 223–24.

12   Ann Cvetkovich considers Sheila Pepe's work at the intersection of craft and public feeling, through her large-scale, interactive installations reclaiming feminist political practices and "literally engaging the senses in a way that makes things feel different." Cvetkovich, *Depression,* 177. John Corso Esquivel's *Feminist Subjectivities in Fiber Art* similarly situates feminist fiber works like that of Sheila Pepe and Shinique Smith in terms of their engagement with a legacy of feminist craft through the lens of affect studies.

13   Lia Gangitano points to this work's queer resistance to representation, and understands her crocheted environments as literal forms of queer "worldmaking." Lia Gangitano, "The Materiality of Shade," in Vicario, *Sheila Pepe,* 29–30.

14   Hammond, "Feminist Abstract Art," 70.

15   Amy Smith-Stewart's introduction to *Harmony Hammond,* 6–23, both situates her work in relation to legacies of postminimalism and feminist craft and also reads her work according to the common corporeal metaphors. My shift away from reading Hammond's work in this way is also notably to read against the artist's own narrative of her work. Hammond has described her practice in overtly corporeal terms, tying abstraction to lesbian content: in her statements, paint is described as skin, and painting is working with the site of a gendered body; wrapped objects "became stand-ins for the female body," "with the fabric as muscle or flesh." At the same time, Hammond also writes of works like *Hunkertime,* composed of multiple units, in terms that

imply intimacy and relationships, in *Lesbian Art in America*, 96. My lifting off from the physical intimacy of this work to consider how else these objects operate beyond a coded female or queer body is not to disregard Hammond's voice, but to take her work seriously today.

16 Bryan-Wilson, *Fray*, 75, 85.

17 Best, *Visualizing Feeling*, 139.

18 Fer is specifically critiquing Lucy Lippard's discussion of Bourgeois's work. Fer, *Infinite Line*, 105.

19 See, for example, Wagner, *Three Artists*; Lippard, "Eros Presumptive"; and Chave, "Minimalism and the Rhetoric of Power."

20 See Latimer, *Harmony Hammond*, 7–25; Haynes, "Going Beneath the Surface"; and Smith-Stewart, "Material Outlaw," in *Harmony Hammond*, 6–23.

21 Lancaster, "Queer Abstraction."

22 Steinberg, *Other Criteria*, 82.

23 DeSimone, "Shinique Smith," 20.

24 Shinique Smith says in an interview with Kymberly Pinder, "The *Bales* are a marriage of two things: the global issue of the reuse and recycling of clothes sent abroad and the formal beauty of bales themselves." Pinder, "Unbaled," 14.

25 Renate Lorenz discusses Smith's work, in particular the 2017 photograph *Untitled (Rodeo Beach Bundle)*, as a form of "radical drag" due to the work's refusal of the categories normally applied to bodies. On the one hand, the photograph suggests an image of a body; on the other, due to the bundling of fabric covering that form, we cannot define it as a person. What this image of an early bundling work, a performance by Smith, does make clear is the kinds of reading practices Westerners engage in to identify difference on the surface of bodies—the semblance of a head scarf that would be commonly identified as both raced and gendered "feminine," the migration suggested by a burden strapped to the back. Lorenz, *Queer Art*, 56.

26 Chave, "Minimalism and the Rhetoric of Power," 44.

27 McClodden is an active practitioner of Santería; see Roffino, "Tionna Nekkia McClodden."

28 Edwards, *Blackness in Abstraction*, 11.

29 On black radical aesthetic practices that disturb such monolithic representation in favor of material engagement, see also Aranke, "Material Matters."

Epilogue

1 To live and work "in the wake," Christina Sharpe tells us, means to reckon with the persistence of Black exclusion from the status of the human—the "wake work" of Black artists and cultural producers reckons with the impos-

sibility of resolution while Black people live and die the legacies of slavery. Sharpe, *In the Wake*, 13–14.

2   Empty because they often do little to address real structural injustices—in fact, they provide an easy cover for the lack of structural changes that would work to dismantle white supremacy. C. Riley Snorton and Hentyle Yapp's *Saturation* volume addresses these issues of racist exclusion within art institutions along with problems of racial representation, understanding, as I do, that representation is not enough to shift cultural structures of oppression, and that we need new methods of accounting for the complexities of race.

3   See Jensen, "The Pink Triangle."

4   See the interview with Baker by curator Michelle Millar Fishar, "MoMA Acquires the Rainbow Flag"; and Campbell, "Gilbert Baker Flag," in *Queer X Design*, 82–83.

5   This history of queer codes is in part what has led scholars to interpret the mid-twentieth-century work of queer artists such as Jasper Johns or Agnes Martin as a kind of closeted symbolic abstraction. See Katz, "Dismembership"; and Butt, "Bodies of Evidence."

6   See Gossett, Stanely, and Burton, *Trap Door*.

7   Puar also importantly works to dismantle the sexual exceptionalism mounted by representational mandates of visibility identity politics and promotes an affective analysis that can work toward unknown queer futurities. Puar, *Terrorist Assemblages*, 204.

8   Berlant and Freeman, "Queer Nationality," 215–16.

9   Butler, "An LGBTQ Micronation Declared War on Australia."

10   Klapeer and Laskar, "Transnational Ways of Belonging," 534.

11   Klapeer and Laskar, "Transnational Ways of Belonging," 528.

12   Laskar, Johansson, and Mulinari, "Decolonising the Rainbow Flag," 206.

13   See Halperin and Traub, *Gay Shame*.

14   For more on the rainbow as prismatic projection, see Casid, "Following the Rainbow," in *Scenes of Projection*, 195–223.

15   In "Black Hair/Style Politics," Kobena Mercer discusses hair as a medium of social significance, a raw material shaped by symbolic value: "If racism is conceived as an ideological code in which biological attributes are invested with societal values and meanings, then it is because our hair is perceived within this framework that it is burdened with a range of 'negative' connotations." Mercer, "Black Hair/Style Politics," 35.

16   Elena Gross discusses the issue of texture in this work and Hennessy's use of black hair across many works. Gross, "When and Where I Enter."

17   Hennessy's *Black Rainbow* statement is included in Wright, "Into the Void."

Ahmed, Sara. "Animated Borders: Skin, Colour and Gender." In *Vital Signs: Feminist Reconfigurations of the Bio/logical Body*, edited by Margrit Shildrick and Janet Price, 45–65. Edinburgh: Edinburgh University Press, 1998.

Ahmed, Sara. *Queer Phenomenology: Orientations, Objects, Others*. Durham, NC: Duke University Press, 2006.

Ahmed, Sara, and Jackie Stacey, eds. *Thinking Through the Skin*. London: Routledge, 2001.

Ahn, Abe. "Forging Queer Identity with Abstraction." *Hyperallergic*, October 19, 2015. https://hyperallergic.com/243093/forging-queer-identity-with-abstraction/.

Alloway, Lawrence. "Classicism or Hard-Edge?" *Art International* 4, no. 2 (1960): 60–71.

Alloway, Lawrence. "Systematic Painting." In *Minimal Art: A Critical Anthology*, edited by Gregory Battcock, 46–55. Berkeley: University of California Press, 1995.

Amin, Kadji, Amber Jamilla Musser, and Roy Pérez. "Queer Form: Aesthetics, Race, and the Violences of the Social." *ASAP/Journal* 2, no. 2 (2017): 227–39.

Anfam, David. *Masters of the Gesture*. Beverly Hills, CA: Gagosian Gallery, 2011.

Aranke, Sampada. "Material Matters: Black Radical Aesthetics and the Limits of Visibility." *e-flux*, no. 79 (2017). https://www.e-flux.com/journal/79/94433/material-matters-black-radical-aesthetics-and-the-limits-of-visibility/.

Barad, Karen. "Re(con)figuring Space, Time, and Matter." In *Feminist Locations: Global and Local, Theory and Practice*, edited by Marianne Dekoven, 75–110. New Brunswick, NJ: Rutgers University Press, 2001.

Barthes, Roland. "Plastic." In *Mythologies*, translated by Annette Lavers, 97–99. New York: Hill and Wang, 1972.

Barthes, Roland. "Style and Its Image." In *The Rustle of Language*, translated by Richard Howard, 90–99. Berkeley: University of California Press, 1989.

Batchelor, David. "Abstraction, Modernism, Representation." In *Thinking Art: Beyond Traditional Aesthetics*, edited by Andrew Benjamin and Peter Osborne, 44–57. London: Institute of Contemporary Arts, 1991.

Batchelor, David. *Chromophobia*. London: Reaktion, 2000.

Batchelor, David, ed. *Colour*. Documents of Contemporary Art. Cambridge, MA: Whitechapel Gallery and MIT Press, 2008.

Batchelor, David. *The Luminous and the Grey*. London: Reaktion Books, 2014.

Belisle, Brooke. "Felt Surface, Visible Image: Lorna Simpson's Photography and the Embodiment of Appearance." *Photography and Culture* 4, no. 2 (July 2011): 157–78.

Berlant, Lauren, and Elizabeth Freeman. "Queer Nationality." In *Fear of a Queer Planet: Queer Politics and Social Theory*, edited by Michael Warner, 193–229. Minneapolis: University of Minnesota Press, 1993.

Berlant, Lauren, and Michael Warner. "Sex in Public." *Critical Inquiry* 24, no. 2 (Winter 1998): 547–66.

Bernstein, J. M. *Against Voluptuous Bodies: Late Modernism and the Meaning of Painting*. Stanford, CA: Stanford University Press, 2006.

Bernstein, Roberta. "Numbers." In *Jasper Johns: Seeing with the Mind's Eye*, edited by Gary Garrels, 44–81. San Francisco: San Francisco Museum of Modern Art and Yale University Press, 2012.

Bersani, Leo, and Adam Phillips. *Intimacies*. Chicago: University of Chicago Press, 2008.

Besemer, Linda. "Abstraction: Politics and Possibilities." *X-Tra Contemporary Art Quarterly* 7, no. 3 (Spring 2005). https://www.x-traonline.org/article/abstraction-politics-and-possibilities.

Besemer, Linda, John Yau, and David Batchelor. *Linda Besemer*. Santa Monica, CA: Angles Gallery and Cohan Leslie and Browne, 2002.

Best, Susan. *Visualizing Feeling: Affect and the Feminine Avant-Garde*. London: I. B. Tauris, 2011.

Betterton, Rosemary. *An Intimate Distance: Women, Artists, and the Body*. London: Routledge, 1996.

Blas, Zach. "Opacities: An Introduction." *Camera Obscura* 31, no. 2 (92) (2016): 149–53.

Blazwick, Iwona, ed. *Adventures of the Black Square: Abstract Art and Society 1915–2015*. London: Prestel and Whitechapel Gallery, 2015.

Boehm, Gottfried. "In-Between Spaces: Painting, Relief, and Sculpture in the Work of Ellsworth Kelly." In *Ellsworth Kelly: In-Between Spaces: Works 1956–2002*, edited by Viola Weigel, 17–43. Basel: Fondation Beyeler, 2002.

Bois, Yve-Alain. *Ellsworth Kelly: The Early Drawings, 1948–1955*. Cambridge, MA: Harvard University Art Museums, 1999.

Bois, Yve-Alain. *Painting as Model*. Cambridge, MA: MIT Press, 1990.

Bois, Yve-Alain, and Rosalind E. Krauss. *Formless: A User's Guide*. New York: Zone Books, 1997.

Bradley, Rizvana. "Introduction: Other Sensualities." In "The Haptic: Textures of Performance," special issue, *Women and Performance: A Journal of Feminist Theory* 24, nos. 2–3 (2014): 129–33.

Bradley, Rizvana. "Living in the Absence of a Body: The (Sus)Stain of Black Female (W)holeness." *Rhizomes: Cultural Studies in Emerging Knowledge*, no. 29 (2016). http://www.rhizomes.net/issue29/bradley/index.html.

Bradley, Rizvana. "Transferred Flesh: Reflections on Senga Nengudi's R.S.V.P." *TDR: The Drama Review* 59, no. 1 (2015): 161–66.

Browne, Simone. *Dark Matters: On the Surveillance of Blackness*. Durham, NC: Duke University Press, 2015.

Bryan-Wilson, Julia. *Fray: Art and Textile Politics*. Chicago: University of Chicago, 2017.

Bryan-Wilson, Julia. "Repetition and Difference: LTTR." *Art Practical* 5, no. 2 (December 2013). https://www.artpractical.com/feature/repetition-and-difference-lttr/.

Buchloh, Benjamin H. D. "The Primary Colors for the Second Time: A Paradigm Repetition of the Neo-Avant-Garde." *October* 37 (Summer 1986): 41–52.

Butler, Josh. "An LGBTQ Micronation Declared War on Australia in 2004 and a Senator Is Still Mad about It." *Huffington Post*, February 28, 2017. https://www.huffingtonpost.com.au/2017/02/27/an-lgbtq-micronation-declared-war-on-australia-in-2004-and-a-sen_a_21726219/.

Butler, Judith. *Bodies That Matter: On the Discursive Limits of "Sex."* New York: Routledge, 1993.

Butler, Judith. "Endangered/Endangering: Schematic Racism and White Paranoia." In *Reading Rodney King/Reading Urban Uprising*, edited by Robert Gooding-Williams, 15–22. New York: Routledge, 1993.

Butler, Judith. *Gender Trouble: Feminism and the Subversion of Identity*. New York: Routledge, 1990.

Butt, Gavin. "Bodies of Evidence: Queering Disclosure in the Art of Jasper Johns." In *Gender, Sexuality, and Museums*, edited by Amy K. Levin, 235–52. Oxford: Routledge, 2010.

Cabañas, Kaira M. "If the Grid Is the New Palm Tree of Latin American Art." *Oxford Art Journal* 33, no. 3 (October 2010): 365–83.

Campbell, Andy. *Queer X Design: 50 Years of Signs, Symbols, Banners, Logos, and Graphic Art of LGBTQ.* New York: Black Dog and Leventhal, 2019.

Casid, Jill H. "Doing Things with Being Undone." *Journal of Visual Culture* 18, no. 1 (2019): 30–52.

Casid, Jill H. "Epilogue: Landscape in, around, and under the Performative." *Women and Performance: A Journal of Feminist Theory* 21, no. 1 (2011): 97–116.

Casid, Jill H. "Handle with Care." *TDR: The Drama Review* 56, no. 4 (2012): 121–35.

Casid, Jill H. "Queer Deformativity: Mark Morrisroe, Jack Pierson, and Jimmy De Sana at Pat Hearn." In *The Conditions of Being Art: Pat Hearn Gallery and American Fine Arts, Co. (1983–2004)*, edited by Jeannine Tang, Anne E. Butler, and Lia Gangitano, 212–37. Brooklyn: Dancing Fox, 2018.

Casid, Jill H. "Queer Expressivity: Or the Art of How to Do It with Louise Fishman." In *A Question of Emphasis: Louise Fishman Drawing*, edited by Amy L. Powell, 47–59. Urbana-Champaign: Krannert Art Museum, University of Illinois Urbana-Champaign, 2021.

Casid, Jill H. *Scenes of Projection: Recasting the Enlightenment Subject.* Minneapolis: University of Minnesota Press, 2015.

Casid, Jill H. "Thanatography: Working the Folds of Photography's Wild Performativity in Capital's Necrocene." *Photography and Culture* 13, no. 2 (2020): 1–26.

Chaich, John, and Todd Oldham. *Queer Threads: Crafting Identity and Community.* Los Angeles: Ammo, 2017.

Chave, Anna. "Minimalism and Biography." *Art Bulletin* 82, no. 1 (2000): 149–63.

Chave, Anna. "Minimalism and the Rhetoric of Power." *Arts Magazine* 64, no. 5 (1990): 44–63.

Cleto, Fabio. *Camp: Queer Aesthetics and the Performing Subject; A Reader.* Ann Arbor: University of Michigan Press, 1999.

Cooke, Lynne, and Karen Kelly, eds. *Agnes Martin.* New York: Dia Art Foundation and Yale University Press, 2011.

Coole, Diana, and Samantha Frost, eds. *New Materialisms: Ontology, Agency, and Politics.* Durham, NC: Duke University Press, 2010.

Cooley, Jessica A. "Crip Materiality: The Art Institution after the Americans with Disabilities Act." PhD diss., University of Wisconsin–Madison, 2021.

Cooley, Jessica A. "An Inartistic Interest: Civil War Medicine, Disability, and the Art of Thomas Eakins." In *Disability and Art History*, vol. 2, edited by Ann Millett-Gallant and Elizabeth Howie. New York: Routledge, 2022.

Cooley, Jessica A. "Introducing Crip Materiality: The Case for Mad Objects and *Soft Screw.*" In *Routledge Companion to Art and Disability*, edited by Keri Watson and Timothy W. Hiles. New York: Routledge, 2022.

Cowan, Sarah Louise. "Texturing Abstraction: Howardena Pindell's Cut and Sewn Paintings." *Art Journal* 79, no. 4 (2020): 26–43.

Cvetkovich, Ann. *Depression: A Public Feeling.* Durham, NC: Duke University Press, 2013.

D'Alessandro, Stephanie. "Through the Eye and Hand." In *Moholy-Nagy: Future Present*, edited by Matthew S. Witkovsky and Carol S. Eliel, 61–104. Chicago: Art Institute of Chicago, 2016.

De Duve, Thierry. *Pictorial Nominalism: On Marcel Duchamp's Passage from Painting to the Readymade*. Minneapolis: University of Minnesota Press, 1991.

Deleuze, Gilles. *The Fold: Leibniz and the Baroque*. Minneapolis: University of Minnesota Press, 1993.

Deleuze, Gilles, and Félix Guattari. *A Thousand Plateaus: Capitalism and Schizophrenia*. Translated by Brian Massumi. Minneapolis: University of Minnesota Press, 1987.

de Lauretis, Teresa. *Freud's Drive: Psychoanalysis, Literature and Film*. Houndmills, UK: Palgrave Macmillan, 2008.

de Lauretis, Teresa. "Queer Theory: Lesbian and Gay Sexualities, an Introduction." *differences: A Journal of Feminist Cultural Studies* 3, no. 2 (Summer 1991): iii–xviii.

Derrida, Jacques. *Archive Fever: A Freudian Impression*. Translated by Eric Prenowitz. Chicago: University of Chicago Press, 1996.

DeSimone, Jaime. "Shinique Smith: An Ongoing Gesture." *International Review of African American Art* 26, no. 3 (2016): 19–23.

Deutch, Helen. "Deformity." In *Keywords for Disability Studies*, edited by Rachel Adams, Benjamin Reiss, and David Serlin, 52–54. New York: New York University Press, 2015.

Doherty, Brigid. "Constructions in Enamel, 1933." In *Bauhaus, 1919–1933: Workshops for Modernity*, edited by Barry Bergdoll and Leah Dickerman, 130–33. New York: Museum of Modern Art, 2009.

Dolphijn, Rick, and Iris van der Tuin, eds. *New Materialism: Interviews and Cartographies*. Ann Arbor: Open Humanities Press, 2012.

Doyle, Jennifer, and David Getsy. "Queer Formalisms: Jennifer Doyle and David Getsy in Conversation." *Art Journal* 72, no. 4 (Winter 2013): 58–71.

D'Souza, Aruna. "Feminist Forms." In *Ulrike Müller: Franza, Fever 103, and Quilts*, edited by Achim Höchdorfer and Barbara Schröder, 37–47. New York: Dancing Foxes, 2012.

Edwards, Adrienne. *Blackness in Abstraction*. New York: Pace Gallery, 2016.

Elderfield, John. "Grids." *Artforum* 10, no. 9 (May 1972): 52–59.

Eler, Alicia. "Queer Art's Not Just about Gender—A Chicago Survey." *Hyperallergic*, November 15, 2012. https://hyperallergic.com/60339/queer-arts-not-just-about-gender-a-chicago-survey/.

Eng, David L. *The Feeling of Kinship: Queer Liberalism and the Racialization of Intimacy*. Durham, NC: Duke University Press, 2010.

Eng, David L., Jack Halberstam, and José Esteban Muñoz. "What's Queer about Queer Studies Now? Introduction." *Social Text* 23, nos. 3–4 (84–85) (Fall–Winter 2005): 1–17.

English, Darby. *How to See a Work of Art in Total Darkness*. Cambridge, MA: MIT Press, 2007.

Enwezor, Okwui. "Social Grace: The Work of Lorna Simpson." *Third Text* 10, no. 35 (Summer 1996): 43–58.

Erharter, Christiane, Dietmar Schwärzler, Ruby Sircar, and Hans Scheirl, eds. *Pink Labour on Golden Streets: Queer Art Practices*. Berlin: Sternberg, 2015.

Esquivel, John Corso. *Feminist Subjectivities in Fiber Art and Craft: Shadows of Affect*. New York: Routledge, 2019.

Fake, Edie. *Memory Palaces*. Brooklyn, NY: Secret Acres, 2014.

Falconer, Morgan. *Painting beyond Pollock*. London: Phaidon, 2015.

Fanon, Frantz. *Black Skin, White Masks*. Translated by Charles Lam Markmann. London: Pluto, 1986.

Fer, Briony. "Color-in-Pieces: The Italian Neo–Avant Garde." In *Part Object, Part Sculpture*, edited by Helen Molesworth, 50–61. Columbus, Ohio: Wexner Center for the Arts and Pennsylvania State University Press, 2005.

Fer, Briony. *The Infinite Line: Re-making Art after Modernism*. New Haven, CT: Yale University Press, 2004.

Fer, Briony. *On Abstract Art*. New Haven, CT: Yale University Press, 1997.

Fishar, Michelle Millar. "MoMA Acquires the Rainbow Flag." *Inside/Out: A MoMA Blog*, June 17, 2015. https://www.moma.org/explore/inside_out/2015/06/17/moma-acquires-the-rainbow-flag/.

Freeman, Elizabeth. *Time Binds: Queer Temporalities, Queer Histories*. Durham, NC: Duke University Press, 2010.

Fried, Michael. *Art and Objecthood: Essays and Reviews*. Chicago: University of Chicago Press, 1998.

Gage, John. *Color and Culture: Practice and Meaning from Antiquity to Abstraction*. Berkeley: University of California Press, 1993.

Gautherot, Franck, Caroline Hancock, and Seungduk Kim, eds. *Lynda Benglis*. Dijon, France: Presses du réel, 2009.

Gay, Peter, ed. *The Freud Reader*. New York: W. W. Norton, 1989.

Getsy, David. *Abstract Bodies: Sixties Sculpture in the Expanded Field of Gender*. New Haven, CT: Yale University Press, 2015.

Getsy, David. "Queer Relations." In "Queer Form," edited by Kadji Amin, Amber Jamilla Musser, and Roy Pérez, special issue, *ASAP/Journal* 2, no. 2 (2017): 254–57.

Getsy, David J., in conversation with William J. Simmons. "Appearing Differently: Abstraction's Transgender and Queer Capacities." In *Pink Labour on Golden Streets: Queer Art Practices*, edited by Christiane Erharter, Dietmar Schwärzler, Ruby Sircar, and Hans Scheirl, 38–55. Berlin: Sternberg, 2015.

Gibson, Ann. *Abstract Expressionism: Other Politics*. New Haven, CT: Yale University Press, 1997.

Gibson, Ann. "Color and Difference in Abstract Painting: The Ultimate Case of the Monochrome." In *The Feminism and Visual Culture Reader*, edited by Amelia Jones, 192–204. London: Routledge, 2003.

Gilroy, Paul. *Against Race: Imagining Political Culture beyond the Color Line*. Cambridge, MA: Harvard University Press, 2000.

Glissant, Édouard. *Poetics of Relation*. Translated by Betsy Wing. Ann Arbor: University of Michigan Press, 2010.

Goldsmith, Kenneth. "The Soft Grid: A Response to Sina Queyra's Lyric Conceptualist Manifesto." *Poetry Foundation*, April 11, 2012. https://www.poetryfoundation.org/harriet-books/2012/04/the-soft-grid-a-response-to-sina-queyrass-lyric-conceptualist-manifesto.

Gossett, Reina, Eric A. Stanely, and Johanna Burton, eds. *Trap Door: Trans Cultural Production and the Politics of Visibility*. Cambridge, MA: MIT Press, 2017.

Greenberg, Clement. *Clement Greenberg: The Collected Essays and Criticism*, vol. 2. Edited by John O'Brian. Chicago: University of Chicago Press, 1986.

Greenberg, Clement. "Modernist Painting." In *Modern Art and Modernism: A Critical Anthology*, edited by Francis Frascina and Charles Harrison, 5–10. New York: Harper and Row, 1982.

Gross, Elena. "When and Where I Enter: Work by Angela Hennessy." In *When and Where I Enter*, by Elena Gross and Valerie Imus. San Francisco: Southern Exposure, 2017. https://soex.org/publications/when-and-where-i-enter.

Halberstam, Jack. *In a Queer Time and Place: Transgender Bodies, Subcultural Lives*. New York: New York University Press, 2005.

Hall, Gordon. "Object Lessons: Thinking Gender Variance through Minimalist Sculpture." *ArtJournal* 72, no. 4 (2013): 47–57.

Halley, Peter. "The Crisis in Geometry." In *The Geometric Unconscious: A Century of Abstraction*, edited by Jorge Daniel Veneciano, 56–71. Lincoln: University of Nebraska Press, 2012.

Halperin, David M., and Valerie Traub, eds. *Gay Shame*. Chicago: University of Chicago Press, 2010.

Hammer, Barbara. "The Politics of Abstraction." In *Queer Looks: Perspectives on Lesbian and Gay Film and Video*, edited by Martha Gever, Pratibha Parmar, and John Greyson, 70–75. New York: Routledge, 1993.

Hammond, Harmony. "Feminist Abstract Art—A Political Viewpoint." *Heresies* 1 (January 1977): 66–70.

Hammond, Harmony. *Lesbian Art in America*. New York: Rizzoli, 2000.

Harper, Phillip Brian. *Abstractionist Aesthetics: Artistic Form and Social Critique in African American Culture*. New York: New York University Press, 2015.

Haynes, Clarity. "Going Beneath the Surface: For 50 Years, Harmony Hammond's Art and Activism Has Championed Queer Women." *ARTnews*, June 27, 2019. https://www.artnews.com/art-news/artists/harmony-hammond-12855/.

Haynes, Clarity. "Queering Abstract Art with Wrapped Up, Grommeted, and Roughed-Up Paintings." *Hyperallergic*, May 12, 2016. https://hyperallergic.com/298095/queering-abstract-art-with-wrapped-grommeted-and-roughed-up-paintings/.

Higgins, Hannah. *The Grid Book*. Cambridge, MA: MIT Press, 2009.

Honkasalo, Julian. "Genderqueer." *Lambda Nordica* 25, no. 1 (2020): 57–63.

Jarman, Derek. *Chroma: A Book of Color.* Woodstock, NY: Overlook, 1995.

Jay, Martin. "Chromophilia: *Der Blaue Reiter*, Walter Benjamin and the Emancipation of Color." Paper presented at the 2011 Yale University Forum on Art, War, and Science in the 20th Century, Hornby Island, British Columbia, Canada, May 19–23, 2011.

Jensen, Erik N. "The Pink Triangle and Political Consciousness: Gays, Lesbians, and the Memory of Nazi Persecution." *Journal of the History of Sexuality* 11, nos. 1–2 (2002): 319–49.

Jones, Amelia. *Body Art: Performing the Subject.* Minneapolis: University of Minnesota Press, 1998.

Jones, Amelia, and Erin Silver, eds. *Otherwise: Imagining Queer Feminist Art Histories.* Manchester: Manchester University Press, 2015.

Jones, Kellie. *Lorna Simpson.* London: Phaidon, 2002.

Joseph, Branden W. "Ulrike Müller: The Old Expressions Are with Us Always and There Are Always Others." *Artforum International* 54, no. 1 (September 2015): 220.

Kafer, Alison. *Feminist, Queer, Crip.* Indianapolis: Indiana University Press, 2013.

Katz, Jonathan D. "Dismembership: Jasper Johns and the Body Politic." In *Performing the Body/Performing the Text*, edited by Amelia Jones, 170–85. London: Routledge, 1999.

Keegan, C. M. "Against Queer Theory." *Transgender Studies Quarterly* 7, no. 3 (2002): 349–53.

Kelly, Ellsworth. "Notes of 1969." In *Ellsworth Kelly*, 30–34. Amsterdam: Stedelijk Museum, 1980.

Klapeer, Christine M., and Pia Laskar. "Transnational Ways of Belonging and Queer Ways of Being: Exploring Transnationalism through the Trajectories of the Rainbow Flag." *Identities: Global Studies in Culture and Power* 25, no. 5 (2018): 524–41.

Koestenbaum, Wayne. *Humiliation.* New York: Picador, 2011.

Krauss, Rosalind. "Agnes Martin: The /Cloud/." In *Bachelors*, 75–89. Cambridge, MA: MIT Press, 1999.

Krauss, Rosalind. "Grids." *October* 9 (Summer 1979): 50–64.

Krauss, Rosalind. *The Originality of the Avant-Garde and Other Modernist Myths.* Cambridge, MA: MIT Press, 1985.

Kristeva, Julia. "Giotto's Joy." In *Desire in Language: A Semiotic Approach to Literature and Art*, 210–36. New York: Columbia University Press, 1980.

Kristeva, Julia. *Powers of Horror: An Essay on Abjection.* New York: Columbia University Press, 1982.

Lancaster, Lex Morgan. "Feeling the Grid: Lorna Simpson's Concrete Abstraction." *ASAP/Journal* 2, no. 1 (2017): 135–59.

Lancaster, Lex Morgan. "Queer Abstraction." *ASAP/J: The open-access platform of ASAP/Journal* (July 2019). https://asapjournal.com/queer-abstraction-lex -morgan-lancaster/.

Lancaster, Lex Morgan. "The Wipe: Sadie Benning's Queer Abstraction." *Discourse: Journal for Theoretical Studies in Media and Culture* 39, no. 1 (Winter 2017): 92–116.

Langsner, Jules. "Four Abstract Classicists." In *Abstract Art in the Late Twentieth Century*, edited by Frances Colpitt, 1–10. Cambridge: Cambridge University Press, 2002.

Laskar, Pia, Anna Johansson, and Diana Mulinari. "Decolonising the Rainbow Flag." *Culture Unbound: Journal of Current Cultural Research* 8, no. 3 (2016): 193–216.

Latimer, Tirza True. *Harmony Hammond: Becoming/Unbecoming Monochrome*. Denver: Redline Art Space, 2014.

Ledesma, Jared. *Queer Abstraction*. Des Moines: Des Moines Art Center, 2019.

Lichtenstein, Jacqueline. *The Eloquence of Color: Rhetoric and Painting in the French Classical Age*. Berkeley: University of California Press, 1993.

Linden, Grace. "Re-enchanting California Hard Edge: Visual Politics in the Glow Paintings of Kelly Brumfield-Woods." *Peripheral Vision* 1 (August 10, 2017). https://www.peripheralvisionarts.org/journal/brumfieldwoods-linden.

Lippard, Lucy. *Changing: Essays in Art Criticism*. New York: Dutton, 1971.

Lippard, Lucy. "Eros Presumptive." In *Minimal Art: A Critical Anthology*, edited by Gregory Battcock, 209–22. Berkeley: University of California Press, 1995.

Lochner, Oona. "Ulrike Müller: Mumok, Vienna, Austria." *Frieze*, no. 23 (March 2016). https://www.frieze.com/article/ulrike-müller.

Lorenz, Renate. "Bodies without Bodies: Queer Desire as Method." In *Mehr(wert) queer: Visuelle Kultur, Kunst und Gender-Politiken*, edited by Barbara Paul and Johanna Schaffer, translated by Lisa Rosenblatt and Charlotte Eckler, 152–64. Bielefeld: Transcript, 2009.

Lorenz, Renate. *Queer Art: A Freak Theory*. New Brunswick, NJ: Transaction, 2012.

Love, Heather. "Queer." In "Postposttranssexual: Key Concepts for a Twenty-First-Century Transgender Studies," edited by Paisley Currah and Susan Stryker, special issue, *TSQ: Transgender Studies Quarterly* 1, nos. 1–2 (2014): 172–75.

Marshall, Richard. *Lynda Benglis*. New York: Cheim and Read, 2004.

Mauzerall, Hope. "What's the Matter with Matter? Problems in the Criticism of Greenberg, Fried, and Krauss." *Art Criticism* 13, no. 1 (1998): 81–96.

McBane, Barbara. "Queer Abstraction." *The Archive: The Journal of the Leslie-Lohman Museum of Gay and Lesbian Art*, no. 53 (Spring 2015): 11–13.

McClure, Michael Jay. "Prima Facie: The Photograph, the Unphotographed, and the Boston School." *Studies in Gender and Sexuality* 15, no. 2 (2014): 103–20.

McNamara, Andrew. "Between Flux and Certitude: The Grid in Avant-Garde Utopian Thought." *Art History* 15, no. 1 (March 1992): 60–79.

McRuer, Robert. "Crip." *Keywords for Radicals: The Contested Vocabulary of Late-Capitalist Struggle*, edited by AK Thompson, Kelly Fritsch, and Clare O'Conner, 119–26. Chicago: AK Press, 2016.

McRuer, Robert. *Crip Theory: Cultural Signs of Queerness and Disability*. New York: New York University Press, 2006.

Meltzer, Eve. *Systems We Have Loved: Conceptual Art, Affect, and the Antihumanist Turn*. Chicago: University of Chicago Press, 2013.

Mercer, Kobena. "Black Hair/Style Politics." *New Formations*, no. 3 (Winter 1987): 33–54.

Mercer, Kobena. *Discrepant Abstraction*. London: Institute of International Visual Arts, 2006.

Meyer, James. "Anthropomorphism." *Art Bulletin* 94, no. 1 (March 2012): 24–27.

Meyer, James. *Minimalism: Art and Polemics in the Sixties*. New Haven, CT: Yale University Press, 2001.

Morris, Robert. "Anti-form." *Artforum* 6, no. 8 (April 1968): 33–35.

Muñoz, José Esteban. *Cruising Utopia: The Then and There of Queer Futurity*. New York: New York University Press, 2009.

Muñoz, José Esteban. *Disidentifications: Queer of Color and the Performance of Politics*. Minneapolis: Minnesota University Press, 1999.

Muñoz, José Esteban. "Introduction: From Surface to Depth, between Psychoanalysis and Affect." *Women and Performance: A Journal of Feminist Theory* 19, no. 2 (2009): 123–29.

Muñoz, José Esteban. "Race, Sex, and the Incommensurate: Gary Fisher with Eve Kosofsky Sedgwick." In *Queer Futures: Reconsidering Ethics, Activism, and the Political*, edited by Elahe Haschemi Yekani, Eveline Kilian, and Beatrice Michaelis, 103–15. Aldershot, UK: Ashgate, 2013.

Namaste, Ki. "Tragic Misreadings: Queer Theory's Erasure of Transgender Subjectivity." *Queer Studies: A Lesbian, Gay, Bisexual, and Transgender Anthology*, edited by Brett Beemyn and Michele Eliason, 183–203. New York: New York University Press, 1996.

Ngai, Sianne. "Visceral Abstractions." GLQ: *A Journal of Lesbian and Gay Studies* 21, no. 1 (2015): 33–63.

O'Neill-Butler, Lauren. "Labor of Love: Lauren O'Neill Butler on the Art of Fierce Pussy." *Artforum* 57, no. 6 (February 2019). https://www.artforum.com/print/201902/lauren-o-neill-butler-on-the-art-of-fierce-pussy-78383.

Phelan, Peggy. *Mourning Sex: Performing Public Memories*. New York: Routledge, 1997.

Phelan, Peggy. *Unmarked: The Politics of Performance*. New York: Routledge, 1993.

Pinder, Kymberly N. "Unbaled: An Interview with Shinique Smith." *Artforum* 46, no. 10 (Summer 2008): 6–17.

Puar, Jasbir K. *Terrorist Assemblages: Homonationalism in Queer Times*. Durham, NC: Duke University Press, 2017.

Richmond, Susan. *Lynda Benglis: Beyond Process*. New York: I. B. Tauris, 2013.

Roffino, Sara. "Tionna Nekkia McClodden with Sara Roffino." *Brooklyn Rail* (December 2019–January 2020). https://brooklynrail.org/2019/12/art/TIONA-NEKKIA-MCCLODDEN-with-Sara-Roffino.

Said, Edward. *Freud and the Non-European*. London: Verso, 2003.

Salamon, Gayle. *Assuming a Body: Transgender and the Rhetorics of Materiality*. New York: Columbia University Press, 2010.

Saltz, Jerry. "Jerry Saltz on '93 in Art." *New York Magazine*, February 1, 2013. https://nymag.com/arts/art/features/jerry-saltz-1993-art/.

Saltz, Jerry, and Rachel Corbett. "How Identity Politics Conquered the Art World: An Oral History." *Vulture*, April 2016. https://www.vulture.com/2016/04/identity-politics-that-forever-changed-art.html.

Sandahl, Carrie. "Queering the Crip or Cripping the Queer? Intersections of Queer and Crip Identities in Solo Autobiographical Performance." *GLQ: Journal of Gay and Lesbian Studies* 9, nos. 1–2 (2003): 25–56.

Schapiro, Meyer. *Mondrian: On the Humanity of Abstract Painting*. New York: George Braziller, 1995.

Sedgwick, Eve Kosofsky. *Tendencies*. New York: Routledge, 1994.

Sedgwick, Eve Kosofsky. *Touching Feeling: Affect, Pedagogy, Performativity*. Durham, NC: Duke University Press, 2003.

Sekula, Alan. "The Body and the Archive." In *The Contest of Meaning: Critical Histories of Photography*, edited by Richard Bolton, 343–89. Cambridge, MA: MIT Press, 1989.

Sharpe, Christina. *In the Wake: On Blackness and Being*. Durham, NC: Duke University Press, 2016.

Sheets, Hillary M. "Black Abstraction: Not a Contradiction." *ARTnews*, June 4, 2014. https://www.artnews.com/art-news/news/changing-complex-profile-of-black-abstract-painters-2452/.

Shiff, Richard. "The Unaccountable." In *Bridget Riley: The Stripe Paintings 1961–2014*, by Paul Moorhouse, Robert Kudielka, and Richard Shiff, 18–39. New York: David Zwirner, 2014.

Sillman, Amy. "AbEx and Disco Balls: In Defense of Abstract Expressionism II." *Artforum* 49, no. 10 (Summer 2011): 314–25.

Simmons, William J. "Betty Tomkins: *Fuck Paintings* (1969–74)." *Flash Art* 48 (303) (July–September 2015): 45–47.

Simmons, William J. "Notes on Queer Formalism." *Big Red and Shiny*, December 16, 2013. http://bigredandshiny.org/2929/notes-on-queer-formalism/.

Simmons, William J. *Queer Formalism: The Return*. Berlin: Floating Opera, 2021.

Simpson, Bennett. *Blues for Smoke*. Los Angeles: Museum of Contemporary Art, Los Angeles, 2012.

Smith, Roberta. "At the Whitney, a Biennial with a Social Conscience." *New York Times*, March 5, 1993. https://www.nytimes.com/1993/03/05/arts/at-the-whitney-a-biennial-with-a-social-conscience.html.

Smith-Stewart, Amy. *Harmony Hammond: Material Witness, Five Decades of Art*. Aldrich Contemporary Art Museum / Gregory R. Miller and Co., 2019.

Snorton, C. Riley, and Hentyle Yapp, eds. *Saturation: Race, Art, and the Circulation of Value*. Cambridge, MA: MIT Press, 2020.

Sontag, Susan. *Against Interpretation and Other Essays*. London: Penguin, 2009.

Spivak, Gayatri Chakravorty. "Imperialism and Sexual Difference." *Oxford Literary Review* 8 (1986): 225–44.

Spivak, Gayatri Chakravorty. *Outside in the Teaching Machine.* New York: Routledge, 1993.

Steinberg, Leo. *Other Criteria: Confrontations with Twentieth-Century Art.* Oxford: Oxford University Press, 1972.

Steinbock, Eliza. *Shimmering Images: Trans Cinema, Embodiment, and the Aesthetics of Change.* Durham, NC: Duke University Press, 2019.

Stryker, Susan. "Transgender Studies: Queer Theory's Evil Twin." *GLQ: Journal of Gay and Lesbian Studies* 10, no. 2 (2004): 212–15.

Taylor, Brandon. *After Constructivism.* New Haven, CT: Yale University Press, 2014.

Taylor, Mark C. *The Moment of Complexity.* Chicago: University of Chicago Press, 2001.

Temkin, Ann, and Briony Fer. *Color Chart: Reinventing Color 1950 to Today.* New York: Museum of Modern Art, 2008.

Vaccaro, Jeanne. "Felt Matters." *Women and Performance: A Journal of Feminist Theory* 20, no. 3 (2010): 253–66.

Vicario, Gilbert, ed. *Sheila Pepe: Hot Mess Formalism.* New York: Prestel, 2018.

Wagner, Anne. *Three Artists (Three Women): Modernism and the Art of Hesse, Krasner, and O'Keefe.* Berkeley: University of California Press, 1998.

Wallace, Maurice O. *Constructing the Black Masculine.* Durham, NC: Duke University Press, 2002.

Williamson, Jack. "The Grid: History, Use, Meaning." *Design Issues* 3, no. 2 (Autumn 1986): 15–30.

Wright, Danielle. "Into the Void: An Interview with Angela Hennessy." *Nat Brut*, no. 10 (Spring 2018). https://www.natbrut.com/angela-hennessy.

Yekani, Elahe Haschemi, Eveline Kilian, and Beatrice Michaelis, eds. *Queer Futures: Reconsidering Ethics, Activism, and the Political.* Farnham, UK: Ashgate, 2013.

Young, Iris Marion. "Gender as Seriality: Thinking about Women as a Social Collective." *Signs* 19, no. 3 (Spring 1994): 713–38.

Note: Page and plate numbers in italics refer to figures.